Reconciling Suffering With Theism

Scan to download PDF of this book.

Scan to download PDF of The Words of Jesus book.

"Truly, truly, I say to you, unless one is born again he cannot see the kingdom of God." Jesus Christ, Son of Man

Reconciling Suffering with Theism

A Theodicy

*Why Does the God of the Bible
Permit Seemingly Senseless
Suffering and Evil?*

Art Hermann

Updated September 2022

Added emphasis on being Born-Again, this time born w/o the power to disobey God.
Added a description of Process Theology and Theodicy
Added Addenda Part VII with 18 Addendum
Made numerous grammatical edits, clarifications, and corrections.
Especially corrections and clarifications regarding libertarian freedom.

ISBN-13: 9798681759737
Imprint: Independently published

To my dear wife Robin
whose wisdom, understanding, help
and moral support made this work possible

Table of Contents

Scan to Email Question or Comment

Scan to go to the Words of Jesus
Online Website

Scan to go to the Words of Jesus
Online Bible Study

*I would like to acknowledge the
person whose comment regarding
'jettisoning' freewill sparked this effort*

Introduction

It is no secret that the Problem of Evil, the problem of seemingly senseless suffering, pain, and hardship in the world, may be the primary obstacle to believing in an all-powerful and good God, especially the God of the Bible. If God created everything out of nothing, how is God not in some way responsible for all the senseless suffering and evil that takes place in the world?

This question almost caused me to reject Jesus, with whom I had a personal encounter. Instead, I put aside my question regarding the problem of evil and began following the person of Jesus over forty years ago.

First, I believed, and then I began to understand. __ *St. Augustine*

Nevertheless, the question of why God permits seemingly senseless suffering and evil remained unanswered. Once retired, I started looking into how Christians and non-Christians alike have tried to answer the questions: Why is there seemingly senseless suffering and evil in the world? Why is there so much of it? And, Why are there such horrifying instances of it?

This book is the result of looking into the literature on this topic for over seven years. *Reconciling Suffering With Theism* may not satisfy anyone else. However, it has provided an outlook on life that has helped me to better manage the frustration of witnessing a world trending into chaos.

Part I is a brief but essential introduction and description of the problem of evil, the problem of seemingly senseless suffering, pain, and hardship in the world.

Part II is the proposed solution to this problem: People must freely ask God that they be born-again, born this time without the power to disobey Him.

Part III is an aggregation of information from different sources regarding the history and development of Augustinian soul-deciding type theodicies.

Part IV is an aggregation of information from different sources regarding the history and development of Irenaean soul-making type theodicies.

Part V is from the Patheos Library of World Religions and Faith Traditions. It includes 15 Christian traditions and their views on suffering and the problem of evil. Written by the world's leading authorities on religion and spirituality, the Patheos Library offers the most accurate and balanced information available on the web. (See: https://www.patheos.com/library/)

Part VI is an aggregation of information from different sources regarding the view of atheism and non-Christian religions on suffering and the problem of evil.

Part VII Addenda - Supplemental material.

Important Note

Much of what is included in Parts I, III, IV, V, VI, and VII was taken directly from other sources. I have tried to credit these sources but admittedly have fallen short of doing so correctly and sufficiently. Nevertheless, I felt it essential to include this material as background and context for Part II.

Part II contains the proposed solution to the Problem of Evil. The main idea is that people must freely ask God that they be born-again without the power to disobey Him this time, then enter the Kingdom of God, Paradise.

Comments can be emailed to:
https://www.thewordsofjesusonline@gmail.com

Synopsis

To escape the suffering, pain, and hardship of evil and enter the Kingdom of God (Paradise), a person must freely ask God that they be born again, born a new creation, a new type of person, one without the power to disobey Him this time.

"He who loves his life loses it, and he who hates his life in this world will keep it to life eternal." (John 12:25 NASB)

Disclaimer

This book does not claim the certainty of its conclusions. Nevertheless, it is an attempt to provide a reasonable, plausible, life-satisfying, Biblically-based, morally sufficient reason as to why the Omni-perfect God of the Bible would permit so much seemingly senseless suffering and evil to take place in the very good world He created out of nothing.

Philosophy is often referred to as studying the fundamental nature of knowledge, reality, and existence. In a broad sense, philosophy is an activity people undertake when they seek to understand fundamental truths about themselves, the world they live in, and their relationship with the world and with one another.

Theology typically means thinking about God. Thinking about what God has revealed about Himself, the world, and people. In Christianity, it usually means studying the sources of Christian beliefs, such as the Bible and the Creeds, and exploring the meaning of Christianity. It has been referred to as faith seeking understanding, which for many is the proper function of Christian theology.

This book is more a philosophical narrative and play of ideas and possibilities than a dogmatic theological statement of indisputable facts and incontrovertible truths.

Part I

Description of the Problem of Evil

There are two kinds of evil problems in the world,
evil itself and the consequence of evil.
__ St. Augustine of Hippo

As understood by most Christians, the Bible presents God as the Omni-perfect (omnipotent, omniscient, omnibenevolent, and so forth) creator of the Universe ex nihilo, out of nothing.

Then how can such an Omni-perfect God permit seemingly senseless suffering and evil to exist in the very good world He created? *(Gen 1:31)*

"The problem of evil is undoubtedly the greatest obstacle to belief in God." (William Lane Craig)

"The sheer crushing weight of the pains suffered by women, children, and men, and the lower animals, including that inflicted by human greed, cruelty, and malevolence, undoubtedly constitutes the most significant obstacle to believing in an all-powerful and loving Creator."
(John Harwood Hick)

"The problem of evil, one of the most fundamental questions of human existence, is universal, universally oppressive, and touches our existence at its very roots." (Karl Rahner)

Alvin C. Plantinga (1932), renowned American religious philosopher and Templeton Prize winner (2017), catalogs the constellation of questions that comprise the problem of evil. Why does God permit evil, why does God permit so much of it, and why does God permit those horrific and seemingly senseless instances of it?

Why God permits evil is known as, The Logical Problem of Evil. Why God permits so much of it is, The Evidential Problem of Evil. Why God permits those horrific and seemingly senseless instances of it is, The Existential Problem of Evil.

Given the problem of evil in all its forms, here are several examples of the argument against the existence of God, especially the Omni-perfect God of the Bible.

Christopher Hitchens, author, and famed atheist, argued that, "If a human creator had deliberately chosen to put hundreds of millions of his fellow humans in a marred place with disasters, bloodshed, famine, and disease, that person would be regarded as a monster. That would mean that if a God with the knowledge and power to stop these things did the same, He would be an even greater monster."

In his book, *Letter to a Christian Nation* (2006), Sam Harris, atheist, neuroscientist, and philosopher, stated. "It is safe to say that almost every person living in New Orleans shared your belief in an omnipotent, omniscient, compassionate God when Hurricane Katrina struck. But what was God doing while Katrina laid waste to their city? Surely, He heard the prayers of those older men and women who fled the rising waters for the safety of their attics, only to be slowly drowned there. These were people of faith. These were good men and women who had prayed throughout their lives. Do you have the courage to admit the obvious? These poor people died talking to an imaginary friend."

In Russian author, Fyodor Dostoyevsky's final novel, *The Brothers Karamazov* (1880), Ivan Karamazov asks his younger brother Alyosha, a cleric: "Imagine that you are creating a fabric of human destiny with the object of making men happy in the end, giving them peace and rest at last, but that it was essential and inevitable to torture to death only one tiny creature . . . and to found that edifice on its unremediated tears, would you consent to be the architect on those conditions? No, I would not, Alyosha replied softly."

Hitchens, Harris, and Dostoyevsky are essentially asking, like Epicurus, the Greek philosopher who lived several centuries before Christ:

1) Is God willing to prevent evil but not able? Then He is not omnipotent.
2) Is He able but not willing? Then He is not omnibenevolent.
3) Is He both able and willing? Then, Whence Cometh Evil?
4) Is He neither able nor willing? Then why call Him God?

This conundrum has come to be known as the problem of evil, in particular, the problem of horrific or gratuitous evil, for which there appears to be no good satisfying reason why an Omni-perfect God would allow such to occur.

Such horrific or gratuitous evil was the point of Ivan's question to Alyosha as he recounted incidents of horrible torment and torture inflicted on little children. He could think of no good reason why an Omni-perfect God would allow such atrocities to be committed against little children, even infants.

Three Forms of the Problem of Evil

Following Alvin Plantinga (p. 2), the Problem of Evil has taken three forms in recent literature. One form addresses the logical problem of evil, the second the evidential problem, and the third the existential problem of evil.

The logical problem of evil asks whether it is logically possible for an Omni-perfect God to coexist with evil in the world. From the work of Alvin Plantinga in his book *God, Freedom, and Evil* (1974&1977), many have come to accept that the answer to this question appears to be, Yes!

Namely, it is logical to think an Omni-perfect God may have a morally sufficient reason for coexisting with evil in the world. Even if we may not know what that reason is, and even if, as skeptics suggest, we may never be able to know. After all, how can mere finite human beings ever expect to understand the ways and means of an infinitely wise and intelligent Omni-perfect God?

However, the evidential problem states that even if it may be logically possible for an Omni-perfect God to coexist with evil in the world, it is nevertheless improbable, given the evidence of the amount and kinds of evil that also exists.

And the existential problem of evil addresses questions raised by specific instances of highly destructive and painful events that have existed in the past and continue to exist throughout the world today, such as the 1755 Lisbon Earthquake and the Jewish Holocaust in World War II. Could not God have prevented these particularly horrible and destructive evil events from occurring without upsetting His plans for humankind?

Furthermore, the evidential problem of evil asks questions from an impersonal perspective, whereas the existential problem of evil asks questions from a more personal point of view.

The evidential problem asks, Why would an Omni-perfect God allow any highly destructive and painful acts of evil to occur? And the existential problem asks, Why did God allow this or that particular instance of evil to occur?

Responses to the logical problem of evil take the form of a defense, whereas responses to the evidential and existential problems of evil take the form of a theodicy.

A defense merely states that it is logically possible that an Omni-perfect God has a morally sufficient reason for allowing evil to exist, but does not attempt to provide such a reason or justification.

A theodicy is more ambitious than a defense. It attempts to provide a morally sufficient and life-satisfying reason and justification as to why an Omni-perfect God would permit evil to exist in the very good world He created out of nothing.

Why This Theodicy?

The Problem of Evil arguably commands more attention than any other issue in the philosophy of religion and will continue to do so because of the obstacle evil presents to believing in a good God, especially the God of the Bible. Numerous Christian theodicies have been proposed during the two millennia of the Christian era, but all have serious and thoughtful detractors, and none have achieved widespread acceptance.

Roger Olsen, commenting on this situation in 2013, states, "My point so far is simply that innocent suffering, the suffering of small children, is a serious challenge to Christian faith in an all-good and all-powerful God, the God of Scripture and Christian tradition. And that Christian thinkers have risen to attempt to meet the challenge in various ways without arriving at consensus or settling on one response, one theodicy, as the total solution."

Reconciling Suffering With Theism (RST) is another attempt to provide a plausible, reasonable, life-satisfying, Biblically-based, morally sufficient reason for which the Omni-perfect God of the Bible permits so much seemingly senseless suffering and evil to exist in the very good world He created out of nothing.

In the proposed RST theodicy, evil is defined as disobedience to God. *(1 John 3:4)* It is also understood that a person obeys God by doing what God has commanded in the Bible should be done, or by not doing what God has commanded should not be done. And a person disobeys by not doing what should be done or by doing what should not be done.

Also proposed is that God has not ordained disobedience to God, nor was disobedience inevitable or essential for the success of God's Creation Project (CP)(p. 14). However, now that evil and suffering are in the world due to humankind's abuse of their freedom to disobey, God can use it, along with the suffering of temptation, which God has ordained, to further His CP.

God uses the consequent suffering caused by disobedience, and the suffering of temptation, to help people realize that to be saved from evil and suffering, they must ask God to remove their power to disobey Him. And this is accomplished in Hades, after the person's death to this present world, by asking God that they be born-again into Paradise without this power.

Experiencing and witnessing acts of evil, from the most commonplace and seemingly harmless to the most horrific, egregious, and destructive, should help people realize the necessity of having their power to disobey God removed. And the more horrible the act of disobedience and its consequences, the more it should bring people to that realization.

For no one is innocent, everyone disobeys God and contributes to the world's evil, pain, suffering, and hardship.

"... for all have sinned and fall short of the glory of God," (Romans 3:23 NASB*)*

The answer to the Problem of Evil provided here is hoped to leave one's sense of reality intact and tell the truth about reality. It is also hoped that it leaves one empowered within the intellectual-moral system in which one lives. Namely, it should not deny God's self-sacrificial love, God's power to do all that is logically possible, and God's perfect goodness.

Note: Both William Lane Craig (p. 43) and Eleanore Stump (p. 125) have expressed ideas that are precursors to the solution of the Problem of Evil presented here.

Part II

Reconciling Suffering with Theism

*Although He was a Son, He learned obedience from
the things [temptations] which He suffered.*
__ *Hebrews 5:8* NASB

The Great Lisbon Earthquake

Many people date the birth of modern atheism to the great Lisbon Portugal earthquake of 1755, which also called into question the general optimism of the Age of Enlightenment (~1685-1815).

On November 1, 1755, All Saints Day in the Roman Catholic faith, the churches in Lisbon were filled to capacity as the faithful worshiped God. Suddenly, the earth began to shake and continued to shake for more than three minutes.

Many ran from the falling buildings to the Tagus River in the center of town, seeking refuge on boats docked in the harbor. Moments later, a gigantic tsunami rushed into the harbor and up the river sweeping away all in its path. The city soon lay in ruins from the quake that caused fissures 15 feet wide in places.

The quake was felt hundreds of miles away, and the tsunami rippled south to North Africa, and north to England and North America. Modern studies rate this quake at 9 on the Richter scale.

Records show that half of Lisbon's population of about 100,000 died in the event, and most of its buildings were destroyed, including those housing great works of art and the records of the Portuguese empire from around the world. In sum, the Lisbon earthquake ranks as one of the worst natural disasters in modern history when measured by loss of life and property.

Historians and literary figures who study theology, philosophy, science, and other academic disciplines see the Great Lisbon Earthquake as much more than a great natural disaster. On the one hand, Christian thinkers of many stripes explained such natural disasters as examples of an all-powerful God exercising power and judgment over His Creation by punishing evildoers.

Yet, the devastation in Lisbon was so great that age-old questions again came to the fore: Why would the omnibenevolent God of the Bible allow such great and seemingly disproportionate suffering to take place in the very good world He created? Why would God permit disasters of such magnitude to afflict both good and bad people indiscriminately?

These questions point to what theologians and philosophers call theodicy. Theodicy is defined as an attempt to provide a morally sufficient and life-satisfying reason or justification for which an Omni-perfect God would permit the kinds and amounts of highly destructive natural and moral evil events to occur throughout the world.

In the wake of the Lisbon earthquake, philosophers and theologians alike wrote hundreds of books and novels about the problem of moral and natural evil. And as might be expected, *The Book of Job* became the focus for many. Job was *"a blameless and upright man, fearing God and turning away from evil," (Job 1:8)* but he still suffered the loss of family and great wealth, forced to endure bodily sickness, festering boils, and more. And the account makes it clear that it is not Job's place to question God but only to endure; God is in charge, testing and refining Job's faith in Him.

8

The philosopher Gottfried Wilhelm Leibniz (1646–1716) suggested seeing such disasters as part of a bigger picture. That, optimistically, given that God is perfect and would create perfectly, this is the best of all possible worlds, and evil is simply part of it and, therefore, must serve some good purpose, whatever that purpose may be, and we must simply learn to live with it.

Famously, Voltaire (1694-1778) ridiculed this optimistic worldview in his novel Candide and other works. He posited that evil is all around us, is not good, and may not serve any good purpose, and therefore this is not the best of all possible worlds. Nevertheless, he agrees we must learn to live with it.

Another figure influenced by the Enlightenment, Immanuel Kant (1724-1804), wrote several pieces on the Lisbon quake, attempting to explain its cause due to massive gaseous changes below the earth's surface, a prime example of a naturalistic explanation. A central point here is that the Lisbon quake unleashed an intellectual conflict over the question of how to explain natural disasters, one that lasted for generations.

Notice that explanations today of such events are primarily in the scientific-naturalistic realm. And while natural explanations are sound and most helpful, satisfying in many ways, they do not preclude even the most ardent naturalistic scientist from wondering, at another level, as to why these events are allowed to occur in the first place if there is a good God. Thus, he joins the rest of humanity, educated and primitive alike, who wonder why a loving good God, if He exists, would allow such suffering to take place.

Inevitably this question turns some who think about it into atheists or agnostics. Yet, like Job, others reaffirm their faith that they ultimately must trust God in all circumstances. Who, after all, can expect to understand the ways and means God uses to provide for and save His wayward children? (1)

Origin of Natural Evil

Events in Nature, such as hurricanes, tornadoes, earthquakes, lightning strikes, and the like, are often considered instances of natural evil that are not caused by either human or fallen angelic agents. However, it is proposed that all such natural evil events find their origin in Adam & Eve's moral disobedience to God in the Garden of Eden.

"Then the LORD God took the man and put him into the garden of Eden to cultivate it and keep it. The LORD God commanded the man, saying, "From any tree of the garden you may eat freely; but from the tree of the knowledge of good and evil you shall not eat, for in the day that you eat from it you will surely die." (Genesis 2:15-17 NASB*)*

When Adam & Eve disobeyed God by eating the forbidden fruit, God declared: *"Cursed is the ground because of you;"* (Genesis 3:17).

Instead of obeying God, Adam & Eve gave in to temptation and obeyed Satan and thereby willfully surrendered and abdicated to Satan their God-given rulership over the Garden *"to cultivate it and keep it."*

"Do you not know that when you present yourselves to someone as slaves for obedience, you are slaves of the one whom you obey, either of sin resulting in death, or of obedience resulting in righteousness?" (Romans 6:16 NASB*)*

Then, Satan and his cohorts were allowed to cause the above-mentioned destructive natural events throughout the world, but only within limits specified by God.

"… do not put forth your hand on him." (Job 1:12 NASB*)*

"I do not ask You to take them out of the world, but to keep them from the evil one. " *(John 17:15* NASB*)*

Furthermore, when Cain killed his brother Able, Satan gained more latitude to make it even more difficult to cultivate the ground, adding to the burden and hardship of evil.

"What have you done? The voice of your brother's blood is crying to Me from the ground. Now you are cursed from the ground, which has opened its mouth to receive your brother's blood from your hand. When you cultivate the ground, it will no longer yield its strength to you; " (Genesis 4:10-12 NASB*)*

Ultimately, the root cause of all natural evil is moral evil, the disobedience of Adam & Eve in the Garden of Eden. When God said,

"Cursed is the ground because of you;" it is understood to mean that the disobedience of Adam & Eve allowed Satan, the newly crowned ruler of the world, to curse the ground.

Through Adam & Eve's obedience to Satan, they allowed Satan to change the nature of this world in ways not presently understood, bringing forth corruption and death upon it. In the same way, when Cain killed his brother Abel, he allowed Satan to curse the ground to an even greater extent.

The Book of Job

The Old Testament assumption is that we live in a divinely governed, just Universe. The prevailing orthodoxy of that time was that God had structured the world so that the righteous and the wicked were rewarded or punished according to what they deserved, a simple principle of moral cause and effect. And although different in many important ways, this is not dissimilar from the Eastern idea of Karma.

However, *The Book of Job* is unorthodox concerning this orthodoxy, for it treats the problematic fact that the justice of God is not confirmed by human experience. A person's circumstances are not necessarily a good or accurate indicator of what they deserve or their standing with God. Thus, this book questions the Old Testament idea of what it means to live in a divinely governed, just Universe.

In a sense, *The Book of Job* is a philosophical debate set in an old folk tale format. It addresses the most perplexing human problem: Why do the innocent suffer? Why do children, even infants, suffer?

According to the story, Job was a morally virtuous and religiously devout ancient patriarch. Nevertheless, all sorts of evils befell him, devastating his once prosperous and flourishing life. So, Job's situation becomes a telling counterexample to the simple moral cause-effect principle.

This Old Testament classic story characterizes the exquisite intermingling of lofty theological ideas with profound psychological anguish. The result is a vision of the value of a relationship with God in a complex world that cannot be explained in simplistic categories or reduced to extrinsic rewards.

11

Many scholars and general readers often interpret the end of the story as depicting a puny human succumbing to divine power or a rebellious sinner admitting wrongdoing. However, the word repents in the context of this Hebrew text means to change one's mind, perhaps with some regret for having held an incorrect opinion in the first place. However, it does not intend to admit moral wrongdoing or spiritual rebellion. In this light, Job is a faithful believer, an honest questioner, a righteous sufferer, and a religious pioneer. (2)

The Evidential Argument From Evil

The evidential argument from evil, an argument for atheism, as advanced by the religious philosopher William L. Rowe (1931-2015) in his celebrated 1979 paper, states:

1) There are instances of intense suffering that an omnipotent, omniscient being could have prevented (... without thereby losing some greater good or permitting some evil equally bad or worse).

2) An omniscient, wholly good being would prevent the occurrence of any such intense suffering it could (... unless it could not do so without thereby losing some greater good or permitting some evil equally bad or worse).

3) Therefore, since such intense suffering is not being prevented, there does not exist an omnipotent, omniscient, wholly good being. (Rowe 1979: 336)

Note: This idea of a 'greater good' arises from the subjective notion that a 'greater good' is a thing whose goodness and value surpasses the badness of that which is required to obtain it.

In 1979 Rowe provided evidence for this argument, a hypothetical but easily conceivable lightning strike in a distant forest resulting in a forest fire. In the fire, a fawn is trapped, horribly burned, and lies in terrible agony for several days before death relieves its suffering.

William Rowe's evidential argument stipulates at least two classes of evil suffering. There is one class, the class of intense evil suffering, that he thinks an Omni-perfect God should prevent while not necessarily preventing a class of less intense evil suffering.

However, consider the following argument. Suppose evil suffering is represented by X in the world, and the varying degrees of evil suffering by X+1, X+2, X+3, and so forth, where the higher the number associated with X, the more intense the suffering.

Then assume that X+5 is the most intense evil suffering imaginable, and it is requested that God prevent X+5. The request is for God to prevent the suffering before it happens, after which there would be no human conception of X+5. That means it will never have been a part of the human experience.

Assuming God prevents X+5, the most intense evil suffering in human experience will now be X+4. However, when the same logical procedure is applied to X+4 as it was to X+5, the most intense evil suffering in human experience is now X+3.

If taken to its logical conclusion, the requests would not stop until God has prevented all evil suffering, which can only be done by God violating or revoking human freedom. However, without the freedom to obey or disobey God, people would not be able to genuinely love God. (3)

People want their freedom to disobey God, and they also want God to prevent all evil and suffering, a mutually exclusive request. Just as it is logically impossible for God to create a square circle or a married bachelor, it is logically impossible for God to create a human freewill that cannot disobey God, or a freewill that can be revoked. A freewill that cannot disobey God, or one that can be revoked, was never really free to begin with.

Regarding Rowe's fawn suffering and dying in a forest fire, such instances of intense suffering are often referred to as gratuitous and unnecessary acts of evil, for which there appears to be no conceivable satisfactory justification. Nevertheless, the purpose of the RST theodicy is to provide such a justification. (4)

Source:

13

(1) https://www.faithandfreedom.com/the-great-lisbon-earthquake-thinking-theology-and-natural-disasters/
(2) Michael L Peterson, *The Problem of Evil* (p. 17-18) University of Notre Dame Press.
(3) *A Creation-Order Theodicy* (2005) by Bruce A. Little
(4) https://iep.utm.edu/evil-evi/#H2

God's Creation Project

RST suggests that from before the beginning, it was in the heart of God the Father to have a Son. So, God bore His one and only Son Jesus, Who had both a Divine Nature and a Human Nature as the Son of God and the Son of Man. And, as a loving parent, Father God desired to provide Jesus, the Son of Man, with a home and a bride, where the Son and His bride could rule and reign over all creation forever.

Therefore, in the beginning, God created the heavens and the earth as their Universe and the Garden of Eden as their home. And in the Garden, God created Adam & Eve, who were intended to be the first of humankind to join Jesus' bride.

Accordingly, God created the Garden of Eden very good in that it was without defect and in good working order, and God also created Adam & Eve very good and without defect. Adam & Eve were tasked with keeping and cultivating the Garden under the authority and direction of Jesus, the Son of Man, as well as being the mother and father of humanity, procreating children of God.

Most importantly, God created Adam & Eve with the ability to love God, and loving God is every person's highest and most important calling.

*"One of them, a lawyer, asked Him a question, testing Him, 'Teacher, which is the great commandment in the Law?' And He said to him, '**You shall love the lord your God with all your heart, and with all your soul, and with all your mind. This is the great and foremost commandment.**'"*
(Matthew 22:35-38 NASB*)*

14

However, love is not real when only love is possible; for love to be real, the possibility of not loving also has to be real. Therefore, Adam & Eve were created open to the possibility of not loving God. They could love God by obeying Him, and they could not love Him by disobeying Him.

"If you love me, keep my commands. ... He who has My commandments and keeps them is the one who loves Me" *(John 14:15,21* NASB*)*

However, only those who would always love and obey God, and never disobey Him, could God consider worthy of being in Jesus' bride.

Therefore, Adam & Eve were created with libertarian freedom (a libertarian will, a freewill) to either obey or not obey God, to love or not love God. As understood here, libertarian freedom means that a person can make choices that are free from being determined by anything other than an act of their will. Internal and external forces acting on a person may strongly influence their choices, but they do not control them with absolute certainty. Likewise, choices made in the past may strongly influence present-day choices, but they do not control them with certainty.

Also, a person's choices are free from being predetermined or foreknown by God. God may know with a high degree of certainty what choices people will make in future situations, but not with absolute certainty. If God knew with absolute certainty what choices people would make in the future, they would not have libertarian freedom. And without libertarian freedom, people could not be held responsible and accountable for their choice to love or not love God, to obey or disobey God.

Adam & Eve, when they chose against obeying God and instead chose to obey Satan, they did so freely, which is evil, and the consequence of their committing evil entered the world.

"... but from the tree of the knowledge of good and evil you shall not eat, for in the day that you eat from it you will surely die." (Gen 2:17 NASB*)*

RST posits that when Adam & Eve disobeyed God and died spiritually and then physically, their souls went to Hades, a place often mentioned by Jesus. Hades is thought to be the temporary dwelling place for the souls of all people following their physical death to this world, and where the soul of Jesus, the Son of Man, is thought to have gone temporarily following His physical death on the Cross.

In Hades, all people can love and obey God by denying themselves their libertarian freewill power to disobey Him by asking God to remove this power from them. And once the person has been fully informed of the consequences, God will remove this power, as it will have served its purpose. Its purpose having been to provide a way for people to love Him by freely denying themselves the power to disobey Him.

Then, once a person has been born-again by God, without the power to disobey Him, He will usher them to Paradise. And with their libertarian freewill power to obey Him, they will be able to obey Him in any of the myriad ways He has provided for them in Paradise.

"The LORD God commanded the man, saying, "From any tree of the garden you may eat freely;" (Gen 2:16, NASB*)*

Therefore, to escape the suffering, pain, and hardship of evil and enter the Kingdom of God, Paradise, a fully informed person may ask God that they be born-again. Born a new creation, a new type of person, one without the power to disobey God this time. And then take their place in the bride of Christ, ruling and reigning forever with Jesus over Father God's creation, helping develop and make it into all He intended for them.

The Problem of Suffering for Theism

Humans experience two kinds of suffering. First, there is the suffering that comes from being tempted to disobey God, and then there is the suffering that comes from actually disobeying Him. People suffer from the temptation to disobey God when becoming impatient, unkind, unfaithful, unloving, and so on. The suffering that comes from temptation is ordained by God and is very good, even essential for the success of God's CP, because it warns people of imminent danger, like a flashing yellow traffic light.

16

However, the suffering that comes from actually disobeying God is not good, was not ordained by God, and was neither essential nor inevitable for God's CP to succeed. First comes the helpful nondestructive suffering of temptation to disobey, and then, if given in to, comes the very unhelpful destructive suffering from actually disobeying God.

Suffering from the temptation to disobey God is a very good part of being human. The suffering of temptation that Adam & Eve experienced in the Garen of Eden was intended to warn and restrain them from disobedience, leading to their death and the death and destruction of the Garden and world around them.

However, more importantly, the suffering of temptation in the Garden was intended to bring Adam & Eve to the point of asking God if they could be born-again. Born-again this time without the power to disobey Him and thereby escape any further suffering from temptation.

"No temptation has overtaken you but such as is common to man; and God is faithful, who will not allow you to be tempted beyond what you are able, but with the temptation will provide the way of escape also, so that you will be able to endure it." (1 Corinthians 10:13 NASB)

It is posited that God had explained to Adam & Eve, even before they were tempted, that when temptation came, they could escape its suffering by being born-again without the power to disobey Him. And even though they could no longer love God by resisting the temptation to disobey Him, they could still love Him by obeying Him, which is all that is required.

Therefore, the suffering of temptation to disobey God is a very good thing for a person to have and is not a defect. God designed it to bring people to the point of wanting to escape this suffering by asking to be born-again without the power to disobey Him. Temptation can no longer affect a person who does not have the power to disobey God.

Christian Theodicies

Theologians and philosophers alike have proposed numerous Christian theodicies during the two millennia of the Christian era. John Harwood

Hick (1922–2012) was a British philosopher of religion and perhaps the twentieth century's most influential philosopher of religion and theodicy.

His framework-setting, discussion-shifting book, *Evil and the God of Love* (1966), details his theodicy, which revolutionized discourse on the Problem of Evil. In it, he describes two basic types of theodicy.

One type is Augustine's (354-430 AD) Western theodicy, and the other is the older Eastern theodicy of Irenaeus (130-202 AD). Hick labeled Augustinian type theodicies as soul-deciding theodicies and Irenaean types as soul-making theodicies.

Soul-making is the idea that a person will gradually be saved to the Kingdom of God, Paradise, through the gradual perfection of their soul, their moral character, by way of making many freewill decisions to obey and receive the grace of God.

Soul-deciding is the idea that a person is saved by making one or, at most, a few freewill decisions to obey and receive the grace of God in this life and then proceed to Paradise following death.

Hick distinguished between the Augustinian type of theodicy, which attempts to clear God of all responsibility for evil, and the Irenaean type, which openly casts God as responsible for evil. However, according to Irenaeus, even though God is responsible for evil, God is justified in using it. Without evil, people would not strive to alleviate the suffering from evil through obedience to God, leading to character development and Christlikeness.

Origen of Alexandria (185-254 AD), who lived about fifty years after Irenaeus, and before Augustine, used two metaphors for this Irenaean worldview. This world is a school and a hospital for souls, with God as Teacher and Physician, in which suffering plays both an educative and healing role in people's lives.

Both families of theodicies are referred to as greater-good theodicies. And both posit that evil arises when people disobey God. And in both, God ultimately brings something good out of every instance of evil, a good which God could not have achieved were it not for that evil, thereby justifying God's permission of that evil. Therefore, people's ability to obey and love God outweighs all the evil that results from people disobeying Him.

And both families typically understand that everything about the future, including human choices, is providentially predetermined by God, and therefore humans are not truly free in a libertarian sense (Calvinism). Or, that human freedom is somehow compatible with all that God has predetermined (Arminianism).

However, from the RST perspective, if God knew in advance what a person would choose in the future, to either love or not love God, to obey or not obey God, they would not have true libertarian freedom. Whatever they chose in the future that God knew beforehand, they could not have chosen otherwise at the moment of choosing. Without the freedom to choose otherwise at the moment of choosing, there is no libertarian freedom and, therefore, no genuine ability to love God.

Therefore, RST posits a libertarian view of human freewill, human freedom, which is incompatible with determinism or compatibilism and therefore differs from typical Augustinian and Irenaean type theodicies.

RST also postulates that human agents have a libertarian freewill that consists of three mutually exclusive parts or modes of operation. There is the libertarian obedient freewill, the libertarian disobedient freewill, and the libertarian non-moral freewill.

The separate obedient freewill and disobedient freewill are seen in operation where Paul talks about his struggle between obeying and disobeying God:

"For what I am doing, I do not understand; for I am not practicing what I would like to do, but I am doing the very thing I hate. But if I do the very thing I do not want to do, I agree with the Law, confessing that the Law is good. . . . For the good that I want, I do not do, but I practice the very evil that I do not want. . . . Wretched man that I am! Who will set me free from the body of this death? Thanks be to God through Jesus Christ our Lord!" (Romans 7:15,16,19,24,25 NASB*)*

And the third part of a person's freewill is the libertarian non-moral freewill, which people use to make choices for their own good pleasure that are neither obedient nor disobedient to God, like choosing between peas and carrots for dinner.

The Paradise Dilemma

Regarding greater-good type theodicies, James F. Sennett argues that if there is freedom in Paradise, then it seems there is also the possibility of evil in Paradise, violating Scripture and standard intuitions. *(1 Cor 6:9, Rev 21:27)*

It appears, then, that there is a dilemma in Paradise. If there is no possibility of evil in Paradise, then Paradise lacks a great good worth the price of great suffering and evil in this world. So then, how can God be justified in omitting such a great good from Paradise?

Following Augustine, Catholicism addresses this dilemma by postulating an afterlife in Purgatory before Paradise for those who do not go directly to Hell. Those entering Purgatory atone for their sins, making them eligible for Paradise, even though they retain their freewill power to disobey God in Paradise.

Some Protestant theodicists, such as Greg Boyd, Kevin Tiempe, and others, address it by appealing to the Irenaean soul-making process where the human soul, a person's moral character, is perfected before entering Paradise. During this life and probably an afterlife before Paradise, a person's moral character is gradually perfected to where disobedience to God is something they would never do. Even though they retain their power to disobey God in Paradise, they will never do so.

RST addresses this dilemma by postulating that the only people in Paradise are those who have demonstrated their love for God by voluntarily having their libertarian disobedient freewill power removed.

Note: Removing a person's libertarian disobedient freewill power does not affect the operation of their other two freewill powers, their libertarian obedient freewill power, and their libertarian non-moral freewill power.

Before Paradise, people love God by obeying Him, and also by resisting the temptation to disobey Him. And they love Him to the greatest extent possible by asking Him to remove their power to disobey. And once it has been removed, it will have served its purpose and is no longer needed to love God in Paradise. In Paradise, people can love God fully by obeying Him in the myriad ways He has provided.

The Skeptical Theist Defense

Following Augustine's argument that finite, intellectually limited humans cannot perceive the ways and means of the infinitely wise and intellectually unlimited Creator God of the Bible, skeptical theism is now a well-known defense against the evidential argument from evil as presented by William Rowe.

Rowe's evidential argument from evil, an argument for atheism, gains traction by claiming that it is likely that at least some intense suffering from evil is gratuitous, not essential for some good to be obtained by God.

The evidential argument from evil postulates that the existence of some intense suffering from evil, for which there seems to be no conceivable good outcome or justification, constitutes evidence against a good God's existence. For example, what possible life-satisfying good outcome can there be for a fawn burned, suffering, and dying a horrible death in a forest fire or for Ivan Karamazov's tortured children?

Therefore an omniscient, omnibenevolent, omnipotent God should prevent these kinds of horrific gratuitous evils. And the fact that they are not prevented is evidence against a good God's existence, in particular, the God of the Bible.

However, as skeptical theists argue, God may perceive and pursue goods from seemingly gratuitous evils that are beyond human comprehension. Skeptical theists Daniel Howard-Snyder and Michael Bergmann are prominent representatives of this response known as the skeptical theist defense.

The primary point of this defense is that the human inability to discern God's good reasons for some evils does not constitute irrefutable evidence that there are no such good reasons. They argue that people have no reason to think that finite human minds can grasp all the connections between evils and goods. Yet such connections may well be known by an infinitely intelligent Omni-perfect God. (1)

Source:
(1) https://plato.stanford.edu/entries/skeptical-theism/

God's Omniscience and Omnipotence

The RST view of God's omniscience is different from the Classic Christian view. The Classic Christian understanding, held by most Augustinians and Irenaeans, is that God is all-knowing, knowing all things past, present, and future with absolute certainty. The RST view holds that God knows all things past and present with absolute certainty, but not the future.
(See: Addendum 10 Freewill Theism p. 281
Addendum 11 The Future Has Not Been Decided p. 294)

However, RST agrees with the Classic Christian view of God's omnipotence in that God can do anything logically possible, but God cannot do the illogical. For example, God cannot create a married bachelor, a square circle, a freewill that can be overruled, or a freewill that can be revoked. As C.S. Lewis said, we may attribute miracles to God, but not nonsense.

The Classic Christian understanding of God's omniscience and omnipotence comes largely from the writings of St. Augustine of Hippo (354-430 AD). He incorporated some of the widely accepted ideas of Greek philosophy, especially Greek Neo-Platonism, into his knowledge of Scripture to make Christianity more acceptable to his time's intelligentsia and upper classes.

However, this Classic view of God's omniscience can be problematic for some Christians. For example, suppose God knew in advance with absolute certainty that a person was about to harm another person, and did not stop them, then, somehow, God would be blameworthy for harm coming to that other person. And since it is known that God helps people, being blameworthy for such harm suggests God's Kingdom is a house divided against itself. *(Matthew 12:25)*

Also, if God knew in advance that a person would love Him, then that person would not have the freedom not to love Him. And without the freedom to not love Him, there can be no genuine love for God, until the freedom to not love Him has been voluntarily relinquished.

However, the Classic view of God's omniscience may be thought of in the following way. Perhaps it is not so much a question of what God can know about the future, but rather what God can choose to know. If God would like to know with certainty people's future choices, then, of course, God could.

However, maybe God created the world so that God's certain knowledge of it is limited to the past and present, but not the future. It may be well within God's omnipotence and intelligence to create a world where God can choose what to know and what not to know about the future.

Therefore, maybe it is more important to God that people should be able to freely love Him than for Him to have absolute and certain knowledge of their future choices. And by God choosing not to have such knowledge, people can have a freewill essential for loving God.

It is proposed then that God created this world so that God's absolute certain knowledge of all things is limited to the past and present, but not the future. And to suggest that God cannot do this is to question God's omnipotence and intelligence to do that which is logically possible. (See: Addendum 11 The Future Has Not Been Decided p. 294)

If that can be accepted, then God cannot be held accountable or responsible for human choices. And then, of the utmost importance, people are genuinely free to choose to love and obey God and fulfill their highest calling, including their freedom to love and obey God by relinquishing their libertarian power to disobey Him.

Source:
https://www.ligonier.org/learn/devotionals/evil-gods-providential-rule/
https://www.ligonier.org/learn/devotionals/house-divided/

Testing and Temptation

From the RST point of view that God has chosen not to have meticulous knowledge of the future, He must test people to determine their willingness to obey Him and join the bride of Christ by giving them commands to obey. And He also had to create them open to temptation to disobey Him to determine their willingness not to disobey Him.

In these two ways, testing and tempting, God can determine who would and who would not be a worthy member of the bride of Christ. Only those who would always obey and never disobey God could God consider worthy of being a member of Jesus' bride. It is important to note that God will test people to determine their willingness to obey, but God will never tempt them to determine their willingness not to disobey Him.

If people thought that God was tempting them to disobey, it would be difficult for them to believe that God would also help them endure the temptation and provide them with *'the way of escape'* from it. There is already enough temptation that arises from the world, the flesh, and the devil, that God does not need to tempt anyone.

"No temptation has overtaken you but such as is common to man; and God is faithful, who will not allow you to be tempted beyond what you are able, but with the temptation will provide the way of escape also, so that you will be able to endure it."
(1 Corinthians 10:13 NASB*)*

Every person struggles with their power to obey God and their separate power to disobey Him, and the focus of this theodicy centers on this struggle.

"For what I am doing, I do not understand; for I am not practicing what I would like to do, but I am doing the very thing I hate. But if I do the very thing I do not want to do, I agree with the Law, confessing that the Law is good. . . . For the good that I want, I do not do, but I practice the very evil that I do not want. . . . Wretched man that I am! Who will set me free from the body of this death? Thanks be to God through Jesus Christ our Lord!" (Romans 7:15,16,19,24,25 NASB*)*

Later in this theodicy, it is suggested that almost everyone will realize that by exercising their freewill to disobey God, they are a source of evil and a source of their own suffering and the suffering of others close to them and far away. And with this realization, they will come to hate their power to disobey God and strongly desire to have it removed by being born-again without it.

"He who loves his life loses it, and he who hates his life in this world will keep it to life eternal." *(John 12:25* NASB*)*

Paraphrasing this verse, "The person who loves their freewill power to disobey God remains apart from God. And the person who hates their power to disobey will give it up by freely asking God that they be born-again into Paradise without it, while still keeping their freewill power to obey, and therefore love God in Paradise."

This act of a person sacrificing their freewill power to disobey God by asking to be born-again without it is considered a decisive act of freely choosing to love God by laying down their life for Him.

"Then Jesus said to His disciples, **'If anyone wishes to come after Me, he must deny himself, and take up his Cross and follow Me. For whoever wishes to save his life will lose it; but whoever loses his life for My sake will find it.'"** *(Matthew 16:24,25* NASB*)*

Further, it is suggested that being born-again is a process that begins when a person believes in their heart that God raised Jesus from the dead and then makes Him their Lord and Savior by inviting the Holy Spirit into their life. And this process can begin in this life or in Hades.

"If you then, being evil, know how to give good gifts to your children, how much more will your heavenly Father give the Holy Spirit to those who ask Him?" *(Lk 11:13* NASB*)*

Then, the born-again process is completed in Hades, with God removing the person's power to disobey, and ushering them to Paradise.

In Hades, everyone can ask to have their power to disobey God removed, and God will remove it. But first, God must fully inform them of the consequences of no longer being able to disobey Him in Paradise.

After which, if they still want to, God will remove this power, as it will have served its purpose. Its purpose having been to provide a way for people to love and obey Him by laying down their life for Him by denying themselves the power to disobey Him.

In Paradise, they will finally be free from the suffering of temptation in that temptation can no longer affect them since they no longer have the power to give in to it.

Further, it is proposed that from the beginning, it was God's plan for Adam & Eve to ask Him to have their freewill power to disobey removed when faced with the excruciating and unrelenting temptation from Satan to disobey in the Garden. Therefore, it is conceivable, and it only seems right and fair, that God had explained to them, in advance of them being tempted, how to escape the suffering of temptation when it came by being born-again without the power to disobey Him.

And if Adam & Eve had accepted God's offer, they would have been the first members of the bride of Christ, and Satan would not have been given rulership of the world. Also, it is thought that if any of Adam & Eve's children disobeyed God, then there would have been consequences for the children, but Satan would not have acquired rulership of the world because only Adan & Eve had it to give away, not their children.

Adam & Eve, having first been born in the image of God, would then have been gradually transformed into a likeness of God, a likeness of Jesus Christ, but without ever becoming perfect like Him. However, instead of obeying God, Adam & Eve, freely, selfishly, and with a complete understanding of the consequences, chose to disobey Him and instead obeyed Satan. And this allowed evil to enter the world, bringing pain, suffering, hardship, and physical death upon themselves, their descendants, and the entire world.

"For the anxious longing of the creation waits eagerly for the revealing of the sons of God. For the creation was subjected to futility, not willingly, but because of Him who subjected it, in hope that the creation itself also will be set free from its slavery to corruption into the freedom of the glory of the children of God. For we know that the whole creation groans and suffers the pains of childbirth together until now. And not only this, but also we ourselves, having the first fruits of the Spirit, even we ourselves

26

groan within ourselves, waiting eagerly for our adoption as sons, the redemption of our body. For in hope we have been saved, but hope that is seen is not hope; for who hopes for what he already sees? But if we hope for what we do not see, with perseverance, we wait eagerly for it." (Romans 8:19-25 NASB)

Following the disobedience and fall of Adam & Eve, God now uses both the suffering that comes from giving in to temptation, and the suffering of temptation itself, to encourage people to love God by laying down their life for Him. And people lay down their life for Him decisively by asking to be born-again without the power to disobey Him.

Familiar Christian Responses to the Problem of Evil

Here are some ways Christians have understood and responded to the Problem of Evil.

1) The great and foremost commandment in the Bible is to love God by obeying God. However, to have a genuine love for God, humans must also have the power to not love Him by disobeying Him, and disobeying Him is the root cause of all moral and natural evil. Therefore, the great value of being able to love and obey God outweighs all the evil and suffering that results from disobeying Him.

2) The testing of our faith through suffering produces endurance, and the one who endures to the end will be saved. *(Jas 1:3, Matt 24:13)*

3) How can finite human beings expect to understand the ways and means of an infinitely wise, intelligent, Omni-perfect God?

4) God sometimes afflicts people with pain and suffering as punishment for their disobedience.

5) God has hidden His good reasons for allowing evil to exist in the world, but in the end, everyone will understand and agree that the acts of evil permitted were for a good purpose. We are in the middle of a long story, and God will answer all questions in the end.

6) O Felix Culpa, O Fortunate Fault. If evil had never entered the world, people would never have known the great salvific love and glory of the Incarnation, Crucifixion, Resurrection, and Ascension of Jesus Christ.

Therefore, people would not have been able to witness and understand the fullness of God's great salvific love and glory, which would have been a great loss to humanity.

7) The answer to the Problem of Evil is mysterious and unknown. Since no one has yet come up with a widely acceptable and satisfactory solution or justification for it, it is not worth pursuing.

8) For the possibility of goodness to exist in the world, the possibility of evil must also exist. Or, for there to be beauty in the world, there must also be the ugly with which to compare it.

9) Ultimately, God is responsible for some evil because it is the best way to accomplish His infinitely good purpose of saving some, if not all, evildoers.

10) God is present with those amid their pain and suffering, making such pain and suffering morally acceptable and even rewarding. The sense of God's presence can more than compensate for any suffering; therefore, experiencing God's presence is a great good worth the price of great suffering.

11) God intervenes and prevents much evil and suffering, but we are unaware of it. God could prevent all evil and suffering but does not so that God's plans and purposes for creation can be fulfilled.

12) God cannot prevent evil and suffering; if God could, God would. Nevertheless, God does exist, and God is good.

13) God is Universally saving all humanity to Paradise; therefore, that great end justifies whatever means God chooses to use.

The RST Response to the Evidential Problem of Evil

In the section The Evidential Argument From Evil (p. 12), William Rowe claims that it is reasonable to think that God could have prevented at least some suffering in the world without losing some good or without allowing an equally bad or worse evil to occur in its place. And since such evils are not prevented, he believes he has reasonable evidence, reasonable grounds for atheism.

Rowe's argument prevails if there has been even one instance of pointless, gratuitous, unnecessary evil in world history. Conversely, if a good reason or justification can be found for God allowing every instance of evil that has ever occurred, then Rowe's argument would seem to fail.

RST proposes that every instance of evil is rooted in human disobedience to God. Therefore, every instance of evil that has ever occurred is there to help people understand that human disobedience to God is its cause. And as people come to this realization, they are to ask God to change them so they can no longer disobey Him.

Such a change in a person is what Jesus might have meant when He said, **"Truly, truly, I say to you, unless one is born again he cannot see the kingdom of God."** *(John 3:3* NASB*)*

If this can be accepted, then every instance of evil, small or great, moral or natural, serves the very good purpose of encouraging people to ask God that they be born-again without the power to disobey. In which case, Rowe's evidential argument for atheism would seem to fail, and the terms gratuitous or unnecessary acts of evil appear a misnomer.

However, in some cases, good things may result from an instance of evil, but they are accidental or incidental to the good of encouraging people to ask God to change them by being born-again without the power to disobey.

Also, it is suggested that people should not think because, *"God causes all things to work together for good to those who love God, to those who are called according to His purpose" (Romans 8:28),* that the good mentioned here is anything other than the good of askng to have their power to disobey God removed.

RST proposes that people can decisively demonstrate their love for God by asking God to remove their power to disobey by being born-again without it. And God will grant their request once they fully understand what it means to live without the power to disobey, and to live only with the power to obey God in Paradise.

Then, in Paradise, a born-again person's character gradually develops and matures into a unique Christlike character as they obey God more and more selflessly, but without them ever becoming perfect like Christ.

It is important to note that a person in Paradise without the power to disobey will not be like a robot, only able to obey God's commands if, when, and as given. Instead, they will be free to choose from among the myriad of ways God has provided for them to obey, ranging from the most selfless to the least selfless of ways.

Of course, some human acts may be neither obedient nor disobedient to God, such as choosing between peas and carrots for dinner or between playing golf or tennis this afternoon. An unlimited number of these non-moral choices may also be available in Paradise for people's enjoyment and well-being.

"Things which eye has not seen and ear has not heard, and which have not entered the heart of man, all that God has prepared for those who love Him." (1 Cor 2:9 NASB*)*

By Adam & Eve's one act of disobedience, they and their progeny became slaves to disobedience. Now those who are enslaved to disobedience can set themselves free with one act of obedience on their part by asking God that they be born-again without the power to disobey this time.

To be made righteous and set free from disobedience is not a matter of the person doing something on their own to set themselves free. It is a matter of them asking God to help them to stop doing something, to stop disobeying Him, and be set free from being a source of evil and suffering.

Jesus has done everything required for people to be made righteous and set free from disobedience. Without the finished atoning work of Christ's perfect obedience to the Father in all things, including His obedience to death on a cross, humanity's freedom from disobedience would not be possible.

But now that Jesus has made the way to freedom from disobedience possible, it is only a matter of people freely choosing to ask God to change them so that they can no longer disobey. The person is only asking to be changed; it is God who is doing the work of changing them.

"And Jesus said to His disciples, **"Truly I say to you, it is hard for a rich man to enter the kingdom of heaven. "Again I say to you, it is easier for a camel to go through the eye of a needle, than for a rich man to enter the kingdom of God. "** *When the disciples heard this, they were very astonished and said, "Then who can be saved?" And looking at them Jesus said to them,* **"With people this is impossible, but with God all things are possible. "** *(Matthew 19:23-26* NASB*)*

Jesus has made salvation from disobedience and evil possible. Therefore, for everyone who suffers, God has put the remedy for their suffering into their own hands. Everyone gets what they want most, an obedient life in Paradise with Jesus free from disobedience and suffering, or a life apart from God enslaved to disobedience and suffering.

What may help a person lay down their life for God by being born-again is to realize that they cannot always control their power to disobey, no matter how hard they try.

"For what I am doing, I do not understand; for I am not practicing what I would like to do, but I am doing the very thing I hate. But if I do the very thing I do not want to do, I agree with the Law, confessing that the Law is good. ... For the good that I want, I do not do, but I practice the very evil that I do not want. ... Wretched man that I am! Who will set me free from the body of this death? Thanks be to God through Jesus Christ our Lord!" (Romans 7:15,16,19,24,25 NASB*)*

Nevertheless, it is good to try hard to resist temptation and to ask for and receive the Holy Spirit's help, thereby reducing the amount of evil and suffering in the world. And as a result of this trying, people's moral character may improve and develop in real and lasting ways, but not to the point of never disobeying God. People must come to see they carry within themselves the seeds of discord and destruction and that they cannot help but sow these seeds wherever they go.

When a person sacrifices any other aspect or attribute of their life for God, like their time, money, or even their body, they still retain in their soul the power to disobey and remain apart from God. Therefore, people must come to hate their libertarian freewill power to disobey God and

31

ask God to remove it by being born-again. This decision is considered the greatest possible act of sacrifice and obedience a person can make for God.

'Samuel said, "Has the LORD as much delight in burnt offerings and sacrifices As in obeying the voice of the LORD? Behold, to obey is better than sacrifice, And to heed than the fat of rams."' (1 Samuel 15:22 NASB)

When people ask God to have their power to disobey removed by being born-again, they fully comply with the command of Jesus to deny themselves by laying down their life for His sake.

"Then Jesus said to His disciples, **'If anyone wishes to come after Me, he must deny himself, and take up his Cross and follow Me. For whoever wishes to save his life will lose it; but whoever loses his life for My sake will find it.'"** *(Matthew 16:24,25* NASB*)*

In the Garden of Eden, before giving in to temptation, Adam & Eve could have escaped the temptation to disobey God by asking God to remove their power to disobey, and God would have granted their request.

Without the power to disobey, temptation could no longer affect them, and they would no longer have been a potential source of evil. Then Adam & Eve could have continued fulfilling God's purpose for their lives by joining them to Christ as His bride and proceeding to transform them into a likeness of Christ without them ever having disobeyed.

Therefore, it was neither essential nor inevitable for evil to enter the world for God's CP to succeed. If Lucifer in Heaven and Adam & Eve in the Garden had asked God to remove their power to disobey when tempted by something inside or outside themselves, God would have granted their request. And if they had done so, evil would not have entered Heaven or the Garden. Instead, they gave in to temptation, disobeyed God, and evil entered Heaven and the Garden of Eden.

Nevertheless, since evil has entered the world, God uses the consequent pain and suffering to help show each person the necessity of asking to have their power to disobey removed by being born-again without it.

And when God grants them their request, they will be ushered by God to Paradise.

In Paradise, the person will receive their new body and their renewed soul within the community of saints in the bride of Christ. There they will enjoy living and working for all eternity in the presence of Jesus, within the beatific vision of God and God's glory.

Of course, libertarian freedom in Hades allows a person to remain there and suffer for as long as they would like or request annihilation. And God will grant their request for annihilation, only after doing everything possible to persuade them to forgo making such a decision, but without going so far as to overrule their freewill power to make that decision. But rather than mercilessly allowing the person to continue suffering in Hades forever, God will grant them their request.

As C. S. Lewis said, 'There are only two kinds of people in the end: those who say to God, 'Thy will be done,' and those to whom God says, 'Thy will be done.' (Lewis, Divorce Chap 9)

In the end, people show their love for God by choosing Paradise and Christlikeness, and they show their hatred of God by choosing to remain apart from God in Hades or by choosing annihilation.

A Real Threat to God's Creation Project

Until the finished work of Jesus Christ on the Cross at Calvary, where He saved and secured His bride and His home forever, there was the possibility of a real threat occurring against God's Creation Project due to human disobedience.

"Then the LORD saw that the wickedness of man was great on the earth, and that every intent of the thoughts of his heart was only evil continually. The LORD was sorry that He had made man on the earth, and He was grieved in His heart. ... Then God said to Noah, The end of all flesh has come before Me; for the earth is filled with violence because of them; and behold, I am about to destroy them with the earth. Make for yourself an ark of gopher wood; ... Thus Noah did; according to all that God had commanded him, so he did. ... Then the LORD said to Noah, Enter the ark, you and all your household, for you alone I have seen to be righteous before Me in this time." (Gen 6:5-6,13-14,22,7:1 NASB)

If Noah had not obeyed God by building and entering the Arc, he and his family would have perished, along with the rest of humanity in the Great Flood, and God's CP would have come to an unsuccessful end.

However, Noah obeyed God and survived, and from his offspring came Jesus Christ, the savior of the world, Whose voluntary sacrificial death on a wooden cross assured the success of God's CP.

And who knows, maybe the same can be said of the Israelites in Deut 20:

"Only in the cities of these peoples that the LORD your God is giving you as an inheritance, you shall not leave alive anything that breathes. "But you shall utterly destroy them, the Hittite and the Amorite, the Canaanite and the Perizzite, the Hivite and the Jebusite, as the LORD your God has commanded you, so that they may not teach you to do according to all their detestable things which they have done for their gods, so that you would sin against the LORD your God.
(Deut 20:16-18 NASB*)*

Maybe through their detestable practices, the people in those cities had become physically infected with some disease that would have presented a real threat to the physical survival of Israel, in which case, God's CP would have failed.

It may be noted that Adam & Eve's disobedience to God in the Garden, as horrific and consequential as it was, was not a threat to God's CP since Jesus the Son of Man was willing to sacrifice Himself on the Cross to atone for their disobedience.

However, as a human being, Jesus the Son of Man also had libertarian freedom to obey or disobey God, and He could have failed God in some way during His Incarnation, in which case God's CP would have failed.

"He existed in the form of God, did not regard equality with God a thing to be grasped, but emptied Himself, taking the form of a bond-servant, and being made in the likeness of men. Being found in appearance as a man, He humbled Himself by becoming obedient to the point of death, even death on a cross." (Phil 2:6-8 NASB*)*

Fortunately, Jesus did not fail to obey God in any way, and He completed the work the Father gave Him to accomplish and was obedient to the Father in all things, including obedience to death on a cross.

"... but so that the world may know that I love the Father, I do exactly as the Father commanded Me." (John 14:31 NASB)

"I glorified You on the earth, having accomplished the work which You have given Me to do." (John 17:4 NASB)

And as proof of His perfect obedience, God raised Jesus the Son of Man physically from the dead, and He ascended physically into Heaven.

Therefore, after Christ suffered and died on the Cross, God's CP was assured that Jesus would have His home, from which He and His bride could rule and reign over all creation forever. It would only be a question of who would choose to join the bride and who would choose to remain in Hades or choose annihilation.

Armageddon and the End of the World

In *The Book of Revelation*, God has revealed that this world will come to an end in a place called Armageddon. Does the question come up as to why God will not prevent this from occurring by doing away with the physical bodies of the perpetrators as God did with the evildoers in Noah's time?

The difference is that the destruction of the world at Armageddon is not a threat to God's CP. God's creation project was secured forever through Christ's death on the Cross. Therefore, following Christ's sacrificial death and finished work on the Cross, God will never again need to do away with the physical body of anyone.

A Response to the Existential Problem of Evil

Stated in broad terms, the existential problem of evil addresses questions regarding specific instances of extremely destructive acts of evil happening to anything or anyone, anywhere in the world. In a more narrow sense, what will be addressed here, are those specific instances of painful, destructive events that happen to people.

In general, the evidential problem of evil asks questions from an impersonal, objective standpoint, whereas the existential problem asks questions from a more personal, subjective standpoint. The evidential problem asks: Why are there any painful acts of evil in the world? And the existential problem asks: Why did those specific incidents of evil happen to that specific person or those specific people?

Also, the response should apply to every instance of evil and suffering that has occurred to anyone in history; everyone's tears should be remediated and made right.

In Paradise, God will *'wipe away every tear from their eyes,'* and every person will confirm that it was good to have lived, no matter what horrific instances of evil they may have experienced before Paradise.

"Then I saw a new heaven and a new earth; for the first heaven and the first earth passed away, and there is no longer any sea. And I saw the holy city, new Jerusalem, coming down out of heaven from God, made ready as a bride adorned for her husband. And I heard a loud voice from the throne, saying, … "Behold, the tabernacle of God is among men, and He will dwell among them, and they shall be His people, and God Himself will be among them, and He will wipe away every tear from their eyes; and there will no longer be any death; there will no longer be any mourning, or crying, or pain; the first things have passed away." (Revelations 21:1-4 NASB)

So those in Paradise will have their tears remediated, made right, by being wiped away by God. But what about the tears of those who choose annihilation? How are their tears made right? It might be said these people have, in their own eyes, made right their own tears by choosing to hate God with all their heart, soul, mind, and strength by asking to be annihilated. And they do so by refusing what would make them happy in the end, even against the best efforts of God to convince them to choose Paradise. In the end, those people place more value on their power to hate and disobey God than they do on a happy existence with God in Paradise.

And what happens to the tears of Innocents who suffer and die before being accountable for their choices? For example, the babies who were aborted? The RST theodicy can only imagine that God has made some provision for them in Hades. Perhaps such Innocents will go to Hades and somehow be nurtured there, and grow, and become accountable for their choices. Then, like everyone else, choose between Paradise, annihilation, or remaining in Hades.

For now, in this world, God will help people endure their tears. The tears of resisting temptation and the consequences of their own disobedience and the disobedience of others as they await rescue in Hades and relief in Paradise.

Answers to a Few Common Questions

Here are answers to a few questions often raised by a person suffering pain or experiencing some loss. It is important to state that answers to personal questions of evil, if not carefully reasoned, can seem remote, cold, and heartless to a person who is suffering. Also, such answers are best expressed with sympathy, empathy, and humility by a family member or someone with a pastoral demeanor.

Question 1: Why doesn't God take this pain away from me? I asked Him to!
A1: He would if He could without harming you or someone else as much or more.

Question 2: Why can't God take this pain away from me without harming me or someone else as much or more?
A2: I'm not sure, but it seems that, in some way, all things in this world are closely interconnected, so much so that a change to one person's situation affects the situation of all other people. For now, try to accept that God is doing all God can do to help you.

Question 3: I thought God was all-powerful and could do anything.
A3: God can do almost anything, but He chose to limit some of His inherent power so people can be truly free to love Him.

Question 4: If that is the way God is, then what good is He?
A4: Ask Him that question; that's a good question. Just know that nothing you could ever think, say, or do can change how God thinks and feels about you and how God wants to help you.

Question 5: Why did this happen to me?

A5: I don't know. Sometimes, terrible things happen to us for such complex reasons that we may never be able to understand why. Just know that God did not cause this to happen to you, and God does not favor one person over another or try to help one person more than another. God is always doing everything possible to help you and everyone else at the same time.

Finally, it may carefully be mentioned to the person who is suffering to remember the words of Jesus: ***"These things I have spoken to you, so that in Me you may have peace."*** *(John 16:33* NASB*)*

Distinguishing Features of the RST Theodicy

1) The most distinguishing feature of the RST theodicy is that the souls of all people go to Hades following their physical death to this present world. And in Hades, people retain their libertarian freedom to either obey or disobey God and can choose between staying in Hades, being annihilated, or going to Paradise.

However, before going to Paradise, the person must voluntarily ask God to remove their power to disobey. And God will remove it once the person has fully understood what it means to be born-again without the power to disobey and with only the power to obey God in Paradise.

In Paradise, with a new body and renewed soul, they will be able to freely choose to obey God from among the myriad of ways God has provided for them to obey in Paradise. They will not be like robots or automatons, only obeying predetermined coded instructions but will obey according to their personal desires and interests.

2) Another distinguishing feature of the proposed theodicy is that in Paradise, as people choose to obey God in more and more selfless ways, God will gradually transform them into a likeness of Christ, a personal individual likeness of Christ, but without them ever becoming perfect like Christ.

Other theodicies mention a process of character development taking place before Paradise. They propose that throughout this life and the life to come, people will eventually become unwilling to disobey God, even though they still retain their inherent power to do so, and then God will usher them to Paradise.

RST agrees that character development can occur in this present life and in Hades. However, it does not agree that anyone with the power to disobey God can ever reach a state where it can be assured they will never do so. If a person has the power to disobey, then disobedience to God is always possible. Therefore, no one with the power to disobey God can enter Paradise.

Likewise, obedience to God is always possible. Therefore, anyone can obey God and choose to have their power to disobey Him removed and enter Paradise. No one can remove their power to obey God or put themselves beyond their ability to obey Him, and God will never remove a person's power to obey Him.

Further, RST posits that the state or condition of a person's character, its degree of selflessness, is not a factor when entering Paradise. All that matters is that the person has voluntarily asked God to be born-again by having their power to disobey removed. Then, in Paradise, the person's character will gradually develop toward Christlikeness by making many selfless decisions, regardless of the state of their character when first entering Paradise.

3) Another distinguishing feature of RST is the proposition that people in this world and in Hades demonstrate their love for God in two distinct ways. They demonstrate their love for God by obeying God, and they also demonstrate their love for God by refusing to give in to the temptation to disobey Him.

Therefore, RST emphasizes the value associated with the suffering of temptation. The suffering of temptation to disobey God is ordained by God and is one of the most important things about the makeup of a person; without temptation, people could not demonstrate their love for God by refusing to give in to it.

And people refuse to give in to temptation, to the greatest extent possible, when they freely ask God to remove their power to give in to it. Once a person is born-again without the power to disobey, temptation can no longer affect them, and temptation will have served its purpose.

If Adam & Eve, while being tempted to disobey God in the Garden, had asked God to remove their power to disobey by being born-again without it, they would no longer have been subject to temptation, and evil would not have entered the world.

They would then have proceeded along their own unique personal path of obedience and transformation into their own particular likeness of Christ in the Garden of Eden by obeying God more and more selflessly. Once a person's power to disobey has been removed, all that is necessary for them to continue loving God in Paradise is to obey Him.

4) The complexity of the interconnectedness of all things is emphasized in RST.

"We might think of ourselves as being, in a sense, entangled with everything and everyone else. We are intimately connected to our family, friends, the entire human race, the plant and animal kingdom, the earth, and the cosmos. We affect – and are affected by – everything and everyone else." (1 p. 50)

"Imagine every free decision ever made and continuously being made, by humans and angels, to be a pebble dropped in a pond producing ripples, representing the ongoing effects of these choices, either good or bad. Each ripple affects the pond, and as these ripples interact with other ripples, they create new interference patterns that, in turn, affect other ripples." (1 p. 91)

"History unfolds like a giant weather pattern – innumerable variables affecting the flow of each part, each part affecting the whole, and the whole affecting each part." (1 p. 91)

From the perspective of this complex interconnectedness of all things, everyone influences events everywhere, for good and bad, through their obedience and disobedience to God. No matter how inconsequential the influence of a person's choices for good or for bad may seem, they are not without some effect, especially when joined together with those of others. And these individual effects may be great or small and may affect people and things close and far away.

In particular, RST emphasizes the importance and necessity of each person being born-again by God, unable to affect and influence people and events contrary to God's will in Paradise.

Source:
(1) *The Cosmic Dance*, by Greg Boyd

Conclusion

It is hoped that this theodicy has put forward a plausible, reasonable, justification, and life-satisfying explanation as to why the Omni-perfect God of the Bible permits evil in the very good world God created out of nothing.

From the beginning, it was in the heart of God the Father to provide a home and a bride for God's one and only Son, Jesus, the Son of Man. And to prepare His bride, people needed to be tested to determine their willingness to always obey Jesus and tempted to determine their willingness never to disobey Him.

The only test that a person must pass if they are going to join the bride of Jesus is the test of demonstrating their love for Him by obeying Him and denying themselves their power to disobey Him.

"Then Jesus said to His disciples, **'If anyone wishes to come after Me, he must deny himself, and take up his cross and follow Me. For whoever wishes to save his life will lose it; but whoever loses his life for My sake will find it.** *'" (Matthew 16:24,25* NASB*)*

And people deny themselves this power decisively by asking God to remove it from them, which God will do in Hades following death to this life.

Further, it is hoped that this theodicy can help people now in two ways: first, by encouraging them to ask the Holy Spirit to help them endure the suffering of temptation, as well as help them endure the suffering that comes from evil. And second, by preparing themselves to give up their power to disobey God in Hades. And people can prepare themselves in several ways; however, none is more important than becoming willing to

41

forgive and love their enemies. What could a person do that is more disobedient to God than not being willing to forgive and love their enemies?

If it is the case that death does not absolve anyone of their responsibility to forgive and love others, then today is the day to begin. Only when someone becomes willing to forgive and love their enemies from their heart are they truly ready to have their power to disobey God removed.

Also, this theodicy applies to all people, Christian and non-Christian alike. It is proposed that all people go to Hades following death to this life where they can choose to remain there, request Paradise, or request annihilation. And people choose to love God by asking to be born-again into Paradise without the power to disobey Him, and people choose to hate God by remaining in Hades or asking to be annihilated.

You Must Be Born Again

Even though everyone goes to Hades following death to this life, and there can make a choice for Paradise, it is thought that the advantage of living well in this present life, and then quickly escaping Hades, goes to the Christian.

Christians, more so than others, have been shown from the Bible how they can experience and enjoy the presence of God in this life through prayer, thanksgiving, praise, worship, service to others, and obedience to God. As well as how they can better prepare themselves to give up their power to disobey God and be born-again into Paradise, because Christians should know better than most:

"He has told you, O man, what is good; And what does the LORD require of you" *(Micah 6:8* NASB*)*

"Now there was a man of the Pharisees, named Nicodemus, a ruler of the Jews; this man came to Jesus by night and said to Him, "Rabbi, we know that You have come from God as a teacher; for no one can do these signs that You do unless God is with him." Jesus answered and said to him, **"Truly, truly, I say to you, unless one is born again he cannot see the kingdom of God."** *Nicodemus said to Him, "How can a man be born when he is old? He cannot enter a second time into his mother's womb and be born, can he?" Jesus answered,* **"Truly, truly,**

I say to you, unless one is born of water and the Spirit he cannot enter into the kingdom of God. "That which is born of the flesh is flesh, and that which is born of the Spirit is spirit. "Do not be amazed that I said to you, 'You must be born again.' "The wind blows where it wishes and you hear the sound of it, but do not know where it comes from and where it is going; so is everyone who is born of the Spirit." Nicodemus said to Him, "How can these things be?" Jesus answered and said to him, "Are you the teacher of Israel and do not understand these things? "Truly, truly, I say to you, we speak of what we know and testify of what we have seen, and you do not accept our testimony." (John 3:1-11 NASB)

RST proposes that when God removes a person's power to disobey, they are born-again into Paradise, a new creation, a new type of human being, but this time with only the power to obey God. And they will not be like robots but can obey God in any of the myriads of ways God has made available to them in Paradise, from the least to the most selfless of ways.

Further, it is suggested that being born-again begins when a person believes in their heart that God raised Jesus from the dead and then makes Him the Lord and Savior of their life by requesting and receiving the Holy Spirit.

And then, the born-again process can be completed in Hades when the person fully understands the consequences of God removing their libertarian freewill power to disobey. Once the fully informed person agrees, God will usher them to Paradise with their libertarian freewill power to obey God intact.

Possible Objections to the Conclusion

Objection 1: Philosophers such as Anthony Flew and J. L. Mackie, along with the great theologian and religious reformer Martin Luther, have argued that an omnipotent God should be able to create a world containing only moral good and no immoral evil. And given that a world with no moral evil is like Heaven, Why didn't God create people directly in Heaven and avoid all the pain and suffering in this life?

A1: In a debate, William Lane Craig was asked this question. He responded that it may not have been possible for God to create a meaningful Heaven of free creatures who will not choose against Him, in isolation from an antecedent world such as ours, which has these same free creatures who have already chosen for Him. The latter meaningful situation in Heaven may have been rendered possible by the fact that it was chosen freely in this world first in the face of great temptation.

Objection 2: Since there will be no temptation to disobey God in Paradise, why can't a person keep their freewill power to disobey since they will not be tempted to do so?

A2: It is agreed that there will be no temptation to disobey God in Paradise that comes from outside a person. However, there is still the potential for temptation to come from within them.

Lucifer was not tempted by anything or anyone outside himself in Heaven, but from pride within himself. And like Lucifer, if a person in Paradise has the power to disobey, then the possibility of them giving in to pride and wanting to be like God is always present. Therefore, a person with the power to disobey God cannot be in Paradise.

Objection 3: Won't people who do not have the power to disobey God in Paradise be like robots or automatons and not be real people able to make real choices?

A3: The key to understanding life in Paradise is that once a person has been born-again without the power to disobey God, they still retain their power to obey Him in any way they want.

The power to obey God allows them to choose from among the myriad ways to obey Him in Paradise. Although God will always gently encourage a person to obey in more and more selfless ways, God will never force them to obey in any particular way. People will be free to obey in any way they wish.

Therefore, it is proposed that the never-ending process of a person being transformed into their own particular likeness of Christ takes place in Paradise as the person chooses the more selfless of ways to obey God from among the wide range of selfless ways available.

Likewise, the non-moral will gives a person the power to choose from among what may be an unlimited number of things and activities to do in Paradise which have nothing to do with either obeying or disobeying God. These things and activities are available for the person's enjoyment and well-being, like choosing between peas and carrots for dinner.

Objection 4: Won't life in Paradise eventually become monotonous or boring?

A4: It is expected that people in Paradise will retain their ability to experience love, joy, and happiness, and love, joy, and happiness make no room for boredom or monotony.

Love and joy are the results of a moral lifestyle. They may be experienced when witnessing or achieving selflessness to the point of personal sacrifice and feeling connected spiritually to God and people.

"In Your presence is fullness of joy; In Your right hand there are pleasures forever."
(Psalms 16:11 NASB*)*

Happiness is based on outward circumstances; happiness can be experienced from any good thing or activity.

"Things which eye has not seen and ear has not heard, and which have not entered the heart of man, all that God has prepared for those who love Him."
(1 Cor 2:9 NASB*)*

And since a person's transformation into a likeness of Christ in Paradise is asymptotic, it is conceivable that their capacity to experience love, joy, and happiness may also increase asymptotically toward the perfect love, joy, and happiness known by Jesus Christ.

Objection 5: There are many sayings of Jesus in the Bible that strongly suggest that people who confess Jesus as their Lord and Savior in this present life are assured of eternal life later in Paradise, with no other decision required on their part following death. Here are a few of these sayings:

"For God so loved the world that He gave His only begotten Son, that whoever believes in Him should not perish but have everlasting life." (John 3:16 NASB)

"He who believes in the Son has everlasting life;" (John 3:36a NASB)

"Truly, truly, I say to you, he who hears My word, and believes Him who sent Me, has eternal life, and does not come into judgment, but has passed out of death into life." (John 5:24 NASB)

"And this is the will of Him who sent Me, that everyone who sees the Son and believes in Him may have everlasting life;" (John 6:40 NASB)

"... but these are written that you may believe that Jesus is the Christ, the Son of God, and that believing you may have life in His name." (John 20:31 NASB)

A5: These sayings would seem to conflict with the main idea of RST that eternal life in Paradise will only come following the fully informed decision of a person in Hades to be born-again by having their power to disobey God removed by God. After which, God will usher them to Paradise. However, this conflict may be resolved if the following can be accepted.

a) Believing in Jesus and being saved by Him requires more than a person's approval and agreement with what He said and did, and more than asking and receiving Him into their life as Lord and Savior. Such are required for salvation but are not sufficient.

b) Believing in Jesus also requires a person's obedience to Him by laying down their life for Him.

c) Repentance, a person changing their mind, changing the direction of their life for the better, and sincere regret and remorse for bad choices made are essential for growth in Christlikeness. However, they are insufficient when it comes to laying down their life for Christ.

d) The only way a person can decisively lay down their life for Jesus and be fit and ready for Paradise is to be born-again without the power to disobey Him.

If these propositions can be accepted, then all that remains for people who have confessed Christ in this present life to enter Paradise is to lay down their life for Him, as mentioned in the following scriptures.

"… but he who does not obey the Son will not see life," (John 3:36b NASB*)*

"He who loves his life loses it, and he who hates his life in this world will keep it to life eternal." *(John 12:25* NASB*)*

"Greater love has no one than this, than to lay down one's life for his friends. You are My friends if you do what I command you." *(John 15:13,14* NASB*)*

"One thing you lack: Go your way, sell whatever you have and give to the poor, and you will have treasure in heaven; and come, take up the cross, and follow Me." *(Mark 10:21* NASB*)*

"Then Jesus said to His disciples, 'If anyone wishes to come after Me, he must deny himself, and take up his cross and follow Me. For whoever wishes to save his life will lose it; but whoever loses his life for My sake will find it.' " *(Matthew 16:24,25* NASB*)*

And RST proposes that people in Hades, following death to this present life, can deny themselves, take up their cross, and follow Him by asking God to remove their power to disobey Him.

Objection 6: If a person believes they can go to Paradise when they die, no matter how they live their life in this world, wouldn't this encourage people to live selfishly now and even encourage suicide to get to Hades quickly, so that they can then quickly request to be born-again to Paradise?

A6: It is thought that the most difficult and most selfless decision a fully informed person can ever make is to lay down their life for God by asking God to remove their power to disobey Him.

"Simon Peter said to Him, "Lord, where are You going?" Jesus answered, **"Where I go, you cannot follow Me now; but you will follow later."** *Peter said to Him, "Lord, why can I not follow You right now? I will lay down my life for*

You." Jesus answered, **"Will you lay down your life for Me? Truly, truly, I say to you, a rooster will not crow until you deny Me three times. "** *(John 13:36-38* NASB*)*

"Peter said to Him, "Even if I have to die with You, I will not deny You." All the disciples said the same thing too." (Matthew 26:35 NASB*)*

And yet, Peter denied knowing Jesus, and the other disciples deserted Him. If it was difficult for Peter and the other disciples to lay down their physical life for Jesus at that time, it might also be difficult for others to lay down their life of disobedience for Him.

And the longer it takes for a person in Hades to lay down their life of disobedience for Him, the more pain and suffering they will have to witness and endure by being present there. Therefore, living selfishly now may not well prepare a person to make the most selfless of all decisions of laying down their life, their power to disobey God, in Hades.

As for encouraging suicide, it may be that suicide can be either a selfish or selfless act. The more selfless the act the more prepared the person will be to selflessly lay down their life for Him in Hades, and more quickly avoid the pain and suffering present there. But the more selfish the act, the more pain and suffering they may have to endure in Hades before they are ready to make the most selfless decision a person can ever make of laying down their life for God by asking Him to o remove their power to disobey Him.

Objection 7: If a person believes they can go to Paradise when they die, no matter how they live their life in this world, might this remove a moral restraint to killing another person?

A7: Like suicide, the killing of another person may be either a selfish or selfless act. The more selfless the act the more prepared the person may be to lay down their own life for Jesus in Hades. But the more selfish the act the more pain and suffering they most assuredly will have to endure in Hades before they are ready to lay down their own life, their power to disobey God. And no one should underestimate the pain and suffering a person may have to endure in Hades before selflessly laying down their own life after selfishly taking the life of another.

Objection 8: Is it possible for a person to be born into this world with a defect that prevents them from making a fully informed rational decision regarding their future?

A8: Although that may be possible, it may also be possible for God to heal or correct that person's defect in this world or in Hades, restoring them to proper working order and enabling them to make a rational, fully informed decision between remaining in Hades, going to Paradise, or being annihilated.

Objection 9: Didn't God overrule the libertarian freedom of the evildoers in Noah's time by destroying them in the Great Flood?

A9: God did destroy the physical bodies of those evildoers, but not their souls and not their libertarian freedom to either obey or disobey God. God took the extraordinary measure of destroying their bodies and sending their souls to Hades because of their extreme and widespread disobedience, which posed a real threat to God's CP.

However, God did not overrule or revoke their libertarian freedom. The souls of those evildoers went to Hades with their freewill power to obey or disobey God intact. In Hades, following the atoning work of Jesus Christ, they could freely decide where they wanted to go.

Following the Atonement, where Jesus saved and secured His bride forever, under no circumstance will God ever again need to take a person's physical life. People today remain free to disobey God without fearing God. It was only before the Atonement, before God's CP was assured, that people should have feared God when tempted to disobey Him.

Objection 10: If God is already doing everything possible to help everyone, everywhere, what is the purpose of prayer?

A10: It is good for people to pray for others and themselves. In prayer, people can have their most profound communion with God. In prayer, people can hear and understand how they can cooperate and co-labor with God to help others and help themselves as well. And from the Sermon on the Mount:

"Pray, then, in this way: 'Our Father who is in heaven, Hallowed be Your name. 'Your kingdom come. Your will be done, On earth as it is in heaven. 'Give us this day our daily bread. 'And forgive us our debts, as we also have forgiven our debtors. 'And do not lead us into temptation, but deliver us from evil. [For Yours is the kingdom and the power and the glory forever. Amen.'] "For if you forgive others for their transgressions, your heavenly Father will also forgive you. "But if you do not forgive others, then your Father will not forgive your transgressions. " (Matthew 6:9-15 NASB)

Objection 11: Why does a person have to wait until Hades to have their freewill power to disobey God removed? Why can't it be removed from them now in this world, and then God usher them to Paradise?

A11: This is a good question that RST struggles to answer. Nevertheless, here is RST's best effort.

The Bible records two instances of God translating someone to Heaven without them first dying physically in this world, Enoch and Elija. So, it may be possible, although seemingly rare, for a person to go to Heaven/Paradise directly from this life.

One possible reason for this rarity might be that it takes time and circumstances in this world for a person to come to the point of asking God to remove their libertarian freewill power to disobey. And then time and circumstances for God to fully inform them of the consequences of making such a decision, and then even more time for personal deliberation. Such time and circumstances may be more available in Hades than in this world.

Nevertheless, given Enoch and Elija, the possibility of God removing a person's power to disobey Him in this world and then ushering them to Paradise, born-again a new creation, can not be discounted.

However, removing a person's power to disobey and then leaving them in this world may not be as reasonable. In that case, the world would seem untenably asymmetric, with some unable to disobey God and others able to.

Comparison of Theodicies

The proposed RST theodicy has elements found in both Augustinian and Irenaean type theodicies and elements not found in either.

1) What Does It Mean To Be Born Again?

The term **'born again'** is taken from what Jesus said to Nicodemus in John 3. However, it is first alluded to by the apostle John in John 1,

"He came to His own, and those who were His own did not receive Him. But as many as received Him, to them He gave the right to become children of God, even to those who believe in His name, who were born, not of blood nor of the will of the flesh nor of the will of man, but of God." (John 1:12-13 NASB)

Then Jesus discusses the necessity of being born-again with Nicodemus, a Jewish Pharisee, a ruler, and the teacher of Isreal:

"Now there was a man of the Pharisees, named Nicodemus, a ruler of the Jews; this man came to Jesus by night and said to Him, "Rabbi, we know that You have come from God as a teacher; for no one can do these signs that You do unless God is with him." Jesus answered and said to him, **"Truly, truly, I say to you, unless one is born again he cannot see the kingdom of God."** *Nicodemus said to Him, "How can a man be born when he is old? He cannot enter a second time into his mother's womb and be born, can he?" Jesus answered,* **"Truly, truly, I say to you, unless one is born of water and the Spirit he cannot enter into the kingdom of God."** *(John 3:1-5* NASB)

The traditional Jewish understanding of the promise of salvation is interpreted as being rooted in 'the seed of Abraham,' the physical lineage from Abraham. Jesus explained to Nicodemus that this doctrine was not correct, that every person must have two births, a natural birth of the physical body (water) and another of the spirit. This discourse with Nicodemus established the Christian belief that all human beings must be born-again of the spiritual seed of Christ to enter the Kingdom of God. (In part from A Bible Dictionary by Samuel B. Emmons)

In RST, it is conjectured that a person being born-again is a process. The person is first involuntarily born into this world with the power to disobey God. And having this power is necessary so that the person can show their love for Him by not disobeying Him when tempted to do so.

Then, in this world or in Hades, the person with a heartfelt desire to stop disobeying God will ask for and receive the Holy Spirit into their life, thereby freely initiating the born-again process by being conceived as a new eternal person within the old temporal person.

Following this conception of the new person within the old, there is a period of gestation. During this period, the person can make marked character improvement and come to understand what it might be like to live in Paradise with only the power to obey God and without the power to disobey Him.

Then, in Hades, following the person's agreement and fully informed understanding of what it means to no longer have the power to disobey God, God will complete the born-again process. They will be born-again a new eternal person with a new eternal body and renewed soul in Paradise, without the power to disobey. Old things have passed away, and all things have become new.

The witness in this world of a caterpillar being born-again into a butterfly is the proverbial example of this process.

Augustinian and Irenaean theologies typically understand being born-again as something that occurs through water baptism when the person makes a public declaration of their faith in Jesus as the Christ, and then God gives them His Spirit.

RST agrees that such an understanding can be the beginning of the born-again process but not the end. It may be how and when the conception of the new person within the old occurs. And where a new life principle is now at work in the person, influencing them in the direction of Christlikeness, self-sacrificial love, service to others, humility, and all the Fruit of the Spirit.

However, in RST, the birthing, the completion of the born-again process, begins in Hades, following the person's fully informed decision to have their libertarian power to disobey God removed. Then they are ushered by God to Paradise, a fully formed new creation with their new body and renewed soul, where maturation toward Christlikeness continues in earnest without the distraction and hindrance of disobedience.

2) Human Freedom, Human Freewill

Augustinian and Irenaean theologians and theodicies subscribe to the notions of determinism (Calvinism, Reformed Theology) and compatibilism (Molinism, Arminian Theology) and reject the notion of libertarian freedom to which RST subscribes.

Libertarian freedom holds that humans can act and choose freely as independent, autonomous beings, regardless of any external or internal forces acting on them. An effective definition of libertarian freedom is that people can freely act differently and choose otherwise at every moment.

Most significant is the libertarian argument that prior events and choices do not completely determine anyone's current choices; they may influence them greatly, but they do not cause them with absolute certainty. Libertarian freedom posits that people can choose independently of forces acting internally or externally on them, whereas determinists argue that people's choices are, in fact, entirely determined by such forces.

Compatibilism attempts to combine libertarianism and determinism. It argues that libertarian freedom and a deterministic universe can be compatible. The main reason behind this approach is the attempt to reconcile the scientific evidence for causality with human moral responsibility.

As originally understood, the scientific principle of causality seems to call into question the idea of any moral responsibility for choices people make. If people are not free to choose otherwise in the moment of choosing, why should they be held responsible for those choices? Whereas, with libertarian freedom, people can freely choose otherwise in the moment and therefore can rightly be held responsible for their choices.

Both determinism and compatibilism hinge on the scientific principle of causality as scientists originally understood it. However, the scientific principle of causality has changed over time.

As initially understood in Classical Newtonian physics, the principle of causality is generally regarded as deterministic or causal, where complete knowledge of the past and present allows for a complete and comprehensive understanding of the future.

However, modern Quantum physics introduced genuine uncertainty into physics and, therefore, uncertainty regarding the future. Given complete knowledge of the past and present, only approximate and probabilistic predictions of the future are possible.

Experiment after experiment has shown that Nature works according to the rules of Quantum physics. Suppose this modern view of physics can be accepted. In that case, the scientific principle of causation might not undermine the notion of libertarian freedom but instead, support it.

RST posits a libertarian view of human freewill, human freedom, which is incompatible with determinism or compatibilism and therefore differs from both Augustinian and Irenaean type theodicies.

Further, it is proposed in RST that the human libertarian freewill is tripartite, consisting of three mutually exclusive parts or modes of operation. There is the obedient freewill, the disobedient freewill, and the non-moral freewill, with each part operating independently of the other two.

3) Greater-Good Type Theodicies

Augustinian and Irenaean type theodicies are types of greater-good theodicies. They state that God permits and even ordains the suffering from evil to bring about something good in people's lives, a good that He could not have brought about without that evil suffering.

The proposed RST theodicy may also be considered a greater-good type theodicy, but with an important distinction. There is a good thing that suffering from evil can help bring about in people's lives, but that kind of suffering was not necessary to achieve that good thing.

If Adam & Eve had obeyed God when suffering temptation in the Garden and had requested their freewill power to disobey God be removed, the suffering from evil would not have entered the world. But now that evil is here, God uses it, along with the suffering of temptation, to help people realize that before entering Paradise, they must be born-again without the power to disobey Him.

"Jesus answered and said to him, **"Truly, truly, I say to you, unless one is born again he cannot see the kingdom of God."** *(John 3:3* NASB*)*

4) Soul-Making vs. Soul-Deciding

Augustinian type theodicies are considered soul-deciding theodicies, where people make one (or a few) essential decisions for Christ in this present life to be saved to Paradise when they die. Decisions, such as being baptized and,

"… if you confess with your mouth Jesus as Lord, and believe in your heart that God raised Him from the dead, you will be saved; for with the heart a person believes, resulting in righteousness, and with the mouth he confesses, resulting in salvation." *(Romans 10:9,10* NASB*)*

Conversely, people who do not make such decisions in this life end up in a literal Hell and suffer there forever.

Irenaean type theodicies are considered soul-making theodicies. Jesus became a person so that people could become like Him. Eventually, everyone's soul or character will be perfected by God to be like Jesus in Paradise by making many morally correct decisions throughout this life and, probably, in the life or lives to come to receive the Grace of God.

The RST theodicy is both a soul-deciding and a soul-making theodicy. At some point in this life or Hades, people may come to realize that they cannot refrain from disobeying God and enter Paradise, no matter how hard they try. At that point, they can decide (soul-deciding) to ask Jesus into their life to help them obey God, and the born-again process commences.

Then in Hades, they can ask God to complete the born-again process by removing their power to disobey, and God will grant their request and usher them to Paradise. In Paradise, with their freewill power to obey God intact, a person's soul or character will continue developing toward the perfection of Christ (soul-making), but without ever becoming perfect like Christ.

Or, when in Hades, instead of choosing to be born-again, people can request and receive annihilation. Or make no decision and remain there for as long as they want. However, it is thought that at some point, Hades will be empty of souls in that everyone will eventually want to escape the suffering present there and choose either Paradise or annihilation, with almost everyone choosing Paradise.

5) Is There a Literal Eternal Place Called Hell?

Irenaean theodicies do not believe in a literal place called Hell, but they believe in the idea of Hell. The idea of Hell spurs people on to obey God and Christlikeness. However, Augustinian theodicies do posit the existence of a literal eternal place called Hell, which was prepared for the devil and bad angels. And people who have refused to accept Jesus in this present life will be sent there and suffer forever.

The RST theodicy, like Augustine, accepts the existence of a literal eternal place called Hell, which was created for the devil and bad angels, however, people are never sent there. Instead, RST posits the existence of a place called Hades, often referred to by Jesus, and where it is thought Jesus went temporarily upon His death on the Cross.

"Therefore it says, "WHEN HE ASCENDED ON HIGH, HE LED CAPTIVE A HOST OF CAPTIVES, AND HE GAVE GIFTS TO MEN." (Now this expression, "He ascended," what does it mean except that He also had descended into the lower parts of the earth? He who descended is Himself also He who ascended far above all the heavens, so that He might fill all things.)" (Ephesians 4:8-10 NASB)

So Hades is thought to be where the souls of Adam & Eve went following their disobedience to God and physical death in the Garden, and where the souls of all people go following their physical death in this world.

6) Who Is Responsible for the Origin of Evil?

The proposed RST theodicy does not agree with either the Augustinian or Irenaean type theodicies in their modern advanced form. They both accept that God has ordained suffering from evil and is ultimately responsible for it but cannot be blamed since suffering is essential to bring about good things and Christlikeness in people's lives.

On the contrary, the proposed RST theodicy relieves God of all responsibility for the origin and existence of evil in the world, placing that blame squarely on Adam & Eve in the Garden of Eden. It is conjectured that God had explained to Adam & Eve, even before they gave in to temptation, that they could escape the suffering of temptation and any possibility of disobedience to Him by being born-again without the power to disobey. However, they selfishly and willfully chose to reject God's offer of escape, wanting instead to be like God and do whatever they wanted.

7) Are There Gratuitous Evils?

The proposed RST theodicy partially agrees with Augustinian and Irenaean theodicies regarding gratuitous evil. RST agrees that there are no gratuitous or pointless evils; however, it differs significantly in its reasoning.

The traditional greater-good type theodicies accept that God can bring something good out of any evil, even though they often cannot specify with satisfaction the exact nature of the good that would justify that evil.

RST states that all evil serves the primary, singular good purpose of bringing people to the realization that they must ask God that they be born-again without the power to disobey, thereby removing them as a source of evil.

Of course, other good things may sometimes occur by chance from an evil act. Still, these are accidental or incidental and can often distract from the primary good by providing a false explanation or justification for the evil.

It is difficult for traditional greater-good theodicies to provide a satisfying reasonable justification for William Rowe's fawn suffering a horrible death in a forest fire or Ivan Karamazov's tortured children. What conceivable satisfying good could justify either example of suffering?

However, from the perspective of RST, all such evil incidents point to the abuse of human freewill power to disobey God. Therefore, the only solution to every kind of evil is for every human to voluntarily have their freewill power to disobey God removed by God by being born-again into Paradise without it.

Therefore, the seemingly ever-present witness of seemingly senseless evil and suffering in the world today should be an ever-present blaring and blazing warning and reminder that *'all have sinned' (Romans 3:23)*, and everyone contributes to evil and suffering and needs to have their power to disobey God removed.

8) Is There Freewill in Paradise?

The traditional greater-good type theodicies of Augustine and Irenaeus propose that a person can be present in Paradise with their freewill power to disobey God intact. They posit that without the power to disobey God, a person cannot genuinely love Him; therefore, the power to disobey Him must be present in Paradise.

Some Augustinians address this question by postulating an afterlife in Purgatory for those who do not immediately go to Hell. Those entering Purgatory atone for their sins, making them eligible for Paradise. And even though they retain their power to disobey God in Paradise, they will never do so.

For Irenaean theodicies, as a person's character matures, they will gradually disobey God less and less. Eventually, everyone's character will be fully mature and perfect like Christ in Paradise and never again disobey. And although different in important ways, this is not dissimilar from ideas espoused by Eastern religions and Darwinian Evolutionary Process theologians.

For RST, any person with the power to disobey God is a potential source of evil and cannot be trusted never to disobey. Therefore, any person with the power to disobey cannot be present in Paradise. However, people in Paradise retain their power to obey and love God in any of the myriad ways God has provided.

Notably, in RST, the state of a person's character, their degree of selflessness, is not a factor for entry into Paradise. Once in Paradise, without the power to disobey, everyone's character will progress toward Christlike selflessness, regardless of the state of their character upon first entering.

9) Does God Have Complete Meticulous Knowledge of the Future?

Traditional Christian theodicies specify that God has meticulous, exhaustive knowledge of everything, past, present, and future. And God has this knowledge of the future by providentially determining everything about it.

Determinism is the doctrine that all future states of existence are completely and precisely determined by the present state of existence, acted upon by unchangeable moral and physical laws, and guided providentially by God down to the smallest detail with no possibility of human libertarian intervention. Therefore, human libertarian freedom is incompatible with the doctrine of determinism, as understood in Calvinism and Reformed Theology.

Another view is that God has this perfect knowledge of the future because God knew beforehand precisely what freewill choices people would make in any given future situation or circumstance. Then, with that knowledge, God providentially arranges all situations and circumstances to achieve a world with the best of all possible freewill outcomes, making this present world the best of all possible worlds where people have freewill. This attempts to make determinism compatible with libertarian freedom, as understood in Arminianism and Molinism.
(See: Addendum 15 - Another Argument Against Molinism p. 308)

The proposed RST theodicy disagrees with both Calvinism and Molinism. In both cases, people do not have the libertarian freedom necessary to obey or not obey God, to love or not love God, no matter what mental exercises its proponents go through to try and prove otherwise.

Instead, the proposed RST theodicy takes the more easily understood approach. God used omnipotence and intelligence to create a world over which He has meticulous, exhaustive knowledge of both the past and present, but not the future. To suggest that God cannot create such a world questions God's omnipotence and intelligence to do so. And modern Quantum physics may support this idea.
(See: Addendum 11 The Future Has Not Been Decided p. 292)

In such a world, people have real and meaningful libertarian freedom to fulfill God's highest calling of loving Him with all their heart, soul, mind, and strength by obeying and not disobeying Him. Without libertarian freedom and the real possibility of choosing not to love God, people cannot genuinely choose to love Him.

Therefore, maybe it was more important to God that people could freely and genuinely choose to love Him than for Him to have meticulous knowledge of everyone's future choices. If God would like to know people's future choices with absolute certainty, then, of course, God could. Therefore, maybe it is not a question of what God is able to know about the future, but instead, what God can choose to know.

RST agrees that God knows all that there is to know about all that exists in the present or has ever existed in the past and is, in that sense, omniscient. However, the future does not yet exist and is therefore unknowable even by God, as purposed by God.

10) Was Evil Inevitable or Essential for the Success of God's CP?

Traditional greater-good type theodicies imply, or state directly, that evil was inevitable, even essential, and even that God ordained evil for God's CP to be successful.

The proposed RST theodicy does not agree with that idea. If Adam & Eve had asked God to be born-again without the power to disobey before giving in to temptation, God would have granted their request, and evil would not have entered the world. And since only Adam & Eve were given rulership of the world, not their children, only they had it to give away. Therefore, evil was not inevitable or essential for God's CP to be successful, in that God provided Adam & Eve with the way to escape temptation and evil. *(1 Cor 10:13)*

11) Was Temptation Inevitable or Essential for the Success of God's CP?

Traditional greater-good type theodicies tend to discuss the suffering of temptation in passing, focusing instead on the suffering resulting from giving in to temptation, which is evil.

However, the proposed RST theodicy focuses on the suffering of temptation itself, which is inevitable and essential to determine who would want to be included in the bride of Christ through love and obedience to God. Love and obedience to Him, not only by resisting temptation, because they cannot always be trusted to do so, but by freely denying themselves their power to disobey by asking to have it removed.

Therefore, God did ordain temptation, which is inevitable and essential for the success of God's CP.

"Woe to the world because of its stumbling blocks! For it is inevitable that stumbling blocks come; but woe to that man through whom the stumbling block comes!" *(Matthew 18:7* NASB*)*

People can struggle mightily and suffer greatly in mind, body, and soul when resisting the temptation to be impatient, unkind, unfaithful, unloving, and so forth; witness Jesus in the Wilderness and in the Garden of Gethsemane.

This theodicy attempts to bring to people's attention what is proposed to be the way God has provided for them to escape and be free from temptation and sin by freely asking to be born-again without the power to disobey Him, and then enter Paradise.

12) Paths to Paradise

In the Irenaean type theodicy, Adam & Eve are not considered to have been literal historical figures. In this type of theodicy, people have always been created as infant children whose character gradually matures through the crucible of evil. Thus the importance and value of evil provided by God; without evil, people would not try to escape its suffering by choosing to obey God and mature toward the perfection of Christ.

Therefore, in this way, Irenaean type theodicies are optimistic about the future in that eventually everyone will become perfect like Christ. However, these theodicies stand against libertarian freedom in that no person can freely choose against becoming perfect like Christ.

Since no one can freely choose not to become perfect like Christ, this begs, Why did God not create everyone directly like Christ in Paradise to begin with, and avoid all the pain and suffering in this present world? In this case, the best that might be said is that people would have freely chosen the way to be perfected, even if they could not choose not to be perfected.

Still, if a person cannot choose against God's will by not becoming perfect like Christ, then they are not truly free in the libertarian sense, and their power to love God is limited to only being able to obey Him. They cannot love Him by freely choosing to deny themselves their power to disobey Him.

Then is this Irenaean outcome not in some way the same as that proposed by RST, where everyone in Paradise can only obey God?

In RST, God could not create a Paradise of free people who will not choose against Him without them first having chosen for Him. And they chose for Him first in Hades by asking to have their power to disobey removed. The latter situation in Paradise was only possible because of what was freely chosen first in Hades.

In Augustinian type theodicies, a literal, historical Adam & Eve were created as adults who could choose to either obey or disobey God. And all they had to do to remain in the Paradise of the Garden of Eden was never disobey God. However, Adam & Eve disobeyed God and died, and their progeny, created as infant children, were tainted, unable to fully obey God, which came to be known as Original Sin.

And following physical death, they would all have to await the Atonement and their redemption by Jesus Christ. Since the Atonement, those who decide for Christ in this life are saved to Paradise through Purgatory, and those who do not will be lost forever in Hell.

Augustinian type theodicies posit God's strong providential influence and control over creation and people, which does not support the idea of genuine libertarian freedom. Also, they are pessimistic about the future, in that not everyone will be saved.

The proposed RST theodicy also considers Adam & Eve to have been literal historical people, created in the image of God in the Garden of Eden; male and female God created them with libertarian freedom.

If Adam & Eve had asked God to remove their power to disobey Him, they could have remained in the Garden. However, they disobeyed God and died physically, and their souls went to Hades with their libertarian freedom intact. And ever since then, when people die, their soul goes to Hades.

Following C. S. Lewis, the gates of Hades are locked on the inside. To escape Hades and go to Paradise, people can ask for and receive the removal of their power to disobey God by being born-again into Paradise without it. Also, because people in Hades have libertarian freedom, they can remain there for as long as they would like or request and receive annihilation.

Those who decide for Paradise follow the gradual character development trajectory of Irenaean theodicies. The difference is that in RST, people in Paradise can only approach but never reach the perfect selfless character of Christ. These proved their love for Him in this world and in Hades by resisting disobedience and, more importantly, by asking that their power to disobey Him be removed.

In RST, because of the finished atoning work of Christ on the Cross, everyone has the libertarian freedom to choose the final destination of their life. In this way, RST is very optimistic about the future, as it is thought almost everyone will eventually choose Paradise over remaining in Hades or annihilation. And importantly, for true love to exist, RST upholds the importance and necessity of people having genuine libertarian freedom to choose if they want to love God, or not.

In the end, people show their love for God by choosing Paradise and Christlikeness, and they show their hatred of God by choosing to remain apart from God in Hades or by choosing annihilation.

13) Arminian Type Theodicies

The proposed RST theodicy both agrees and disagrees with Arminian theology and theodicy:
RST agrees that evil is not essential to bring about good.
RST disagrees that there are gratuitous evils.
RST disagrees that God knows the future, as in Molinism.
RST disagrees that God might inflict punishment for sin.
RST disagrees that there was no temptation in Heaven.
RST agrees that God graciously enables depraved and corrupt sinners to respond to the grace of God, and the name of that response is faith.

14) Wesleyan Type Theodicies

The proposed RST theodicy does not agree with John Wesley (1703-1791) and Methodism, where God permits evil to bring forth a fuller manifestation of His glory than could have been achieved otherwise.

This concept, O Felix Culpa, O Fortunate Fault, is paradoxical. It looks at the fortunate consequence of an unfortunate event, which would never have been possible if not for the unfortunate event in the first place.

The fortunate consequence is the bringing forth of a fuller manifestation of God's great glory to humanity. The unfortunate event is the suffering, tortured life and death of Jesus Christ.

However, RST disagrees that the suffering life and death of Jesus Christ was the only or best way that a fuller manifestation of God's great glory could be revealed to humanity.

"The heavens are telling of the glory of God; And their expanse is declaring the work of His hands." (Psalm 19:1 NASB*)*

"For since the creation of the world His invisible attributes, His eternal power and divine nature, have been clearly seen, being understood through what has been made, so that they are without excuse." (Romans 1:20 NASB*)*

"Father, glorify Your name." *Then a voice came out of heaven: "I have both glorified it, and will glorify it again." (John 12:28* NASB*)*

These Scriptures aside, the human inability to conceive of another way for God to reveal a fuller manifestation of His great glory to humanity does not mean there is no other way. People have no good reason to think that finite human minds can grasp all the ways in which God could manifest His great glory.

Therefore, it is proposed that God, with His infinite wisdom, intelligence, and omnipotence, has the means of manifesting His great glory to humanity without torturing to death on a wooden cross the Human Nature of His one and only Son of Man, Jesus Christ.

Also, the proposed RST theodicy does not agree with Wesley's Universalism that, in the end, God will save everyone to Paradise. RST does agree that all who want to be saved will be saved, but some may insist on not being saved, which libertarian freedom allows. Libertarian freedom allows for annihilation, which God will grant a person following their well-informed, insistent, and most sincere request, rather than mercilessly consigning them to endure endless suffering in Hades.

15) Process Theology and Theodicy

The more recent development of Process Theology, and the associated Process Theodicy, although a derivative of Irenaeanism, presents a challenge to both the Irenaean and Augustinian positions.

As presented by Augustine, freewill is considered incompatible with divine omniscience. Humans cannot have freewill if God is omniscient. If God is truly omniscient, He will know infallibly what people will do, meaning they cannot be free to do otherwise.

Also, since God created all things ex nihilo, out of nothing, original sin, as conceived by Augustine, must itself be sourced in God, rendering any punishment unjust. And Irenaean soul-making theodicies, which suppose that God inflicts pain on people for His own good ends, and the good ends of people, is regarded as immoral.

The Process Doctrine proposes that God is benevolent and feels the world's pain (both physically and emotionally) but suggests that His power is restricted to persuasion and so is unable to prevent certain evil events from occurring.

Ultimately, God is not omnipotent. Not that He limits Himself in some way for the sake of His creation, but His power is limited in a metaphysical sense; God has all the power it is possible for Him to have.

Process Theology accepts God's indirect responsibility for evil but maintains that He is blameless since He does everything within His limited power to prevent it. However, in the end, because of God's goodness, perseverance, and persuasiveness, all will be saved to Paradise.

However, some process theologians hold a more nuanced view of God's power. For them, the process deity is not even a personal being and therefore does not resemble the God of the Bible as understood by the community of faith. And although different in important ways, this nuanced view is similar to the Natura naturans form of atheism.

Natura naturans is natural creative power. Natural creative power is a universal; as such, it is an abstract object. This power is natural, immanent, ultimate, and thus at work in every natural thing. For religious naturalists, it is an atheistic concept of the divine; it is an atheistic concept of the sacred or holy.

Natural creative power is not the theistic deity and certainly not the Christian or Abrahamic God. After all, any theistic deity is a thing, a particular, while natural creative power is a universal, it is not a particular. As the ultimate immanent power of being, natural creative power is being-itself. It is being-as-being, the power of existence itself, the power to be rather than to not be.

The existence of being-itself is certainly consistent with natural science. It's obviously not supernatural and fits perfectly well into the scientific study of the nature of reality. The same line of reasoning that justifies the existence of scientific universals, like energy, mass, and charge, can be extended to justify the existence of an abstract power like being-itself.

The existence of natural creative power is hardly a radical idea. Being-itself is simply what all beings have in common. If you affirm that many distinct beings exist, then you also affirm that they have existence in common; they all share existence, being-itself, as their ultimate universal or power of being.

Natural creative power participates in explanatory relations: Why is there something rather than nothing? Because the natural creative power of being must be; it cannot fail to create; it necessarily generates.

Natural creative power is not a thing; therefore, it is not a god. But it is holy, sacred, and divine. Atheists are not prohibited from affirming the existence of holy, sacred, or divine powers. Religious naturalists revere and admire natural creative power, especially as it manifests in the myriad forms of life on earth.

Theologically, RST is about as far away as one can get from Process Theology and Theodicy.

"And Jesus said to them,
"Render to Caesar the things that are Caesar's, and to God the things that are God's. " *(Mark 12:17* NASB*)*

In the same way,
"Render to Science the things that are Science, and to God the things that are God's."

(See: Addendum 3 The Family of God p. 258
Addendum 4 The Genders of God p. 259
Addendum 5 Jesus The Son of Man p. 260
Addendum 6 The Personhood of God p. 262
Addendum 16 Process Theology p. 312
Addendum 17 Theodicy in Process Theology p. 319
Addendum 18 When Did Sin Begin in Process Theology? p. 333)

Additional Remarks

It is not sufficient for a person to demonstrate their love for another by only stating a willingness to lay down their life for them. For a person to demonstrate their love for another decisively, they must freely lay down their life for them in the most meaningful way possible.

It is proposed that the most meaningful way for a person to love and lay down their life for God is to freely ask Him that they be born-again without the power to disobey Him this time. For a person to lay down their power to disobey God is a far more meaningful demonstration of love than laying down any other part of their life for Him, including laying down their physical body.

It also seems that God the Father first demonstrated His love for humanity by denying Himself the ability to have exhaustive meticulous knowledge of the future. And it is thought that God did this so that human beings, including Jesus the Son of Man, could genuinely and meaningfully be free to choose to love Him in return, or not.

Even though this sacrifice was a sufficient demonstration of God's great love for humanity, to make it even more clear, it was followed by the voluntary incarnation and sacrificial death of Jesus Christ, the Son of Man. And it only seems right that God the Father would not have asked His Son to sacrifice something of Himself without Him first sacrificing something of Himself.

God the Father asked Jesus to lay down His physical life to atone for and rescue humankind from disobedience. But first, the Father laid down His ability to foreknow the future so that His Son Jesus, and all humanity, could have genuine libertarian freedom to love Him in return, or not.

"Father, glorify Your name." *Then a voice came out of heaven: "I have both glorified it, and will glorify it again." (John 12:28* NASB)

What makes the sacrifice of God's knowledge of the future even more admirable is that He did so without the assurance that Jesus, the Son of Man, would succeed in His mission of always being obedient and never disobedient to Him. Given that Jesus, the Son of Man *'being made in the likeness of men' (Phil 2:7)*, also had libertarian freedom, He could have disobeyed God or failed to obey Him in some way during His incarnation.

Therefore, God's Creation Project was at risk of failure by the Father making it possible for Jesus the Son of Man to fail Him. And if the Son of Man had failed God in any way, God's CP would have failed, and all humanity would have been lost, including the Human Nature of Jesus, the Son of Man. But the Divine Nature of Jesus, the Son of God, would not have been lost.

A sacrificial act of love for another to attain the highest level of admiration must involve the risk of failure and even death in some way. People know this intuitively because of their respect and admiration for a firefighter who runs into a burning building to rescue someone, knowingly risking injury, even death. However, if the firefighter knew beforehand that there was no real risk of such, only the appearance of the possibility of it, then the firefighter's choice would be less admirable and could even be considered disingenuous.

Fortunately, it is known with absolute certainty, with everything in God the Father's Creation at risk, Jesus, the Son of Man, did not fail God in any way. And this was attested to by God the Father resurrecting Him physically from the dead, followed by His physical ascension into Heaven, among other things.

Jesus, the Son of Man, obedient to Father God to the point of death, even death on a cross, assured the success of God's CP by securing His bride and home in Paradise. Therefore, the sacrifice of God the Father's knowledge of the future was not in vain.

The Uneven Distribution of Suffering and Hardship

When Adam & Eve disobeyed God and obeyed Satan, they abdicated their God-given rulership of the world over to him. And in ways not well understood, Satan was able to upset the good working order of God's creation. For example, if Jesus can calm the wind and the waves, then maybe Satan can stir them up to some extent.

Nevertheless, when Adam & Eve disobeyed God, they condemned themselves, their progeny, and the entire world to pain, suffering, hardship, and physical death. And since then, all humanity has been enslaved to Satan. And as people enslaved, they have been complicit in

69

spreading death and destruction throughout the world. However, some think this suffering and hardship has been unevenly and unfairly distributed.

Greg Boyd offers an explanation for such an uneven distribution in his book *The Cosmic Dance* (2016). Following and expanding on his idea, imagine every disobedient act ever committed and being committed today by humans and bad angels to be a pebble dropped in a pond. And the ripples produced represent the onward outgoing painful effects of these evil acts.

Each ripple interacts with other ripples to create new interference patterns affecting other ripples. And it may be that some ripples caused by obedient acts mitigate the effects of these disobedient ripples adding to the complexity and unevenness of their impact.

In this way, we might think of ourselves as being, in a sense, entangled with everyone and everything else. We are connected intimately to our family, friends, the entire human race, the plant and animal kingdom, the earth, and the cosmos. We affect and are affected by everything and everyone else, and modern Quantum physics seems to support this idea of entanglement.

From this perspective, the seemingly uneven occurrence of some instances of suffering and hardship may result from the unfathomably complex interaction of an innumerable number of disobedient acts, occurring now and ever since Adam & Eve first disobeyed, mitigated by acts of obedience.

Following Boyd, this may be analogous to how the unfathomably complex interaction of an innumerable number of weather-related variables unevenly distributes rain and snow across the landscape. Many people have seen it rain on one side of a street but not on the other, which may help explain why some people get hurt or healed, and others do not. (1)

In this way, suffering and hardship may be understood as the result of the complex interaction of free agents acting today and from time immemorial, obeying and disobeying God.

God has always done everything possible to prevent all instances of evil and suffering, but necessarily within the boundary of never forcefully overruling or revoking the libertarian freedom of anyone to disobey Him. To override the freewill of someone to disobey, to interfere with their disobedient ripples, would be to nullify the possibility of them being able to love God genuinely, their highest calling, and His greatest desire for them. And if God was to override the freewill of one person's power to disobey, why not everyone's?

If God were ever going to overrule the freewill of someone, it would have been when Adam & Eve were first going to disobey Him in the Garden. This first, worst, and most consequential freewill act of disobedience ever committed was allowed by God. However, within this self-imposed limit of nonintervention, God strives to influence people everywhere to do good and never give in to temptation, even by influencing others, to influence others to do good.

Source:
(1) Greg Boyd, *The Cosmic Dance*

How Are People To Obey and Therefore Love God Today?

People in this world have the libertarian freedom to obey and therefore love God today in two mutually exclusive ways. First, people can love God by obeying Him in the ways He has commanded in the Bible. And second, they can love God by not disobeying Him in the ways He has commanded.

So, people love God when they obey and do what God has commanded them to do, and they also love God when they obey and do not do what God has commanded them not to do. (See: The Ten Commandments)

But how are people to obey God in all the ways commanded in the Old and New Testaments? The proposed answer begins in the Old and ends in the New.

"Teacher, which is the great commandment in the Law? And He said to him, **'You shall love the Lord your God with all your heart, and with all your soul, and with all your mind. This is the great and foremost**

**commandment. *The second is like it, You shall love your neighbor
as yourself. On these two commandments depend the whole Law
and the Prophets. "'** *(Matthew 22:36-40* NASB*)*

Therefore, beginning with the Old Testament, people keep and obey
'the whole Law and the Prophets' when they love God first; and
second, when they love their neighbor as they love themselves.

The second commandment was given initially in Leviticus 19:18, *'you shall
love your neighbor as yourself;'* However, in John 13:34, Jesus gave the new
second commandment,

**"A new commandment I give to you, that you love one another,
even as I have loved you, that you also love one another. "**

Then, in John 15:9, Jesus says how He loves people, **"Just as the Father
has loved Me, I have also loved you;"**

Therefore, Jesus the Son of Man loves people in the same way that God
the Father loves Him, and now people are to love one another as Jesus
loves them, which is how the Father loves Him.

As Jesus the Son of Man redefined other Old Testament Laws, imagine
Him redefining the second commandment by saying,

'You have heard that it was said, you shall love your neighbor as yourself,
but I say to you, you shall love your neighbor as the Father loves Me.'

With this in mind, what Jesus said in Matthew 22:37-40 could be
reworded as follows:

'You shall love the Lord your God with all your heart, and with all your
soul, and with all your mind. This is the great and foremost
commandment. The second is like it, You shall love your neighbor as the
Father loves Me. On these two commandments depend the whole Law
and the Prophets, and all of My commandments to you.'

And taking this approach with the Great Commission given by Jesus in
Matthew 28:19-20:

'Go therefore and make disciples of all the nations, baptizing them in the name of the Father and the Son and the Holy Spirit, teaching them to observe all that I commanded you, to love themselves and one another in the same way that the Father loves Me; and lo, I am with you always, even to the end of the age.'

To some extent, each of us can understand and imagine how Father God must love Jesus, the Son of Man, the perfect Son, the perfect Person, and what Father God must think and feel about Him. Then put yourself in Jesus' place. He put Himself in our place on the Cross so that we could put ourselves in His place in the heart of Father God.

Source:
(1) http://thewordsofjesusonline.com/

How Then Shall We Live Now, Today?

"God is love, and the one who abides in love abides in God, and God abides in him."
(1 John 4:16 NASB*)*

"He who has My commandments and keeps them is the one who loves Me; and he who loves Me will be loved by My Father, and I will love him and will disclose Myself to him. *Judas (not Iscariot) said to Him,* **"Lord, what then has happened that You are going to disclose Yourself to us and not to the world?"** *Jesus answered and said to him,* **"If anyone loves Me, he will keep My word; and My Father will love him, and We will come to him and make Our abode with him. He who does not love Me does not keep My words; and the word which you hear is not Mine, but the Father's who sent Me."** *(Jn 14:21-24* NASB*)*

"Do not work for the food which perishes, but for the food which endures to eternal life, which the Son of Man will give to you," "This is the work of God, that you believe in Him whom He has sent." "Man shall not live by bread alone, but by every word that proceeds from the mouth of God." "... the words that I have spoken to you are spirit and are life."
(John 6:27,29, Matthew 4:4, John 6:63 NASB*)*

"I am the true vine, and My Father is the vinedresser. Every branch in Me that does not bear fruit, [love, joy, peace, patience, kindness, goodness, faithfulness, gentleness, self-control] He takes away; and every branch that bears fruit, He prunes it [of fear, uncertainty, and doubt] so that it may bear more fruit. You are already clean because of the word which I have spoken to you.

"Abide in Me, and I in you. As the branch cannot bear fruit of itself unless it abides in the vine, so neither can you unless you abide in Me. I am the vine, you are the branches; he who abides in Me and I in him, he bears much fruit, for apart from Me you can do nothing. If anyone does not abide in Me, he is thrown away as a branch and dries up; and they gather them, and cast them into the fire and they are burned.

"If you abide in Me, and My words abide in you, ask whatever you wish, and it will be done for you. My Father is glorified by this, that you bear much fruit, and so prove to be My disciples. Just as the Father has loved Me, I have also loved you; abide in My love.

"If you keep My commandments, you will abide in My love; just as I have kept My Father's commandments and abide in His love. These things I have spoken to you so that My joy may be in you, and that your joy may be made full.

"This is My commandment, that you love one another, just as I have loved you. Greater love has no one than this, that one lay down his life for his friends. You are My friends if you do what I command you. No longer do I call you slaves, for the slave does not know what his master is doing; but I have called you friends, for all things that I have heard from My Father I have made known to you.

"You did not choose Me but I chose you, and appointed you that you would go and bear fruit, and that your fruit would remain, so that whatever you ask of the Father in My name He may give to you. This I command you, that you love one another."
(John 15:1-17 NASB)

Part III

Augustinian
Soul-Deciding Type Theodicies

Part III is an aggregation of information from different sources
regarding the history and development of Augustinian
Soul-Deciding Type Theodicies.

A Biography of St. Augustine of Hippo (354–430 AD)

Augustine of Hippo also known as Saint Augustine, was a
theologian, philosopher, and the bishop of Hippo Regius in
Numidia, Roman North Africa. His writings influenced the
development of Western philosophy and Western Christianity, and he is
viewed as one of the most important Church Fathers of the Latin Church
in the Patristic Period.

His many important works include *The City of God, On Christian Doctrine*,
and *Confessions*. According to his contemporary, Jerome, Augustine
"established anew the ancient Faith." In his youth, he was drawn to the
major Persian religion, Manichaeism, and later to Greek Neo-Platonism.

After his baptism and conversion to Christianity in 386 AD, Augustine
developed his own approach to philosophy and theology,
accommodating a variety of methods and perspectives. Believing the

grace of Christ was indispensable to human freedom, he helped formulate the doctrine of original sin and made seminal contributions to the development of 'just war theory.'

When the Western Roman Empire began to disintegrate, Augustine imagined the Church as a spiritual City of God, distinct from the material Earthly City. His thoughts profoundly influenced the medieval worldview. The segment of the Church that adhered to the concept of the Trinity as defined by the Council of Nicaea and the Council of Constantinople closely identified with Augustine's *On the Trinity*.

Augustine is recognized as a saint in the Catholic Church, the Eastern Orthodox Church, and the Anglican Communion. He is also a preeminent Catholic Doctor of the Church and the patron of the Augustinians. Many Protestants, especially Calvinists and Lutherans, consider him one of the theological fathers of the Protestant Reformation due to his teachings on salvation and divine grace.

Protestant Reformers generally, and Martin Luther in particular, held Augustine in preeminence among early Church Fathers. In the East, his teachings are more disputed and were notably attacked by John Romanides. But other theologians and figures of the Eastern Orthodox Church have shown significant approbation of his writings, chiefly Georges Florovsky.

The most controversial doctrine associated with him, the filioque, was rejected by the Orthodox Church. Filioque is a Latin term "and from the Son" added to the original Nicene Creed, and which has been the subject of great controversy between Eastern and Western Christianity. The Latin term is not in the original text of the Creed, which says that the Holy Spirit proceeds "from the Father", without additions of any kind, such as "and the Son" or "alone." Other disputed teachings include his views on original sin, the doctrine of grace, and predestination. Nevertheless, though considered to be mistaken on some points, he is still considered a saint and has influenced some Eastern Church Fathers, most notably Gregory Palamas.

Historian Diarmaid MacCulloch has written: "Augustine's impact on Western Christian thought can hardly be overstated; only his beloved example, Paul of Tarsus, has been more influential, and Westerners have generally seen Paul through Augustine's eyes."

In late August of 386 AD, at the age of 31, having heard of Ponticianus's and his friends' first reading of the life of Anthony of the Desert, Augustine converted to Christianity. As Augustine later told it, his conversion was prompted by hearing a child's voice say "take up and read." Resorting to the Sortes Sanctorum, casually opening the Holy Scripture and reading the first words to come to hand, he opened a book of St. Paul's writings at random and read:

"Let us behave properly as in the day, not in carousing and drunkenness, not in sexual promiscuity and sensuality, not in strife and jealousy. But put on the Lord Jesus Christ, and make no provision for the flesh in regard to its lusts." (Romans 13: 13–14 NASB)

He later wrote an account of his conversion in his *Confessions*, which has since become a classic of Catholic and Protestant theology and a key text in the history of autobiography. This work is an outpouring of thanksgiving and penitence. Although it is written as an account of his life, *Confessions* also talks about the nature of time, causality, freewill, and other important philosophical topics. The following is taken from that work:

"Belatedly I loved thee, O Beauty so ancient and so new, belatedly I loved thee. For see, thou wast within and I was without, and I sought thee out there. Unlovely, I rushed heedlessly among the lovely things thou hast made. Thou wast with me, but I was not with thee. These things kept me far from thee; even though they were not at all unless they were in thee. Thou didst call and cry aloud, and didst force open my deafness. Thou didst gleam and shine, and didst chase away my blindness. Thou didst breathe fragrant odors and I drew in my breath; and now I pant for thee. I tasted, and now I hunger and thirst. Thou didst touch me, and I burned for thy peace."

The Vision of St. Augustine by Ascanio Luciano

Ambrose baptized Augustine and his son Adeodatus, in Milan on Easter Vigil, 24–25 April 387 AD. A year later, in 388, Augustine completed his apology *On the Holiness of the Catholic Church*. That year, also, Adeodatus and Augustine returned home to Africa. Augustine's mother Monica died at Ostia, Italy, as they prepared to embark for Africa. Upon their arrival, they began a life of aristocratic leisure at Augustine's family's property. Soon after, Adeodatus, too, died. Augustine then sold his patrimony and gave the money to the poor. He only kept the family house, which he converted into a monastic foundation for himself and a group of friends.

In 391 Augustine was ordained a priest in Hippo Regius (now Annaba), in Algeria. He became a famous preacher (more than 350 preserved sermons are believed to be authentic), and was noted for combating the Manichaean religion, to which he had formerly adhered. In 395, he was made coadjutor Bishop of Hippo and became full Bishop shortly thereafter, hence the name "Augustine of Hippo;" and he gave his property to the church of Thagaste. He remained in that position until his death in 430. He wrote his autobiographical *Confessions* in 397–398. His work *The City of God* was written to console his fellow Christians shortly after the Visigoths had sacked Rome in 410.

Augustine worked tirelessly to convince the people of Hippo to convert to Christianity. Though he had left his monastery, he continued to lead a monastic life in the episcopal residence. Much of Augustine's later life was recorded by his friend Possidius, bishop of Calama (present-day Guelma, Algeria), in his Sancti Augustini Vita. Possidius admired Augustine as a man of powerful intellect and a stirring orator who took every opportunity to defend Christianity against its detractors. Possidius also described Augustine's personal traits in detail, drawing a portrait of a man who ate sparingly, worked tirelessly, despised gossip, shunned the temptations of the flesh, and exercised prudence in the financial stewardship of his see. (1) He followed the Manichaean religion (Dualism, the power of good and the power of evil are equal) during his early life, but converted to Christianity in 386 at the age of 31.

Augustine himself never formally constructed what today would be called a theodicy. However, from all that he wrote regarding the problem of suffering, especially in his two major works, *Confessions* and *The City of God*, the key elements of a theodicy can be derived.

In *Confessions*, Augustine wrote that his previous work was dominated by materialism and that exposure to Neo-Platonic thought enabled him to consider the existence of a non-physical substance. This understanding from Greek thought helped him develop a response to the problem of evil from a theological (and non-Dualist) perspective, in light of his interpretation of the first few chapters of Genesis and the writings of Paul the Apostle.

It is important to note that Augustine lived, and early Christianity developed, in a Greek intellectual and social environment. Any endeavor to understand the development of Christianity in the time of Augustine must take into account the influence of Neo-Platonism in that period.

Confessions by Augustine

At the time Augustine wrote *Confessions*, Christianity was still in its infancy. Its' main body of followers were peasant class, for it had no philosophical foundations with which to attract the upper class intellectuals. Augustine, however, was ambitious and was faced with the dilemma of substantiating the Christian religion in the eyes of the intelligentsia. How might he do this? Necessarily; he was forced to draw upon available sources, the same ones that the intellectuals of his time were familiar with and to which they subscribed. Augustine relied upon the authors of the Old Testament and the New Testament, but also, Virgil, Cicero, and Anaximenes, and none more so than the Neo-Platonists.

Neo-Platonism is a modern term used to designate the period of Platonic philosophy beginning with the work of Plotinus (203-270 AD) and ending with the closing of the Platonic Academy by the Emperor Justinian in 529 AD. The great third century thinker Plotinus, is responsible for the grand synthesis of progressive Christian and Gnostic ideas with the traditional Platonic philosophy. Even though it is highly unlikely that St. Augustine had direct access to either Socratic or Platonic modes of thought, he did make use of the Neo-Platonic ideals as they were set forth by Plotinus. Augustine ascertained that the Neo-Platonic and Christian doctrines ran parallel on several very important dogmas.

The Neo-Platonists conceptualized a prime mover which they called "the One" or "the good." A modern definition of this enigma could be "the Absolute." They believed that from this One all things came into being and to this One all things will one day return. The One is both omniscient and omnipotent and exists merely because it is, and the object of its love is itself. Because of the One's all-powerful nature no human can ever hope to grasp either its meaning, purpose, cause, or its effects, and it is eternal, within which lays the beginning and the end of all things. The Neo-Platonists also thought that the One cannot be thought of as a physical entity, for it has no bounds. Augustine easily incorporates most of these views into his concept of the Christian God who is an all-knowing, all-powerful, benevolent deity.

The Neo-Platonists also had a central belief in the human soul. They saw the soul as eternal and capable of change. The Neo-Platonic soul was in constant motion, beginning at a state of oneness with all other souls. Its journey proceeds from the realm of oneness with others downward to the realm of material being only to reverse its motion and return again to oneness with others after being "educated" on the material plane of existence. The Neo-Platonic idea of perpetual circular motion of the soul also works for Augustine, but only up to a point. It breaks down for Augustine at the point in time when the perpetual comes into play. Augustine's concept of the soul makes one trip through the cycle and then assumes its place in the eternal paradise. Augustine is very careful in his wording of this particular passage of *Confessions*.

Augustine takes great care to mirror the Neo-Platonic view of the One when describing the characteristics of the Christian God. And this is done for two purposes, the first being the fact that Neo-Platonism was one of the predominant philosophical views of the time period in which *Confessions* was written, and Augustine was trying to show that Christianity had a valid base with respect to the beliefs and views of the time. The second point that Augustine was trying to make was that from the Neo-Platonic progression of thought the Christian doctrine naturally followed, thereby attempting to entice Neo-Platonists into conversion to the Christian faith. By doing this, Augustine pushes a fledgling Christian religion over the edge into a much wider range of acceptance as he has shown that Christianity has appeal to not only the lower class of society but also to the upper classes as well. Therefore, Augustine made extremely valuable use of his Neo-Platonic predecessors in his writing of *Confessions*. He not only used their philosophy, he used it to expound on his own ideas of God and meshed the two together into a more coherent and wider ranging theory than either had been before he altered them.

His use of Neo-Platonic teachings served to give credibility to the Christian doctrine and spread the Christian faith not only to the Neo-Platonists but also to the greater majority of the upper classes of Roman society. And his usage worked with outstanding results. He accomplished his goals of expanding Christianity and of building the level of acceptance and credibility of the Christian religion to such an extent that it continues in effect today more than a millennia and half later. Thus, by examining Augustine's background and training in Greek philosophy and Neo-Platonic thought, his interaction with and evaluation of Platonism and Neo-Platonism to Christianity in his own writing, and the parallel between Neo-Platonic philosophy and his philosophical theology, it would be easy to conclude that his theology was too heavily influenced by Neo-Platonism.

However, Augustine's thoughts, even though influenced by Neo-Platonism, must not be disregarded as tainted or secular as most of his thought still aligns with Saint Paul. Overall, history has shown that the philosophical principles of Neo-Platonism were not detrimental to Augustine's theology and his positive impact upon the church. Additionally, Augustine's thought led to the development of the theology of the Reformed thinkers beginning with John Calvin, who was heavily influenced by Augustine. And other reformers held high Augustine's soteriological position on God's direct revelation to mankind and the powerful psychological notion of the individual self. These themes would later captivate Protestantism and evangelical Christianity. Thus, the implications of the doctrines of Augustine have left an overwhelmingly positive impact on the church.

The City of God by Augustine

In *The City of God*, Augustine developed his 'theodicy' as part of an attempt to trace human history and describe its conclusion. Augustinian type theodicies typically assert that God is perfectly good and that He created the perfectly good world out of nothing. He then created Adam out of the dust of the earth, and then Eve out of Adam. Entry of both moral and natural evil into the world is explained as Adam and Eve's abuse of their God-given morally freewill by disobeying God. And they disobeyed God when they ate fruit from the tree of the knowledge of good and evil in the Garden of Eden. Consequently, God was fully justified by punishing them with death and banishment from the Garden.

81

And because Augustine believed that all humanity is "seminally present in the loins of Adam", he argued that all of humanity inherited Adam's sin and like Adam is deserving of punishment.

Augustine proposed that evil could not exist within God, nor be created by God, and is instead a by-product of God's creativity. He rejected the notion that evil exists in itself, proposing instead that it is a privation of good or falling away from good, and therefore is a corruption of nature. He wrote that evil has no positive nature; but the 'loss of good' has received the name 'evil.' Augustinian theologians argue that the sin of Adam and Eve corrupted their morally freewill and the morally freewill of their descendants leaving them unable to resist sin. Therefore, God is blameless and good, and not Himself responsible for evil. However, in spite of his belief that a morally freewill can be corrupted, Augustine maintained that it was vital for humans to have one, because they could not live well without it. And even though humans contained no evil, he argued that evil could originate with them because, like other good things, they could be corrupted.

Augustine believed that a physical Hell exists, but that the Grace of Jesus Christ provides humans with the ability to choose to follow God and be forgiven and avoid Hell, and he maintained that humans can only be saved if they choose to receive God's Grace in this life. Accepting that even those who will be saved continue to sin in this life, Augustine proposed that they will still go to Hell for a time to be purged of their sin, before going to Heaven.

Also, the felix culpa, or the fortunate fault theme, which is common to various Christian orientations, comes out of Augustine's writings. It affirms that sin is essentially linked to God's great redemptive activity of the Incarnation, Christ's Sinless Life, Crucifixion, Resurrection, and Ascension. Without the presence of sin in the world humans would not have seen and therefore not known of these great demonstrations of God's love toward fallen humanity. Therefore, His Glory would have shown less brightly which would have been a great loss for both humankind and God. Thus it was not only inevitable that sin enter the world but also essential in order for the fullness of God's Glory to be revealed.

What is at stake for Augustine is not so much "the problem of evil," but rather the related problem of wondering how evil can exist on the assumption that God is Omni-perfect. The Augustinian reply is that evil occurs because God permits it, and God permits it because of a greater-good that He derives from it. Augustine sees the grand narrative of world history as one that begins with Adam's fall and culminates with Christ's return. It has a beneficent beginning, in which God creates everything good, and it has a beneficent ending, in which Christ restores all things to perfection, with the exception of those who are damned. What is between the beginning and the end, might seem to have no meaning or purpose or goal, but we have the hope, through the Gospel of Christ, that a greater-good will come out of it all. (2)

Source:
(1) https://en.wikipedia.org/wiki/Augustine_of_Hippo
(2) Neoplatonic Influences in Augustine's Confessions 2 PDF
Kraley, Shon H. (1990) "Neoplatonic Influences in Augustine's Confessions," Anthós (1990-1996): Vol. 1: No. 1, Article 6.
http://pdxscholar.library.pdx.edu/anthos_archives/vol1/iss1/6
Neoplatonism and Christianity – Wikipedia
Neo-Platonism: iep.utm.edu/neoplato
Augustine's Philosophical Theology and Neo-Platonism
http://apologetics.com/blog/jlivermore/augustines-philosophical-theology-a-neoplatonism/
God and the Problem of Evil: Chad Meister

John Calvin (1509 – 1564)

John Calvin and Martin Luther were the two most important Reformers, and along with the others were influenced by the works of Augustine. In 1536, Calvin brought out the first edition of his *Institutes of the Christian Religion*, the first systematic, theological treatise of the new Reform movement. Calvin agreed with Luther's teaching on justification by faith. However, he found a more positive place for law within the Christian community than did Luther.

Calvin's tradition merged eventually with Zwingli's into the Reformed tradition, which was given theological expression by the *Second Helvetic Confession* of 1561. Zwingli and Calvin agreed with most of the Christian tradition that the Universe was created from nothing by God. This is the doctrine of creation ex nihilo. This belief emphasizes God's complete sovereignty. It also carries as a consequence the fact that anything wrong with the Universe cannot be attributed to matter or the material of the Universe, since this too was created by God and it was created very good. (Genesis 1:31)

Unlike Augustine, but like Luther, Calvin was willing to accept that God is responsible for evil and suffering. However, unlike Luther, he maintained that God cannot be blamed for it, since He uses evil to bring about good in life, the directing of people back to Himself. And modern Reformers believe that God not only allows or permits evil, but that God ordains evil, and that all evil glorifies God by revealing God's goodness toward undeserving sinners. That is, evil is essential if the glory of God is to be perfectly and completely displayed.

Calvin continued the Augustinian approach that the origin of sin in the world was the disobedience of Adam & Eve in the Garden, and argued that as a result of this disobedience the human mind, will, and affections have been corrupted. And he believed that only the Grace of God is able to provide humans with ongoing ethical guidance, arguing that human reason is blinded by their corrupt human nature.

Calvin proposed that humanity is double predestined, it is divided into the elect and the reprobate: the elect are those who God has chosen to save and the reprobate are those who God has chosen to be damned. For Calvin (as for Zwingli and Luther), once you are saved you cannot lose your salvation. Humans do not have it in their power to damn themselves, just as they do not have it in their power to save themselves.(1)

With all the other Reformers Calvin teaches that a person enjoys the benefits of the death of Christ through God-given faith in Christ. Can such a believer know and be assured that Christ has saved him by his death? Calvin held that it was possible for a person to be assured of his own salvation, and normal to expect this. It was monstrous to teach that such assurance was impossible. But he recognized that saving faith is often accompanied by periods of doubt which eclipse assurance, and that even assured faith is never totally free from doubt. Again, this will distinguish Reformed theologies from Catholic and Methodist theologies. Calvin and Zwingli are willing to pay any theological price to protect the doctrine of God's absolute and Fatherly sovereignty. (2)

Calvinists argue all humans are sinful and in and of ourselves we are unable to freely choose to believe in Christ. Though we are naturally able to believe, we are morally unable to believe; we are bent by sin so that we are always choosing contrary to God's best. When the elect hear the gospel, the Holy Spirit restores their moral ability to believe through the regeneration of the Holy Spirit. Most Calvinists believe this results in immediate faith in Christ. This view is an orthodox option and is the dominant view in the Reformed tradition and is held by many Southern Baptists as well. (3)

In his book, *Calvin's Theodicy and the Hiddenness of God*, Paolo de Petris explores the origin, structure, and strategies of John Calvin's defense of divine providence. His study helpfully summarizes Calvin's conception of the nature of evil. First, Calvin defines evil primarily as moral evil, or sin. Second, he argues that God does not author evil directly, which shifts the blame from God to humanity. Third, as an extension of his doctrine of double-predestination, he argues that God ordains evil; but again, cannot be blamed for it.

Calvin situates his doctrine of evil within the cosmic drama where evil complicates the plot until the dénouement, when the hidden narrative arc of providence becomes revealed to all, much to their delight. God's providential arrangement of the Universe entails the positive function of evil: it is not simply a negation. It must further God's mysterious plan for creation in ways that elude us, as the book of Job illustrates.

Calvin, like Augustine, affirms the original goodness of creation, including Lucifer and all the angels before their fall, and attributes the fall to their misuse of freedom, and believes that God ultimately brings good out of evil. Unlike Augustine, Calvin rooted his conceptions in the Bible and focused on God's providential employment of evil, but did not share the speculative and Neo-Platonic aspects of Augustine's thought.

Like Aquinas and Augustine before him, Calvin was unable to answer the question of the ultimate origin of evil: How does it arise in the first place, given creations original goodness? Calvin seemed disinterested in the question, perhaps because it intrudes on the mystery of providence, or perhaps because it distracts from more pressing theological concerns about divine and human culpability for evil. Divine sovereignty and human freedom stand in uneasy tension in Calvin's theodicy.

Like Augustine and Aquinas, Calvin clears God from moral culpability, assigning blame to creation, particularly to the misuse of freedom. Unlike Augustine and Aquinas, however, Calvin does not focus on God's permission of evil as much as on his co-option of evil to further his mysterious providential ends. Calvin does not see God as the victim of his own creation, like a failed cosmic experiment. Nor does he think evil takes God by surprise or thwart his inscrutable sovereign will. God has not, Calvin insists, lost control of the Universe. Rather, evil fits within God's larger designs for creation, and so expresses the divine will even as it resists it. Calvin's paradoxical stance on providence and evil reflects his Augustinian heritage and his commitment to God's omnipotent sovereignty over the Universe.

In all this we see the influence of the medieval nominalists and their arguments that we cannot reason or speculate our way to knowledge of God, and we cannot draw analogies from human experience or from nature to God. All we know about God is what we learn in scripture. Calvin did not ask the question, "Why is creation the way it is?" He observed the fact of evil and suffering in the world, and the Biblical account in Genesis of the Fall. The elect are given the gift of faith, which brings, along with assurance that our sins are forgiven, the confidence that while we may not know why God does what God does, God surely does know. (4)

Source:
(1) https://en.wikipedia.org/wiki/Augustinian_theodicy
Presbyterian – Suffering and the problem of evil
https://www.patheos.com/library/presbyterian/beliefs/suffering-and-the-problem-of-evil
(2) http://the-highway.com/articleJuly02.html
(3)https://www.fbcdurham.org/wp-content/uploads/2015/08/Doctrines-of-Man-Christ-the-Holy-Spirit-3-Humanitys-Sin.pdf
(4) Scott, Mark S. M.. Pathways in Theodicy: An Introduction to the Problem of Evil (p. 35-37). Fortress Press

---

Luis de Molina (1535 – 1600)

Luis de Molina was a 16th-century Spanish Jesuit theologian and philosopher who lived about thirty years after John Calvin, and he took exception to Calvin's teaching on divine sovereignty and human libertarian freedom. Calvin believed that God's omniscience included perfect knowledge of all events past, present, and future. That is, God, from His perspective, sees the past, present and future of the world as altogether one thing, an eternal now.

Rational thinking would lead people to reject a good and just God who predestines and foreknows every event and yet condemns people to Hell. How could the good God of the Bible know beforehand that a human would commit an evil act, then not prevent it, and yet in some way not be responsible for it? Calvin's response was his willingness to accept that God is responsible for the entry of evil into the world. However, he maintained that God cannot be blamed for it, since He uses evil to bring about some greater-good, like directing people back to Himself.

Molina Was Critical of Calvin

Molina states in his *Concordia*: "In fact, if the method of predestining some adults and not others was the one which has been gleaned from the theory of these authors with their predeterminations, then I do not see in what sense it is true that God wills that all human beings be saved if they themselves do not prevent it, or in what sense it is true and not fictitious that all human beings without exception have been created by God for eternal life. Nor do I see how God could justifiably reproach the non-predestinate for not living in a pious and holy manner and for not attaining eternal life; indeed I do not see how it is true that God has placed human beings in the hand of their own counsel, so that they might direct their actions as they will. To the contrary, given this method of predestination and predeterminations, the freedom of the created faculty of choice perishes, and the justice and goodness of God with respect to the reprobate are greatly obfuscated and obscured. Thus, this theory is neither pious nor in any way safe from the point of view of the faith."

Consequently, Molina proposes to go further than Calvin and attempts to remove from God all responsibility for evil, since to think otherwise would detract from God's glory.

Kenneth Keathley, author of *Salvation and Sovereignty: A Molinist Approach*, writes that Molinists argue that God perfectly accomplishes His will in the lives of genuinely free creatures through the use of His omniscience. That is, Molinism is an attempt to hold fast the attribute of God's meticulous foreknowledge regarding all future human choices, while at the same time maintaining libertarian freedom for those same humans. William Lane Craig and Alvin Plantinga are prominent contemporary advocates of Molinism.

A Molinist Understanding of God's Knowledge

Molinism proposes God's knowledge consists of three types:

The first type is God's knowledge of necessary truths or "natural knowledge." These truths are independent of God's will and are non-contingent. This knowledge includes the full range of logical possibilities. Examples include such logical statements as "All bachelors are unmarried."

The second is called "middle knowledge" and contains the full range of possible things that would happen given certain circumstances.

The third kind of knowledge is God's "free knowledge" which consists of contingent truths that are dependent upon God's will, or truths that God brings about, that He does not have to bring about. Examples might include statements such as "God created the earth" or something particular about this world which God has actualized. This is called God's "free knowledge" and it contains the future or what will happen.

In between God's natural and free knowledge is His middle knowledge by which God knows what His free creatures would do under any circumstance. These are "truths" that do not have to be true, but are true without God being the primary cause of them. In the *Internet Encyclopedia of Philosophy*, John D. Laing has provided an example of middle knowledge: "If John Laing were given the opportunity to write an article on middle knowledge for the *Internet Encyclopedia of Philosophy*, he would freely do so." This viewpoint is difficult for some to grasp but is the basis of Molinist opinion.

William Lane Craig points out that God's middle knowledge plays an important role in the actualization of the world. But by placing middle knowledge before the creation decree God allows for freedom in the libertarian sense. The placing of middle knowledge logically after necessary truths, but before the creation decree also gives God the possibility to survey all possible worlds and decide which world to actualize.

Craig calls Molinism one of the most fruitful theological ideas ever conceived, because it serves to explain not only God's meticulous foreknowledge of the future, but divine providence and predestination as well. Under it, God retains a measure of divine providence without hindering humanity's freedom. Because God has middle knowledge, He knows what an agent would freely choose to do in a particular situation. So for example, God knows that agent A, if placed in circumstance C, would freely choose option X over option Y. Therefore, if God wanted to accomplish X, all God would have to do is, using his middle knowledge, actualize the world in which A was placed in C, and then A would freely choose X. God retains an element of providence without nullifying A's choice, and God's purpose is accomplished.

Thus, if God wanted to accomplish something in particular, all God would have to do is, using his middle knowledge, actualize the one world from among all possible worlds, where that something was freely chosen by His creatures. And conversely, if God did not want something to happen, then all God would have to do is, using his middle knowledge, actualize the world in which that something was not freely chosen. This is not to say that God is pleased or satisfied with everything that takes place in the world. It has been suggested that possibly an event like the Holocaust could not have been omitted by God without something equally bad or worse occurring. Therefore, given human libertarian freedom, the world we live in is the best of all possible worlds.

What Are Counterfactuals?

A counterfactual claim is a hypothesis or other belief that is contrary to the facts. It is a hypothetical statement of what the world might be like had the hypothetical statement been true. In other words, it is a conditional statement in which the conditional clause is false, as in, "If I had only arrived on time, then ... ..., but of course I did not arrive on time."

Again, counterfactual thinking is a concept in psychology that involves the human tendency to create possible alternatives to life events that have already occurred; something that is contrary to what actually happened. Counterfactual thinking is, as it states: "counter to the facts." These thoughts consist of the "What if?" and the "If I had only..." that occur when thinking of how things could have turned out differently. Counterfactual thoughts include things that in the present–now could never happen in reality because they solely pertain to events that have occurred in the past. (2)

Biblical Texts for Molinism

Molinists have supported their case scripturally with Christ's statement in Matthew 11:23: "And you, Capernaum, will not be exalted to heaven, will you? You will descend to Hades; for if the miracles had occurred in Sodom which occurred in you, it would have remained to this day." The Molinist claims that in this example, God knows what his free creatures would choose under hypothetical circumstances, namely that the Sodomites would have responded in a way that Sodom would still have been in existence in Jesus' day, given that hypothetical situation. Matthew 11:23 contains what is commonly called a "counterfactual" of creaturely freedom. But counterfactuals are to be distinguished from foreknowledge. The Bible contains many examples of foreknowledge such as Deut 31:16-17, where God tells Moses that the Israelites will forsake God after they are delivered from Egypt. (1)

Molinists have often argued that their position is the Biblical one by indicating passages they understand to teach God's middle knowledge. Molina advanced the following three texts: 1 Samuel 23:8-14, Proverbs 4:11, and Matthew 11:23. Other passages which Molinists use are Ezekiel 3:6-7, Jeremiah 38:17-18, 1 Corinthians 2:8, Deuteronomy 28:51-57, Matthew 23:27-32, Matthew 12:7, Matthew 24:43, Luke 16:30-31, and Luke 22:67-68.

William Lane Craig has argued at length that many of Christ's statements seem to indicate middle knowledge. Craig cites the following passages: Matthew 17:27, John 21:6, John 15:22-24, John 18:36, Luke 4:24-44 and Matthew 26:24.

Thomas Flint claims the twin foundations of Molinism are God's providence and man's freedom. Molinism harmonizes texts teaching God's providence (such as Acts 4:28 or Ephesians 1:11) with texts emphasizing man's choice (such as Deuteronomy 30:19 or Luke 13:34).

Critics of Molinism

Molinism has been controversial and criticized since its inception in Molina's *Concordia*. The "grounding objection" is at present the most debated criticism of Molinism and is often considered the strongest.

The argument claims that there are no metaphysical grounds or good reasons to believe in the truthfulness of counterfactuals of creaturely freedom.

As Hugh McCann puts it, "Perhaps the most serious objection against it [Molinism] is that there does not appear to be any way God could come by such knowledge [the truth of counterfactuals].

As we have seen, knowledge is not merely a matter of conceiving a proposition and correctly believing it to be true. It requires justification: one must have good reasons for believing. But what justification could God have for believing the propositions that are supposed to constitute middle knowledge [the truth of counterfactuals]?"

It has been said, "God cannot do that which is logically impossible to do." To be "omniscient" (all-knowing) is to "know all there is to know." If something is not knowable, that does not detract from "omniscience." If the future does not exist, then God cannot logically know it. But since God knows all there is to know past and present, he is omniscient (all-knowing).

Molinism Defended

Defenders of Molinism summarize their beliefs as follows:

Mankind is free in a libertarian sense, otherwise God is the author of evil.

The Bible (and common sense) affirms that if people had been in different circumstances, they would have behaved in certain ways. In other words, it affirms counterfactuals.

God is omniscient, and therefore He knows all counterfactuals.

And based on this knowledge of counterfactuals, God is able to sovereignly guide history by strongly and weakly actualizing various states of affairs in order to accomplish his purposes.

Lastly, this understanding helps make sense of various passages in Scripture.

In the end, there are two main reasons defenders of Molinism state for their beliefs. First, Scripture implies it exists by affirming God's sovereignty, man's freedom, the reality of counterfactuals, and God's omniscience — Molinism almost has to be true if those things are true. Second, it helps Christians read Scripture and make sense of what's happening in the text. (3)

Is Molinism as Bad as Calvinism? By Jerry L. Walls

The essence of Molina's view of providence is that God arranges the world as He will, in light of what He knows by middle knowledge. God's providence covers free choices in the sense that He brings it about that freewills are placed in such and such circumstances knowing they will make such and such free choices. God's concurrence, of course, underlies all aspects of providence, including free choice. All good actions are specifically intended by God while evil actions are permitted by God's providence for the sake of some greater-good. Predestination should be understood as one aspect of God's overall providence. That is to say, God predestines specific persons to salvation and damnation only in the sense that He brings about or permits the circumstances in which He knows those persons will freely choose either salvation or damnation.

It is important to recognize that Molina had a number of connected motives for developing his view of middle knowledge. In the first place, he was concerned to maintain that God's knowledge of the future is both detailed and absolutely certain. In a similar way, he wanted to insist that God exercises particular, not merely a general, providence over all of creation. To think otherwise would detract from God's glory. Molina is also interested to defend middle knowledge for the simple reason that he thinks it is clearly implied in certain passages of scripture, including the words of Christ.

But there is another fundamental motivation at work, namely, Molina's desire to preserve libertarian freedom. This is necessary in order to make sense of the notion that God justly rewards or punishes us for our actions. Without libertarian freedom, it is difficult if not impossible to make sense of the claim that some are damned even though God wishes to save all persons. For if persons are not free in the libertarian sense, it would seem to follow that if God wishes to save all of them, then all in fact will be saved. For if freedom is compatible with determinism, then God could save all persons, and do it in such a way that all would freely choose salvation.

In Molina's view, it is not possible to maintain both human freedom and a strong view of providence without resorting to middle knowledge. If we want to hold an adequate view of divine foreknowledge and providence, we have a choice: we must either accept middle knowledge or a conception of absolute predestination which totally destroys human freedom. For Molina the choice is obvious. If we accept middle knowledge we can maintain that God's knowledge of the future is absolutely certain and that our choices are altogether free, just as if there were no foreknowledge.

Now then, is Molina's view as triumphant as he imagines? Or is Calvinism, or something as bad, lurking beneath the surface, as some critics think? Let us try to state what the critics have in mind. It seems to be something like this: Molinism is just as bad as Calvinism because according to it, God puts people, or allows them to be put, in circumstances in which He knows they will choose evil and be damned. If this is so, the Calvinist may urge, the seeming moral superiority of Molinism is really an illusion.

Source:
(1) https://en.wikipedia.org/wiki/Molinism
https://craigcfisher.wordpress.com/2014/02/09/the-theory-behind-omniscience-the-ugly-side-of-calvinism/
Is Molinism as Bad as Calvinism – Jerry L. Walls
(2) https://en.wikipedia.org/wiki/Counterfactual_thinking
(3) http://evangelicalarminians.org/acceptingrejecting-calvinism-pt-11-molinism-defended/

Jacobus Arminius (1560–1609)

Jacobus Arminius was a Dutch theologian from the Protestant Reformation period whose views became the basis of Arminianism and the Dutch Remonstrant movement. He lived about twenty years after Molina and about fifty years after Calvin, and he was taught by Theodore Beza, Calvin's hand-picked successor. The greater-good theodicies of Irenaeus, Augustine, Calvin, and others, teach that the entry of evil into the world was inevitable, and that evil serves a purpose in the plan of God from which He will bring about a greater-good than would have been possible without it.

Arminianism does not accept this teaching since it indicates that evil is essential to bring about good. God does not need evil to bring about good; sin and evil are not essential in God's plan. A greater-good theodicy renders sin and evil essential, thereby making God responsible for evil. God is not responsible for evil; it is humans and fallen angels who are responsible. However, even though God is not responsible for evil, the Arminian theodicy maintains that God does 'allow' evil, even gratuitous evil for which there seems to be no purpose, which keeps God's sovereignty as well as human libertarian freewill intact.

God is so strongly sovereign over evil that no evil will occur that does not serve God's purpose or to which God does not attach some specific meaning or significance. Nothing happens, according to Arminius, by chance or accident. Also, there is no possible explanation as to why God does not prevent gratuitous evil, and no explanation is necessary apart from the fact that God is sovereign. However, God undoubtedly does prevent many individual instances of pain and suffering in ways not obvious to anyone. It is important to note that God never intended or needed evil to occur for His creation plan to be successful, but now that evil is present in the world He can use it in furtherance of His plan.

Arminian theology, the theology of the early Church, gives human beings, created in the image of God, the God-given power of moral choice in a way that is authentic. The classic Arminian view affirms that the future is perfectly foreknown by God and yet is, in principle and practice, 'open' and 'undetermined.' That is, future free decisions made by people are 'certain' but not 'necessary.' The person who makes a moral choice is free, in a libertarian sense, either to make that choice or to make a different choice.

In Arminianism loving God is the highest function of a created being to which all people are called. Any form of deterministic philosophy, such as Calvinism, deprives people of an authentic expression of love toward God and destroys the image of God within them. Further, there is libertarian freewill in Heaven, but since there will be no temptation to sin in Heaven, there will be no sin. Adam & Eve had freewill, but since their natures were pure and good in the Garden, and not inclined to sin, without temptation, they would not have sinned.

However, according to Arminian theology, when you have a self at all, as Adam & Eve did, there is a possibility of being tempted to put yourself first, a wanting to be like God. It was with this that Satan tempted Adam & Eve, and out of this hopeless attempt to be like God that evil came into the world. And this sin of Adam & Eve brought God's judgment upon creation, subjecting humanity to pain, suffering, hardship, and death and corrupted the perfect working order of the world. Instances of pain and suffering from natural causes are often the result of living in a world that no longer functions as it was intended.

Arminius believed the abuse of freewill brings pain and suffering, and when pain and suffering happens, God can then use it for various good purposes. For instance, suffering can lead people to turn to God for help; it can bring growth in their character; and it can provide an opportunity for virtue, both in the person who suffers and others who help the suffering person. However, according to Arminius it is also true that God might inflict pain and suffering directly as punishment for sin or to accomplish any of the goods just mentioned; but, God never commits moral evil and He never does anything without there being a justifying 'good' result. Again, these things are not God's ideal will. He would have much preferred that evil had never entered the world in the first place.

Why Do Bad Things Happen to Relatively Good People?

From a Christian point of view, no one is fully good or sin-free, and all suffer pain as a result of living in a sin-cursed world. Thankfully, Jesus Christ took the punishment for all human sin when He died on the cross, so that anyone who trusts in Him as Lord and Savior will be forgiven and made right with God and have eternal life now in this life, and eventually eternal life in Heaven. However, most Christians believe if we do not trust in Jesus in this life, we are doomed to eternal separation from God forever in Hell.

Human beings want their freedom, to think and to behave in whatever manner they desire, and they also want God to prevent all evil and prevent them from going to Hell. This is a logical contradiction, like asking God to create a square circle. Arminian theology posits that God, through His Holy Spirit and by the life, death, and resurrection of Jesus Christ, graciously enables depraved and corrupt sinners to respond to that grace, and the name of that response is faith.

In the beginning, why didn't God simply create Heaven instead of this world and forego all the pain and suffering? Philosophers such as Anthony Flew and J. L. Mackie, along with Martin Luther, have argued that an omnipotent God should be able to create a world containing moral good and no immoral evil.

In a debate, William Lane Craig was asked this question and responded that it may not have been possible for God to create a meaningful Heaven of free creatures who will not choose against Him, in isolation from an antecedent world such as ours which has these same free creatures who have already chosen for Him. The latter meaningful situation in Heaven may have been rendered possible by the fact that it was chosen freely in this world first in the face of great temptation. So Craig suggests we will love God with libertarian freewill in Heaven, and with the lack of temptation in Heaven, in combination with our glorified/perfected natures, it can be assured that we will never forsake the love of God again. (1)

Source:
(1) https://en.wikipedia.org/wiki/Jacobus_Arminius
https://en.wikipedia.org/wiki/Arminianism
http://evangelicalarminians.org/remonstrance-episode-16-open-theism-part-2/
http://evangelicalarminians.org/brian-abasciano-answering-the-problem-of-evil-from-an-arminian-perspective by Brian Abasciano

---

The Progression of Theology and Theodicy from Augustine to Calvin to Molina to Arminius

Augustine

In *Confessions*, Augustine wrote that his previous work was dominated by materialism and that exposure to Neo-Platonic thought enabled him to consider the existence of a non-physical substance. It is important to note that Augustine lived, and early Christianity developed, in a Greek intellectual and social environment. Any endeavor to understand the development of Christianity in the time of Augustine must take into account the influence of Neo-Platonism in that period.

At the time Augustine wrote *Confessions*, Christianity was still in its infancy. Its' main body of followers were peasant class, for it had no philosophical foundations with which to attract the upper class intellectuals. Augustine, however, was ambitious and was faced with the dilemma of substantiating the Christian religion in the eyes of the intelligentsia. How might he do this? Necessarily; he was forced to draw upon available sources, the same ones that the intellectuals of his time were familiar with and to which they subscribed. Augustine relied upon the authors of the Old Testament and the New Testament, but also, Virgil, Cicero, and Anaximenes, and none more so than the Neo-Platonists. Neo-Platonism is a modern term used to designate the period of Platonic philosophy beginning with the work of Plotinus (203-270) and ending with the closing of the Platonic Academy by the Emperor Justinian in 529 AD. Even though it is highly unlikely that St. Augustine had direct access to either Socratic or Platonic modes of thought, he did make use of the Neo-Platonic ideals as they were set forth by Plotinus. Augustine ascertained that the Neo-Platonic and Christian doctrines ran parallel on several very important dogmas.

The Neo-Platonists conceptualized a prime mover which they called "the One" or "the good." A modern definition of this enigma could be "the Absolute." They believed that from this One all things came into being and to this One all things will one day return. The One is both omniscient and omnipotent and exists merely because it is, and the object of its love is itself. Because of the One's all-powerful nature no human can ever hope to grasp either its meaning, purpose, cause, or its effects, and it is eternal, within which lays the beginning and the end of all things. The Neo-Platonists also thought that the One cannot be thought of as a physical entity, for it has no bounds. Augustine easily incorporates most of these views into his concept of the Christian God who is an all-knowing, all-powerful, benevolent deity.

The Neo-Platonists also had a central belief in the human soul. They saw the soul as eternal and capable of change. The Neo-Platonic soul was in constant motion, beginning at a state of oneness with all other souls. Its journey proceeds from the realm of oneness with others downward to the realm of material being only to reverse its motion and return again to oneness with others after being "educated" on the material plane of existence. The Neo-Platonic idea of perpetual circular motion of the soul also works for Augustine, but only up to a point. It breaks down for Augustine at the point in time when the perpetual comes into play. Augustine's concept of the soul makes one trip through the cycle and then assumes its place in the eternal paradise. Augustine is very careful in his wording of this particular passage in *Confessions*.

Augustine takes great care to mirror the Neo-Platonic view of the One when describing the characteristics of the Christian God. And this is done for two purposes, the first being the fact that Neo-Platonism was one of the predominant philosophical views of the time period in which *Confessions* was written, and Augustine was trying to show that Christianity had a valid base with respect to the beliefs and views of the time. The second point that Augustine was trying to make was that from the Neo-Platonic progression of thought, the Christian doctrine naturally followed, thereby attempting to entice Neo-Platonists into conversion to the Christian faith. By doing this, Augustine pushes a fledgling Christian religion over the edge into a much wider range of acceptance as he has shown that Christianity has appeal to not only the lower class of society but also to the upper classes as well. Therefore,

Augustine made extremely valuable use of his Neo-Platonic predecessors in his writing of *Confessions*. He not only used their philosophy, he used it to expound on his own ideas of God, and meshed the two together into a more coherent and wider ranging theory than either had been before he altered them.

His use of Neo-Platonic teachings served to give credibility to the Christian doctrine and spread the Christian faith not only to the Neo-Platonists but also to the greater majority of the upper classes of Roman society. His usage worked with outstanding results. He accomplished his goals of expanding Christianity and of building the level of acceptance and credibility of the Christian religion to such an extent that it continues in effect today more than a millennia and half later. Thus, by examining Augustine's background and training in Greek philosophy and Neo-Platonic thought, his interaction with and evaluation of Platonism and Neo-Platonism to Christianity in his own writing, and the parallel between Neo-Platonic philosophy and his philosophical theology, it would be easy to conclude that his theology was too heavily influenced by Neo-Platonism.

However, Augustine's thoughts, even though influenced by Neo-Platonism, must not be disregarded as tainted or secular as most of his thought still aligns with Saint Paul. Overall, history has shown that the philosophical principles of Neo-Platonism were not detrimental to Augustine's theology and his positive impact upon the church. Additionally, Augustine's thought led to the development of the theology of the Reformed thinkers beginning with John Calvin, who was heavily influenced by Augustine. And other reformers held high Augustine's soteriological position on God's direct revelation to mankind and the powerful psychological notion of the individual self. These themes would later captivate Protestantism and evangelical Christianity. Thus, the implications of the doctrines of Augustine have left an overwhelmingly positive impact on the church.

John Calvin

Augustine's thought led to the development of the theology of the Reformed thinkers beginning with John Calvin, who was heavily influenced by Augustine. John Calvin and Martin Luther were the two most important Reformers, and along with the others were influenced by the works of Augustine. Unlike Augustine, but like Luther, Calvin was willing to accept that God is responsible for evil and suffering. However, unlike Luther, he maintained that God cannot be blamed for it, since He uses evil to bring about good in life, as directing people back to Himself. And modern Reformers believe that God not only allows or permits evil, but that God ordains evil, and that all evil glorifies God by revealing God's goodness toward sinners. Evil is essential if the glory of God is to be perfectly and completely displayed through the life, death, and resurrection of Jesus Christ.

Calvin continued the Augustinian approach that the origin of sin in the world was the disobedience of Adam & Eve in the Garden, and argued that as a result of this disobedience the human mind, will, and affections have been corrupted. Calvin, like Augustine, affirms the original goodness of creation, including Lucifer and all the angels before their fall, and attributes the Fall of Adam & Eve to their misuse of freedom, He believes that God ultimately brings good out of evil. Unlike Augustine, Calvin rooted his conceptions in the Bible and focused on God's providential employment of evil, but did not share the speculative and Neo-Platonic aspects of Augustine's thought.

Like Aquinas and Augustine before him, Calvin was unable to answer the question of the ultimate origin of evil: How does it arise in the first place, given creations original goodness? Calvin seemed disinterested in the question, perhaps because it intrudes on the mystery of providence, or perhaps because it distracts from more pressing theological concerns about divine and human culpability for evil. Divine sovereignty and human freedom stand in uneasy tension in Calvin's theodicy.

Like Augustine and Aquinas, Calvin clears God from moral culpability, assigning blame to creation, particularly to the misuse of freedom. Unlike Augustine and Aquinas, however, Calvin does not focus on God's permission of evil as much as on His co-option of evil to further His mysterious providential ends. God is not the victim of His own creation, like a failed cosmic experiment, and evil does not take God by surprise or thwart His inscrutable sovereign will. God has not, Calvin insists, lost control of the Universe. Rather, evil fits within God's larger designs for creation, and so expresses the divine will even as it resists it. Calvin's paradoxical stance on providence and evil reflects his Augustinian heritage and his commitment to God's omnipotent sovereignty over the Universe.

In all this we see the influence of the medieval nominalists and their arguments that we cannot reason or speculate our way to knowledge of God, and we cannot draw analogies from human experience or from nature to God. All we know about God is what we learn in scripture. That is, Calvin did not ask the question, "Why is creation the way it is?" He observed the fact of evil and suffering in the world, and the Biblical account in Genesis of the Fall. The elect are given the gift of faith, which brings, along with assurance that our sins are forgiven, the confidence that while we may not know why God does what God does, God surely does know.

Luis de Molina

Luis de Molina was a 16th-century Spanish Jesuit theologian and philosopher who lived about thirty years after John Calvin, and he took exception to Calvin's teaching on divine sovereignty and human libertarian freedom. Calvin believed that God's omniscience included perfect knowledge of all events past, present, and future. That God sees the past, present and future of the world as altogether one thing, an eternal now.

Rational thinking would lead people to reject a good and just God who predestines and foreknows every event and yet condemns people to Hell. How could the good God of the Bible know beforehand that a human would commit an evil act, then not prevent it, and yet in some way not be responsible for it? Calvin's response was his willingness to accept that God is responsible for the entry of evil into the world. However, he maintained that God cannot be blamed for it, since He uses evil to bring about some greater-good, as directing people back to Himself. Consequently, Molina proposes to go further than Calvin and attempts to remove from God all responsibility for evil, since to think otherwise would detract from God's glory. William Lane Craig calls Molinism one of the most fruitful theological ideas ever conceived, because it serves to explain not only God's meticulous foreknowledge of the future, but divine providence and predestination as well.

The essence of Molina's view is that God is able to arrange any and all circumstances in the world in any way He sees fit. And God knows what every person would freely choose to do, or not do, when faced with a decision in any and all of these circumstances. According to Molina God knows the truth of all counterfactuals. A counterfactual is a conditional statement in which the conditional clause is false, as "If I had done this instead of that, then something else would have happened." And, God knows what that 'something else' is in every case where this could have been done instead of that. Therefore, in light of this 'middle knowledge' God has arranged all the circumstance in the world to bring about the best of all possible worlds in which people have libertarian freewill.

In Molina's theology, God's providence covers free choices in the sense that He brings it about that people with freewill choices are placed in such and such circumstances knowing they will make such and such free choices. Thus, if God wanted to accomplish something in particular, all God would have to do, using his middle knowledge, is actualize the one world from among all possible worlds, where that something was freely chosen by His creatures. And conversely, if God did not want something to happen, then all God would have to do is, using His middle knowledge is providentially actualize the world in which that something was not freely chosen. This is not to say that God is pleased or satisfied with everything that takes place in the world. It has been suggested that possibly an event like the Holocaust could not have been omitted by God without something equally bad or worse occurring. Therefore, given human libertarian freedom, the world we live in is the best of all possible worlds.

Molinism has been controversial and criticized since its inception in Molina's *Concordia*. The "grounding objection" is at present the most debated criticism to Molinism, and often considered the strongest. The argument claims that there are no metaphysical grounds for the truthfulness of counterfactuals of creaturely freedom. As Hugh J. McCann puts it:

"Perhaps the most serious objection against it [the truth of counterfactuals] is that there does not appear to be any way God could come by such knowledge. Knowledge, as we have seen, is not merely a matter of conceiving a proposition and correctly believing it to be true. It requires justification: one must have good reasons for believing. But what justification could God have for believing the propositions that are supposed to constitute middle knowledge?"

Jacobus Arminius

Jacobus Arminius was a Dutch theologian from the Protestant Reformation period whose views became the basis of Arminianism and the Dutch Remonstrant movement. He lived about twenty years after Molina and about fifty years after Calvin, and he was taught by Theodore Beza, Calvin's hand-picked successor.

The greater-good theodicies of Irenaeus, Augustine, Calvin, and others, teach that the entry of evil into the world was inevitable, and that evil serves a purpose in the plan of God from which He will bring about a greater-good than would have been possible without the evil. Arminianism does not accept this teaching since it indicates that evil is essential to bring about good, but God does not need evil to bring about good; sin and evil are not essential in God's plan. A greater-good theodicy renders sin and evil essential, thereby making God in some way to some degree responsible or dependent upon evil. Arminius objects saying that God is not responsible or dependent upon evil; it is humans and fallen angels who abused their freewill who are responsible, and evil was not essential for God's plan to succeed.

However, even though God is not responsible for evil, the Arminian theodicy maintains that God does 'allow' evil, even gratuitous evil for which there seems to be no purpose, which keeps God's sovereignty as well as human libertarian freewill intact.

God is so strongly sovereign over evil that no evil will occur that does not serve God's purpose or to which God does not attach some specific meaning or significance. Nothing happens, according to Arminius, by chance or accident.

Also, there is no possible explanation as to why God does not prevent gratuitous evil, and no explanation is necessary apart from the fact that God is sovereign.

However, God undoubtedly does prevent many individual instances of pain and suffering in ways not obvious to anyone. It is important to

Arminius that God never intended or needed evil to occur for His creation plan to be successful, but now that evil is present in the world He can use it in furtherance of His plan. Arminian theology, the theology of the early Church, gives human beings, created in the image of God, the God-given power of moral choice in a way that is authentic.

The classic Arminian view affirms that the future is perfectly foreknown by God, in the way understood by Luis de Molina, and yet is, in principle and practice, 'open' and 'undetermined.' That is, future free decisions made by people are 'certain' but not 'necessary.' The person who makes a moral choice is free, in a libertarian sense, either to make that choice or to make a different choice.

Loving God is the highest function of a created being to which all people are called. In Arminian theology, any form of deterministic philosophy, such as Calvinism, deprives people of an authentic expression of love toward God and destroys the image of God within them.

St. Anselm of Canterbury (1033-1109)

St. Anselm (1033-1109) was a theologian and philosopher of the Catholic Church and was one of the most important Christian thinkers of the eleventh century. He lived about 600 years after Augustine and was heavily influenced by him. He is famous in theology for drawing a relationship between believing and understanding with his maxim, "I do not seek to understand so that I may believe, but I believe so that I may understand" which is based on a saying of Augustine, "believe so that you may understand."

Augustine believed that knowledge of God comes before faith in God, but faith in God brings with it a constant desire for deeper understanding. Christians earnestly want to understand what they believe.

In the preface to his *Proslogion*, St. Anselm declares: "I have written the following short work...from the point of view of someone trying to raise his mind to the contemplation of God, and seeking to understand what he believes."

And he is most famous in philosophy for having discovered and articulated the so-called ontological argument in the *Proslogion*. With the ontological argument St. Anselm is advancing the idea of the existence of a necessary and non-contingent being, from the concept of "a being than which nothing greater can be conceived." And he does so from reason alone, rather than from observation, but from the human notion of a perfect being in whom nothing is lacking.

St. Anselm reasoned that, if such a being fails to exist, then a greater being, namely, "a being than which nothing greater can be conceived," and which does exist, can be conceived. But this would be absurd: nothing can be greater than a being than which nothing greater can be conceived. So a being than which nothing greater can be conceived, God, exists. Anselm's intention in the *Proslogion* was to offer a single argument that would establish not only the existence of God but also define the various attributes that Christians believe God possesses, such as the Omni-perfect attributes of the God of the Bible.

For example, God must be omnipresent, for if He was not, a greater being than He could be conceived. But God is that than which no greater can be conceived, so He must be omnipresent. The ontological argument thus works as a sort of divine-attribute-generating machine. Admittedly, although the ontological argument tells us that God has whatever characteristics it is better or greater to have than to lack, it does not tell us what these characteristics are. We must have some independent way of identifying them before we can plug them into the ontological argument and generate a full-blown conception of the divine nature. Anselm identifies these characteristics in part by appeal to human intuitions about value, and in part by independent argument. And his intuitions about value are shaped by the Neo-Platonic/Augustinian tradition of which he was a part. Augustine took from the Neo-Platonists the idea that the greatest and best of beings are stable, uniform, and unchanging.

Thus Augustine took from the Neo-Platonists ideas of what attributes are the greatest and best of attributes for a greatest of all possible beings to have. Through Augustine (and others) these ideas, and the conception of God to which they naturally lead, became the common view of Christian theologians for well over a millennium. To illustrate, an omnipotent God would be greater than a God who was not omnipotent, with the following clarification from C. S. Lewis. "His omnipotence means the power to do all that is intrinsically possible to do, not to do the intrinsically impossible, and this is not in some way a limitation of his omnipotence. You may attribute miracles to him, but not nonsense. For example, it is intrinsically or logically impossible for God to create a square circle or a married bachelor, as that would be nonsense." The ontological argument, which is the concept of "a being than which nothing greater can be conceived" turns out to be one of the most marvelously fertile and fascinating arguments for understanding and defining the attributes of a non-contingent being who necessarily exists.

However, one of the earliest recorded objections to Anselm's argument for the existence of God was raised by one of Anselm's contemporaries, Gaunilo of Marmoutiers. He offered a criticism suggesting that the "notion" of God cannot be conceived, as Anselm had asserted. He argued that many theists would accept that God, by nature, cannot be fully comprehended and therefore cannot be fully conceived. Therefore, if humans cannot fully conceive of God, the ontological argument fails.

Anselm replied to Gaunilo that the ontological argument applied only to concepts with necessary existence. Anselm suggested that only a non-contingent being who necessarily exists can fulfill the remit of "a being than which nothing greater can be conceived."

However, even if Gaunilo's criticism succeeds, and Anselm's argument to prove the necessary existence of God fails, it does not negate the value of the argument for establishing the various attributes that Christians believe God possesses.

In the interest of completeness, it will be mentioned here that there are three other classical proofs for the existence of the Omni-perfect God of the Bible: (1) the cosmological argument; (2) the teleological argument; and (3) the fine-tuning argument.

(1) The "cosmological" argument is an argument for the existence of God which claims that all things in nature depend on something or someone else for their existence, and that the whole cosmos must therefore itself depend on something or someone else for its existence.

The history of this argument goes back to Parmenides who claimed that "nothing comes from nothing." It was developed in Neo-Platonism and early Christianity and later in medieval Islamic theology during the 9th to 12th centuries, and re-introduced to medieval Christian theology in the 13th century by Thomas Aquinas.

The Kalām cosmological argument is a modern formulation of the argument named for the kalam (medieval Islamic scholasticism), which was popularized by William Lane Craig in his *The Kalām Cosmological Argument* (1979). The Kalam argument's underpinning is the impossibility of an actual infinite and/or the traversing of infinite time. This is what distinguishes it from other cosmological arguments such as that of Thomas Aquinas, which rests on the impossibility of an essentially ordered infinite regress. According to atheist philosopher Quentin Smith, "a count of the articles in the philosophy journals shows that more articles have been published about Craig's defense of the Kalam argument than have been published about any other philosopher's contemporary formulation of an argument for God's existence."

(2) The "teleological argument," also known as the argument from design, or the intelligent design argument, is an argument for the existence of God based on perceived evidence of deliberate design in the natural world.

(3) And the "fine-tuning" argument depends on the empirical claim that, as a matter of natural law, life could not have developed if certain fundamental properties of the Universe were to have differed even slightly from what they are. (1)

Source:
(1) https://www.iep.utm.edu/anselm/
https://www.iep.utm.edu/ont-arg/
https://plato.stanford.edu/entries/anselm/
https://plato.stanford.edu/entries/ontological-arguments/#StAnsOntArg
https://courses.lumenlearning.com/sanjacinto-philosophy/chapter/ontological-argument-criticisms/
https://en.wikipedia.org/wiki/Cosmological_argument
https://en.wikipedia.org/wiki/Kalam_cosmological_argument

https://themajestysmen.com/obbietodd/anselm-v-aquinas-is-gods-existence-self-evident/

St. Thomas Aquinas (1225–1274)

Thomas Aquinas, a thirteenth-century scholastic philosopher and theologian heavily influenced by Augustine, proposed a form of the Augustinian theodicy in his *Summa Theologica*. Aquinas began by attempting to establish the existence of God, through his Five Ways, and then attested that God is good and must have a morally sufficient reason for allowing evil to exist. Aquinas proposed that all goodness in the world must exist perfectly in God, and that, existing perfectly, God must be perfectly good. He concluded that God is goodness, and that there is no evil in God. Aquinas supported Augustine's view that evil is a privation of goodness, maintaining that evil has existence as a privation intrinsically found in good. The existence of this evil, Aquinas believed, can be completely explained by freewill. Faced with the assertion that humans would have been better off without freewill, he argued that the possibility of sin is necessary for a perfect world, and so individuals are responsible for their sin. Good is the cause of evil, but only owing to fault on the part of the agent.

In his theodicy, to say something is evil is to say that it lacks goodness which means that it could not be part of God's creation, because God's creation lacked nothing. Aquinas noted that, although goodness makes evil possible, it does not necessitate evil. This means that God (who is good) is not cast as the cause of evil, because evil arises out of a defect in an agent, and God is seen to be without defect. Philosopher Eleonore Stump, considering Aquinas' commentary on the Book of Job, argues that Aquinas has a positive view of suffering: it is necessary to contrast Earth with Heaven and remind humans that they still have the propensity to commit evil.

Aquinas believed that evil is acceptable because of the good that comes from it, and that evil can only be justified when it is required in order for good to occur. Attempting to relieve God of responsibility for the occurrence of evil, Aquinas insisted that God merely permits evil to happen, rather than willing it. He recognized the occurrence of what seems to be evil, but did not attribute to it the same level of existence that he attributed to spirituality. Like Augustine, Aquinas asserted that humans bear responsibility for evil owing to their abuse of freewill.

The Difference between Anselm and Aquinas

St. Thomas Aquinas lived a century after St. Anselm of Canterbury, and in these two Medieval thinkers there is the replaying of the age old rivalry between Plato and Aristotle. Plato highly regarded knowledge gained a priori from the power of the human mind alone. Whereas Aristotle highly regarded evidence gained a posteriori from a person's ability or power to observe or experience the world. A proposition is knowable a priori if it can be shown to be true independently of evidence acquired by observation or experience. That is, a priori knowledge derives from the power of the human mind to reason that some truths are self-evident truths and require no additional evidence for validation. For example, the proposition that all bachelors are unmarried is a self-evident truth knowable a priori. If the truth of a proposition is not self-evident, then it can be shown to be true a posteriori on the basis of evidence gained by observation or experience. For example, the proposition that it is raining outside is not self-evident and is knowable a posteriori if what is happening outside can be observed.

Regarding the truth of the proposition that God exists, Anselm, the Christian Platonist, offers his ontological argument for the existence of God from the concept of "a being than which nothing greater can be conceived." And he does so from reason alone; that is, from the human notion of a perfect being in whom nothing is lacking. Whereas, for Aquinas the Christian Aristotelian, the truth that God exists is not self-evident, and therefore requires further evidence for validation. He therefore offers his version of a cosmological argument for the existence of God which is a concerted attempt to discern divine truth from within the order of the natural world.

The history of the cosmological argument goes back to Parmenides who claimed that "nothing comes from nothing." That is, all things in nature depend on something or someone else for their existence, and that the whole cosmos must therefore itself depend on something or someone else for its existence.

Anselm offers compelling support from the Bible that the existence of God should be self-evident to the human mind. In Romans 2:15 it says that God's Law is "written on their hearts, while their conscience also bears witness." This then would seem to support Anselm's ontological argument that the existence of God is self-evident. If so, then Anselm's ontological argument isn't so much based on a Platonic worldview as it is a Biblical worldview. But Aquinas' cosmological argument also offers a compelling Biblical response as to whether or not God exists. In Romans 1:20, "For since the creation of the world His invisible attributes, His eternal power and divine nature, have been clearly seen, being understood through what has been made, so that they are without excuse." Therefore, Aquinas' cosmological argument regarding God's existence is not so much an Aristotelian world view as it is a Biblical worldview.

Anselm's reading of Psalm 14:1, "The fool has said in his heart, There is no God," leads Anselm to conclude that the fool is not simply ignorant of a God who has revealed Himself to our hearts and minds, he is not simply blind, he is simply a complete fool. However, Aquinas is more kind and understanding toward Anselm's fool. While not rejecting Anselm's argument outright, Aquinas believes that the existence of God's is not simply self-evident, and must be further validated by means of observation or experience.

The difference between these two Medieval thinkers is then not so much the difference between Plato and Aristotle, as it is between Romans 2:15 and Romans 1:20. In Romans 2:15, St. Paul says, "they show the work of the Law written in their hearts, their conscience bearing witness," supporting Anselm's claim that the existence of God is self-evident. And in Romans 1:20, it says, "For since the creation of the world His invisible attributes, His eternal power and divine nature, have been clearly seen, being understood through what has been made," supporting Aquinas' claim that the existence of God can be known by observing all that God has made. It would seem then that the ontological and cosmological arguments work well together, and stand better together than either can stand alone. (1)

Source:
(1) https://themajestysmen.com/obbietodd/anselm-v-aquinas-is-gods-existence-self-evident/

110

https://www.iep.utm.edu/apriori/

Martin Luther (1483-1546)

Martin Luther was a German theologian and religious reformer who was the catalyst of the 16th-century Protestant Reformation. The Reformation is said to have begun when Martin Luther posted his Ninety-five Theses on the door of the Castle Church in Wittenberg, Germany, on October 31, 1517.

Through his words and actions, Luther precipitated a movement that reformulated certain basic tenets of Christian belief and resulted in the division of Western Christendom between Roman Catholicism and the new Protestant traditions, mainly Lutheranism, Calvinism, the Anglican Communion, the Anabaptists, and the Anti-Trinitarians. He is one of the most influential figures in the history of Christianity.

One of Luther's foremost achievements was the translation of the New Testament into the German vernacular. This task was an obvious ramification of his insistence that the Bible alone is the source of Christian truth and his related belief that everyone is capable of understanding the biblical message.

Certain key tenets of Luther's theology have shaped Protestant Christianity since the 16th century. They include his insistence on the Bible, the Word of God, as the only source of religious authority, a dogma known as sola Scriptura; his emphasis on the centrality of grace, appropriated by faith, as the sole means of human salvation; and his understanding of the church as a community of the faithful, a priesthood of all believers, rather than as a hierarchical structure with a prominent division between clergy and laity.

Like all monotheists Luther confronted the dilemma on the subject of evil and suffering. Does God want to relieve suffering, but is unable? In that case God is good but not all-powerful. Is God able to relieve suffering but unwilling or too unconcerned? Then God is all-powerful but not good. It is debated among Lutherans whether Martin Luther actually provided a theodicy, that is, justifying that God is good and just despite the existence of evil in this world,.

111

Luther agreed with most of the Christian tradition that the Universe was created from nothing by God. This belief emphasizes God's complete omnipotence. That is, God's power is unlimited even by the laws of logic because, as they say, God can do what is logically impossible. It also carries as a consequence the fact that anything wrong with the Universe cannot be attributed to matter or the material of the Universe, since this too is created by God.

Also, if the entrance point for evil and suffering in the world is the work of Satan, resulting in human sin, then this simply pushes the problem back to square one. That is, could not God have created humans in such a way that they would not sin? One option for Christians has been to argue that God created humans with freewill, so that there was a possibility that they would not sin. In that case, the buck for sin would stop squarely on the desk of humans.

But Luther rejected this option. For him, humans do not have the freewill to choose to accept or reject salvation (this is in contrast to John Wesley and Thomas Aquinas). For Luther, the buck for sin and salvation ultimately stops with God.

Why would God set the Universe up in such a way? Some Christians have argued that God sets it up this way because God's power and glory are more clearly shown in allowing and then saving from sin than if sin had never entered the world. (This is the tradition of O felix culpa! O happy sin!) Luther also rejected this argument. Sin and evil, the causes of suffering, were finally for Luther a mystery. For Luther all the possible ways of explaining it or getting God off the hook for it (called in theology "theodicy," literally, "justifying God") are inappropriate speculation.

Luther inherited from the medieval nominalists the belief that God is completely hidden from us. The only exception is what God has chosen to reveal in scripture. Scripture is not intended to satisfy our curiosity; it tells us only what we need to know to be saved. One thing it tells us (and this, according to Luther, is absolutely necessary to be saved) is that God's ways are not ours.

We ought not wonder why God did not set things up differently, or try to make sense of the way things are set up. We are born into the middle of the set-up, and our only hope is to cling to the promise of salvation from sin, evil, and suffering through Christ found in the Bible.

In Luther's 1530 sermon On Cross and Suffering, based on Christ's passion in the Gospels, Luther showed his pastoral response to the Christian who suffers under God's hand., he wrote, "Christ had no need at all for this suffering, but we and the whole human race needed this suffering.....Therefore we must note in the first place that Christ by his suffering not only saved us from the devil, death, and sin, but also that his suffering is an example, which we are to follow in our suffering.

Though our suffering and cross should never be so exalted that we think we can be saved by it or earn the least merit through it, nevertheless we should suffer after Christ, that we may be conformed to him. For God has appointed that we should not only believe in the crucified Christ, but also be crucified with him... 'He who does not take his cross and follow me,' He says, 'is not worthy of me.' (1)

Source:
(1) https://www.britannica.com/biography/Martin-Luther
http://lutherantheologystudygroup.blogspot.com/2012/05/did-luther-do-any-theodicy.html
The Problem of Evil, by Peterson
https://www.patheos.com/library/lutheran/beliefs/suffering-and-the-problem-of-evil

---

Gottfried Wilhelm Leibniz (1646–1716)

Gottfried Wilhelm Leibniz was a prominent German polymath and one of the most important logicians, mathematicians and natural philosophers of the Enlightenment (1685–1815). (In philosophy, Leibniz is most noted for his optimism, his conclusion that our Universe is, in a restricted sense, the best possible one that God could have created, an idea that was often lampooned by others such as Voltaire, following the Great Lisbon Earthquake in 1755. Of importance, Leibniz coined the term "theodicy" in 1710 in his work *Théodicée*, in an attempt to justify God's existence in light of the apparent imperfections of the world.

Theodicy and Optimism

The *Theodicy* tries to justify the apparent imperfections of the world by claiming that it is optimal among all possible worlds. It must be the best possible and most balanced world, because it was created by an all-powerful and all-knowing God, who would not choose to create an imperfect world if a better world could be known to Him or possible to exist. This follows from Anselm (1033-1109) where in his *Proslogium* Ch II he stated, "And indeed, we believe that thou art a being than which nothing greater can be conceived." In effect, apparent flaws that can be identified in this world must exist in every possible world, because otherwise God would have chosen to create the world that excluded those flaws.

The *Theodicy* is Leibniz's attempt to reconcile his personal philosophical system with his interpretation of the tenets of Christianity. This project was motivated in part by Leibniz's belief, shared by many conservative philosophers and theologians during the Enlightenment, in the rational and enlightened nature of the Christian religion as compared against its purportedly less-advanced non-Western counterparts. It was also shaped by Leibniz's belief in the perfectibility of human nature (if humanity relied on correct philosophy and religion as a guide), and by his belief that metaphysical necessity must have a rational or logical foundation, even if this metaphysical causality seemed inexplicable in terms of physical necessity (the natural laws identified by science). According to Leibniz, since reason and faith must be entirely reconciled, any tenet of faith which could not be defended by reason must be rejected.

Leibniz then approached one of the central criticisms of Christian theism: if God is all good, all wise, and all powerful, then how did evil come into the world? The answer (according to Leibniz) is that, while God is indeed unlimited in wisdom and power, his human creations, as creations, are limited both in their wisdom and in their will (power to act). This predisposes humans to false beliefs, wrong decisions, and ineffective actions in the exercise of their freewill. God does not arbitrarily inflict pain and suffering on humans; rather He permits both moral evil (sin) and physical evil (pain and suffering) as the necessary consequences of metaphysical evil (imperfection), as a means by which humans can identify and correct their erroneous decisions, and as a contrast to true good. Further, although human actions flow from prior causes that ultimately arise in God and therefore are known to God as metaphysical certainties, an individual's freewill is exercised within natural laws, where choices are merely contingently necessary and to be decided in the event by a "wonderful spontaneity" that provides individuals with an escape from rigorous predestination. (1)

Source:
(1) https://en.wikipedia.org/wiki/Gottfried_Wilhelm_Leibniz

John Wesley (1703–1791)

John Wesley was an English cleric, theologian and evangelist who was a leader of a revival movement within the Church of England known as Methodism. The societies he founded became the dominant form of the independent Methodist movement that continues to present. Educated at Charterhouse and Christ Church, Oxford, Wesley was elected a fellow of Lincoln College, Oxford in 1726 and ordained as an Anglican priest two years later. He led the "Holy Club", a society formed for the purpose of study and the pursuit of a devout Christian life; it had been founded by his brother, Charles, and counted George Whitefield among its members. In contrast to Whitefield's Calvinism, Wesley embraced Arminian doctrines. (1)

The Theodicy of John Wesley

From time immemorial to the present theologians have debated the question of theodicy, by which is meant the justification of divine providence, the reconciliation of the existence of evil with the goodness and sovereignty of God. It is not surprising then to find that John Wesley attempts a solution to this problem in his sermon entitled "God's Love to Fallen Man," using as his text Romans 5:15: "Not as the offence, so also is the free gift." Near the beginning of the sermon Wesley declares that it is exceedingly strange that hardly anything had been written on the subject. This is a bit surprising from a man so well read as the founder of Methodism. The question was raised in Job, it was debated by Plato and the Stoics, by Plotinus, Augustine, Giordano Bruno and Jakob Boehme, all of whom lived before Wesley's day. The matter was raised by Kant and Hegel, who were more or less contemporary with him. Could it be to one of these Wesley refers when he writes in the sermon "that plausible account of the origin of evil, published to the world some years ago, and supposed to be unanswerable: that, 'it naturally results from the nature of matter, which God was not able to alter'? It is very kind of this sweet-tongued orator to make an excuse for God! But there is really no occasion for it: God hath answered for himself."

Wesley follows by stating that man abused his liberty, produced evil; brought pain into the world. This God permitted in order to bring forth a fuller manifestation of his wisdom, justice and mercy, to bestow an infinitely greater happiness than could have been obtained unless Adam had fallen. But let us permit Wesley to develop his own argument. Wesley says there has been more happiness and holiness in the world than there could have been had not Adam sinned, for, then, Christ would not have died, thus, not showing his amazing love to mankind, as an Advocate with the Father. There could have been no justification by faith and no redemption in the blood of Christ; He could not have been made God to us. Further, continues Wesley, there would have been no room for love; we could not have known the power of the resurrection, nor the love of the Holy Spirit. Weslsey concludes that tragic error of our first parents opened the way for God's Son to die for us, and without this we would have lost the motive of brotherly love.

Wesley proposed that the entrance of evil into the world became the cause of suffering, yet, what are called "afflictions" in the language of men are, in the thought of God, blessings. If there had been no suffering then one of the most excellent parts of our religion would have been missing, the noblest of all Christian graces, love enduring all things. The sight worthy of God is to see a man struggling with adversity, and superior to it. By affliction our faith is tried, made acceptable to God. By the coming of evil we cultivate the quieter virtues: patience, meekness, gentleness, longsuffering; otherwise, there would have been no returning good for evil. Adam's fall gave all posterity the opportunity of exercising the passive virtues and doing good in numberless instances, for, the more good we do the happier we will be. If Adam had not fallen, then each individual would have been personally responsible for his wrongdoing to God; but by the death of Christ, to break the power of evil, every man now rests on the covenant of grace. By the Fall, God was compelled to send his Son into the world, otherwise we could not have known Christ in the flesh. By the birth, life and death of our Lord we have come to know the "unsearchable riches of Christ." Mercy now rejoices over judgment.

Having canvassed the earthly virtues that Wesley considers to have come through evil, he now proceeds to delineate the eternal values so derived. The most holy are those who have most successfully opposed sin, thus, they will shine brightest in heaven. Evil brought a train of woe which God's children have helped to combat by their good works, the reward for which they will receive in heaven. Wickedness entails suffering, but those who suffer with Christ shall also reign with him.

To sum up, and in conclusion, Wesley preaches that God permitted Adam's transgression in order that He might more fully manifest his wisdom, justice and mercy. By mankind conquering wickedness through the merits of Christ's death, the race has found a source of greater holiness and happiness than it could otherwise have known. While the ways of God may be unsearchable to us we can discern the general scheme of the divine plan running through all eternity.

A Criticism of Wesley's Theodicy

It seems surprising that Wesley, so well versed in Scripture, did not see his argument answered from the Book. It is only necessary to refer to two texts: Romans 9:14, "What shall we say then? Is there unrighteousness with God? God forbid." Galatians 2:17b, "Is Christ therefore the minister of sin? God forbid." Other verses could be cited.

Dr. Daniel Curry, in an editorial in *The Methodist Review*, November, 1888, answered the founder of Methodism. "John Wesley theodicy is a theological heresy, an unconscious variation from the truth. The doctrine of sin as taught in Sermon LXIV is obnoxious in its accumulated assumptions, a perversion of the Scriptures adduced to support it, and if adopted as explanatory of the world's irregularities must logically legitimate man's disaster and render atonement unnecessary and void, or a makeshift for mischief which might have been prevented. To declare the "unspeakable advantage" of the Fall, to speculate on the innumerable benefits of natural and moral evil; to condemn our repining of Adam's transgression as the source of earth's woes; and to insist that man should glorify God because He instituted sin as the instrument of suffering, and by suffering of final elevation, is a doctrine to be rejected....If evil is constitutionally or instrumentally good, or it can be established that a sinful world is provisionally happier, it might be well to introduce the disciplinary regime of sin among the angels, for they are imperfect and distant from the perfections of God. A whiff of polluted atmosphere might sweep over the hills of immortality to good effect upon those who inhabit the heights. ... Sin is the essential opposition to God, He hates it, we hate it, and any defense of it savors of the pit whence it came." (2)

A Comment on Wesley's Theodicy by Jerry L. Walls

John Wesley explained the existence of evil in moral rather than metaphysical terms. His understanding of the fall was fairly typical of western theology and he also enthusiastically embraced a version of the felix culpa theme as essential for theodicy. Unlike many influential western theologians, he also relied heavily on libertarian freedom to account for evil. His most striking proposal for theodicy involves his eschatological vision of the future in which he believed the entire world living then will be converted. I argue that his theodicy is implicitly universalist, especially in its eschatological speculations, and show that this is in tension with his strong libertarian commitments. (3)

Source:
(1) https://en.wikipedia.org/wiki/John_Wesley
(2)G.F.Hubbartt:place.asburyseminary.edu/asburyjournal/vol12/iss2/3/
(3) The abstract from: "As the Waters Cover the Sea": John Wesley on the Problem of Evil by Jerry L. Walls

---

David Hume (1711-1776)

David Hume, a Scottish philosopher and historian, was in the end 'weakly deistic.' He claimed that it is not possible to infer the existence of a good God from the facts of evil but that the concomitant presence of good also blocks an inference to a completely malicious being. Since the world contains a perplexing mix of good and evil, the most reasonable inference is to a creator that is completely indifferent to his sentient creatures.

John Leslie Mackie (1917-1981)

Taking Hume's claims further, J. L. Mackie, a moral skeptic, in his book *Evil and Omnipotence* (1955), published his argument that was designed to expose a logical contradiction between the existence of God and the existence of evil; an argument which, if valid, is a direct disproof of theism. Mackie claimed that religious beliefs not only lack rational support, but are positively irrational, in that several parts of the essential theological doctrine of the nature of God are inconsistent with one another, as the omnipotence of God and the benevolence of God. In its simplest form, following Epicurus, the problem of evil is this: God is omnipotent; God is wholly good; and yet evil exists; therefore God does not exist. Beginning in the second half of the twentieth century, atheologians (persons who try to prove the non-existence of God) commonly claimed that the problem of evil was a problem of logical inconsistency which became known as the 'logical problem of evil.'

Alvin C. Plantinga (1932)

The Freewill Defense

Alvin Plantinga, in *God, Freedom, and Evil* (1974&1977) presented a response to the logical problem of evil as stated by Mackie. This has become known as the 'freewill defense' to the logical problem of evil. In it he demonstrated that the coexistence of an omnipotent benevolent God and of evil is logically consistent. Such a defense (not a "theodicy" proper) does not demonstrate the existence of God, or the probable existence of God, but only attempts to prove that the existence of God and the presence of evil in the world are not logically inconsistent. He argued that if evil is the result of the actions of free, rational, fallible human beings, then the existence of God and evil are consistent.

This argument is supported by claiming that there are some things that an omnipotent God could not do, yet remain omnipotent; for example, He could not create a square circle or a married bachelor. Specifically, if God grants a kind of freewill to humans that is incompatible with any form of determinism, then it is not within God's power to control the outcome of their choices, thus allowing the possibility for evil.

Plantinga's version of the defense embraces Augustine's view of freewill, that it is a good thing for people to have because they could not live well without it. Theologian Alister McGrath has noted that, because Plantinga only argued that the coexistence of God and evil are logically possible, he did not present a theodicy, but a defense. Plantinga did not attempt

119

to demonstrate that his proposition is true or plausible, just that it is logically possible.

Given that many theists and non-theists came to agree that the freewill defense of Plantinga shows that the logical argument against theism, as exemplified in Mackie, fails, many atheistic and nontheistic professional philosophers developed a different type of argument to show why evil is still a problem for theism. That is, even though it is 'logically possible' that a 'good' God can coexist with evil, it is still highly improbable that an omnipotent and omnibenevolent God exists given the preponderance of 'evidence' of evil in the world.

What became known as the 'evidential argument from evil' claims that some fact or facts about the evidence of evil in the world count against the credibility or probability of theistic belief. This argument assumes both that a 'good' God would prevent or eliminate any 'gratuitous evil' which does not lead to a greater-good and also, therefore, that a greater-good for every evil or type of evil must be specified in order for the theodicy to be adequate.

One critical issue in the ongoing discussion concerns the concept of gratuitous evil, that is, any evil that is not necessary to achieve some greater-good or to prevent another evil that is equally bad or worse. The controversy pertains to two key questions: whether it is rational to believe that gratuitous evils exist and whether standard theism requires God to prevent them.

O Felix Culpa Theodicy

Departing from his usual defensive stance that the logical argument against theism fails, Alvin Plantinga articulates a 'felix culpa' or 'fortunate fault' theodicy similar to Augustine and Wesley. Based on this ancient theme, the human fall into sin is an exceedingly fortunate event because, in addressing sin, God enacts a plan of redemption that involves the incomparable good of the Incarnation and Atonement. So, if God's intention is to create a highly valuable world that includes not only the good of His own existence but the good of Incarnation and Atonement, then, logically, He must will that the world contain sin, suffering, and evil.

Kevin Diller responds by questioning Plantinga's strategy of interpreting evil as a means to God's far greater ends. Diller argues that this makes evil a functional good, somehow rational and fitting in God's economy, thus distorting its true theological significance as needless and harmful but permitted rebellion and damage.

William L. Rowe (1931-2015)

William L. Rowe, a philosopher of religion and an atheist, formally postulated his version of the 'evidential argument from evil' in 1979, but its roots are ancient. Rowe claims that it is reasonable to think that at least some of the intense suffering in our world could have been prevented without losing a greater-good or without allowing an equally bad or worse evil. Since Rowe assumes that theism entails that God is justified in permitting evils only if they are essential to a greater-good, he believes he has good grounds for atheism.

For William Rowe and others who advance the evidential argument from evil, God reveals to human beings neither the specific reasons nor the fact that he even has reasons for permitting gratuitous evil. If then, there is any true analogy between God's ways and human ways, then given the good-parent analogy, it is reasonable to think that the goods for the sake of which a loving, self-revealing God allows evils would not be totally beyond our ken.

The version of the evidential argument from evil offered by Paul Draper frames the matter as follows: although theism may offer an explanation for evil that has some degree of plausibility on its own, there may be a competing hypothesis that explains evil better by comparison. Draper argues that atheism explains the actual pattern of pain and pleasure in the world better than theism does. The focus here is not on our inability to see a justifying reason but on our supposed ability to see that an atheistic explanation is superior to a theistic one.

Peter van Inwagen (1942)

Peter van Inwagen in the book *The Problem of Evil*, discusses various senses of the term, "problem of evil." Not surprisingly, the problem of evil he will be addressing is the problem of answering the argument from evil, the argument, or rather arguments, against the existence of God based on the facts about evil. And in it he accepts the views that in some circles are coming to be known as 'open theism,' though he does not himself use that term. The answers to different versions of the argument from evil take the form of 'defenses' rather than 'theodicies.' Defenses are stories which are such that they might be true if God exists and which, if they were true, would show that God has morally adequate reasons for permitting various sorts of evils. As will be seen these defenses may well constitute at least the core of a modest theodicy

He first addresses the "global argument from evil," which points out that the world contains vast amounts of truly horrendous evil, and claims that this would not be the case if there were a God. Van Inwagen's answer to that is a fairly elaborate free-will defense, including a state of original righteousness in which humans enjoyed the 'beatific vision' of God in the Garden of Eden and also possessed preternatural powers which enabled them to protect themselves against natural evils. There would of course be no moral evils in such a state. The fall of the original group of humans into sin led to the loss both of the beatific vision and of the preternatural powers. Therefore, humans became subject to destruction by the random forces of nature, and also to an ever-worsening series of man-made evils in the horrific treatment of humans by other humans.

God, in his love and mercy, put into operation a plan to rescue human beings from this predicament, and draw them back into the love-relationship with Himself that is their only true happiness. This however requires voluntary cooperation from the human beings involved; love cannot be forced. So, for human beings to cooperate with God in this rescue operation, they must know that they need to be rescued. They must know what it means to be separated from him. And what it means to be separated from God is to live in a world of horrors. If God simply "canceled" all the horrors of this world by an endless series of miracles, He would thereby frustrate his own plan of reconciliation.

If He did that, we should be content with our lot and should see no reason to cooperate with him. Van Inwagen proposes that God does in fact prevent a great deal of the evil and suffering that would otherwise result from the rebellion against Him which is the present state of the human race. But for the reasons given, He cannot prevent all of it.

Van Inwagen goes on to attend to "local" arguments from evil, arguments from particular evils that are not deflected by his response to the global argument. The first of these is an argument from horrors that lead to no greater-good, or none that an omnipotent being could not have obtained without permitting the horror in question. The response is that horrors are an inevitable consequence of the separation of humans from God; by preventing all horrors God would prevent humans from becoming aware of their need to be reconciled with him. Van Inwagen contends that in general there is no minimum number of horrors that must be permitted in order to make human beings aware of the evils of their present state. That is, if 'n' horrors would suffice to accomplish a certain purpose, then n - 1 horrors would accomplish the same purpose. God cannot prevent all horrors, because that would frustrate his plan for reuniting human beings with himself. But wherever God draws the line on the number of horrors permitted, it will be an arbitrary line. In view of this, the moral requirement that God should prevent every horror that does not lead to a greater-good is unsound and should be rejected.

The other local argument from evil is based on the suffering of animals. This suffering, in a great many cases, cannot be seen as the consequence of wrong-doing by human beings, and thus is untouched by the free-will defense deployed thus far. The answer to this involves several important claims: The existence of "higher-level sentient creatures" (animals that are conscious in a way comparable to the higher non-human mammals) is a great good. Any world containing such creatures either contains a great deal of animal suffering, or else is "massively irregular" due to frequent divine intervention in the ordinary course of nature. But for a world to be massively irregular is a defect at least as great as the defect of containing large amounts of animal suffering. In view of these things, God is not morally at fault for having created a world such as ours, which does indeed contain a great deal of animal suffering.

Van Inwagen maintains that this "anti-irregularity defense," when conjoined with the free-will defense, constitutes "a composite defense that accounts for the sufferings of both human beings and beasts", and also may after all constitute at least the core of a modest theodicy. (1)

Van Inwagen states elsewhere in his essay "The Place of Chance in a World Sustained by God:" If what I have said is true, it yields a moral for students of the problem of evil: Do not attempt any solution to the problem that entails that every particular evil has a purpose, or that, with respect to every individual misfortune, or every devastating earthquake, or every disease, God has some special reason for allowing it. Concentrate rather on the problem of what sort of reasons a loving and providential God might have for allowing His creatures to live in a world in which many of the evils that happen to them for no reason at all. (2)

Source:
(1) https://ndpr.nd.edu/news/the-problem-of-evil/
(2) http://andrewmbailey.com/pvi/Chance.pdf

Marilyn McCord Adams (1943-2017)

In addition to philosophical work on the logical and evidential versions of the problem of evil, some work has also been done on what we might call the 'existential version of the problem of evil.' The 'existential problem of evil' calls attention to the personal 'real-life' dimension of the problem in addition to the more impersonal abstract and general lines of reasoning that are typically pursued when discussing the logical and evidential problem of evil. Marilyn Adams explores the redemptive or salvific nature of human suffering, providing what we might consider to be a forthrightly spiritual solution to the existential problem of evil. Adams advocates 'the logic of compensation' for the victims of evil, a postmortem healing of divine intimacy with God. This goes so deep, she believes, that eventually victims will see the horrors they suffered as points of contact with the incarnate, suffering God and cease wishing they had never suffered them. (1)

She was an avowed Christian universalist, believing that ultimately all will receive salvation and restoration in Christ. Traditional doctrines of Hell err again by supposing either that God does not get what God wants with every human being ("God wills all humans to be saved" by God's antecedent will) or that God deliberately creates some for ruin. To be sure, many human beings have conducted their ante-mortem lives in such a way as to become anti-social persons. Almost none of us dies with all the virtues needed to be fit for heaven. Traditional doctrines of hell suppose that God lacks the will or the patience or the resourcefulness to civilize each and all of us, to rear each and all of us up into the household of God. They conclude that God is left with the option of merely human penal systems, namely liquidation or quarantine. (2)

When confronted by horrendous evil, even the most pious believer may question not only life's worth but also God's power and goodness. A distinguished philosopher and a practicing minister, Marilyn McCord Adams has written a highly original work on a fundamental dilemma of Christian thought—how to reconcile faith in God with the evils that afflict human beings. Adams argues that much of the discussion in analytic philosophy of religion over the last forty years has offered too narrow an understanding of the problem. The ground rules accepted for the discussion have usually led philosophers to avert their gaze from the worst-horrendous-evils and their devastating impact on human lives. They have agreed to debate the issue on the basis of religion-neutral values, and have focused on morals, an approach that Adams claims is inadequate for formulating and solving the problem of horrendous evils. She emphasizes instead the fruitfulness of other evaluative categories such as purity and defilement, honor and shame, and aesthetics. If redirected, philosophical reflection on evil can, Adams's book demonstrates, provide a valuable approach not only to theories of God and evil but also to pastoral care.

Source:
(1) https://en.wikipedia.org/wiki/Marilyn_McCord_Adams
(2) https://www.amazon.com/Horrendous-Goodness-Cornell-Philosophy-Religion/dp/0801486866

Eleanore Stump (1947)

The problem of evil traditionally has been understood as an apparent inconsistency in theistic beliefs. Orthodox believers of all three major monotheisms, Judaism, Christianity, and Islam, are committed to the truth of the following claims about God: (1) God is omnipotent; (2) God is omniscient; (3) God is perfectly good. Reasonable people of all persuasions are also committed to this claim: (4) There is evil in the world; and many theists in particular are bound to maintain the truth of claim (4) in virtue of their various doctrines of the afterlife or the injunctions of their religion against evil. As other philosophers have pointed out, there is a logical inconsistency in (1)-(4). To show such an inconsistency, one would need at least to demonstrate that this claim must be true: (5) There is no morally sufficient reason for God to allow instances of evil.

Plantinga's presentation of the freewill defense is a landmark in contemporary discussions of the problem of evil. As Plantinga expounds it, the freewill defense rests on these two philosophical claims, which it adds to the theological assumptions: (6) Human beings have freewill; (7) Possession of freewill and the use of it to do more good than evil is a good of such value that it outweighs all the evil in the world.

Besides (1)-(7), there are three Christian beliefs that seem to me especially relevant to the problem of evil. They are these: (8) Adam fell. (9) Natural evil entered the world as a result of Adam's fall. (10) After death, depending on their state at the time of their death, either (a) human beings go to heaven or (b) they go to hell. It is clear that these beliefs themselves raise a host of problems, partly because they seem implausible or just plain false and partly because they seem to raise the problem of evil again in their own right.

According to the Christian beliefs summarized as (8), (9), and (10), all human beings since Adam's fall have been defective in their freewills, so that they have a powerful inclination to will what they ought not to will, to will their own power or pleasure in preference to greater-goods. It is not possible for human beings in that condition to go to heaven, which consists in union with God; and hell understood in Dantean terms is arguably the best alternative to annihilation. A good God will want to fix such persons, to save them from hell and bring them to heaven; and as the creator of these persons, God surely bears some responsibility for fixing and saving them if He can. How is He to do so?

It seems to me clear that He cannot fix the defect by using his omnipotence to remove it miraculously. The defect is a defect in freewill, and it consists in a person's generally failing to will what he ought to will. To remove this defect miraculously would be to force a person's freewill to be other than it is; it would consist in causing a person to will freely what he ought to will. But it is logically impossible for anyone to make a person freely will something, and therefore even God in his omnipotence cannot directly and miraculously remove the defect in freewill, without destroying the very freedom of the will He wants to fix.

126

If God cannot by his omnipotence directly fix the defect in freewill, it seems that human beings must fix it themselves. Self-repair is a common feature of the natural world, but I do not think self-repair is possible for a person with post-fall freewill. People, of course, do sometimes reform their lives and change their habits and will something different from what they previously willed. To reform the will requires willing something different from what one previously willed; that is, it requires a change of will. But how to change the will is the problem in the first place. If we want to know whether a man himself can fix a defect in his will, whether he himself can somehow remove his tendency to will what he ought not to will, it is no help to be told that of course he can if he just wills to change his will.

We know that a man can change his will for the better; otherwise his will would not be free. The problem with a defect in the will is not that there is an inability to will what one ought to will because of some external restraint on the will, but that one does not and will not will what one ought to will because the will itself is bent towards evil. Consequently, changing the will is the end for which we are seeking the means; if one were willing to change one's will by willing what one ought to will, there would be no problem of a defect in the will. Self-repair, then, is no more a solution to the problem of a defective will than is God's miraculous intervention.

If God cannot and human beings will not fix the defect in their wills, what possible cure is there? Christianity suggests what seems to me the only remaining alternative. Let a person will that God fix his defective will. In that case, God's alteration of the will is something the person has freely chosen, and God can then alter that person's will without destroying its freedom. It is a fact well-attested in religious literature that people who find it next to impossible to will what (they believe) they ought to will may nonetheless find it in themselves to will that God alter their wills. Willing to have God save one from one's sin is willing to have God bring one to a state in which one is free from sin, and that state depends essentially on a will which wills what it ought to will.

What role God plays in man's coming to will that God fix his will is controversial in the history of Christian thought. Some Protestant theologians have argued that God bears sole responsibility for such willing; Pelagius apparently argued that all the responsibility belongs to man. Perhaps the correct view here too consists in postulating a cooperative divine and human effort. At any rate, if a man does will that God fix his will or save him from his sins, then I think that God can do so without detriment to freewill, provided that He does so only to the extent to which the man freely wills that God do so. And so, in general, God's fixing the will seems to be a lengthy process, in which a little willing produces a little fixing, which in turn promotes more willing of more fixing. On Christian doctrine, this is the process of sanctification, which is not finally completed until after death when it culminates "in the twinkling of an eye" in the last changes which unite the sanctified person with God.

The fixing of a defective freewill by a person's freely willing that God fix his will is, I think, the foundation of a Christian solution to the problem of evil. With considerable diffidence, then, I want to suggest that Christian doctrine is committed to the claim that a child's suffering is outweighed by the good for the child which can result from that suffering. This is a brave (or foolhardy) thing to say, and the risk inherent in it is only sharpened when one applies it to cases in which infants suffer, for example, or in which children die in their suffering.

On the solution to the problem of evil which I have been developing in this paper, if God is good and has a care for his creatures, his overriding concern must be to insure not that they live as long as possible or that they suffer as little pain as possible in this life but rather that they live in such a way as ultimately to bring them to union with God. I think, then, that it is possible to produce a defensible solution to the problem of evil by relying both on the traditional theological and philosophical assumptions in (1)-(4) and (6), and on the specifically Christian doctrines in (8)-(10).

Like other recent attempted solutions, this one also rests fundamentally on a revised version of (7), namely, this: (7''') Because it is a necessary condition for union with God, the significant exercise of freewill employed by human beings in the process which is essential for their being saved from their own evil is of such great value that it outweighs all the evil of the world. That is, (7''') constitutes a morally sufficient reason for evil and so is a counter-example to (5), the claim that there is no morally sufficient reason for God to permit instances of evil.

128

Furthermore, although I have argued for one particular good as the good which justifies moral and natural evil, nothing in my account rules out the possibility that either sort of evil may produce other goods as well. On my account, however, what ultimately gives exercise of freewill its main value is its necessary role in producing union with God; and it is this significant exercise of freewill, a bent freewill cooperating in its own cure, which I have argued outweighs all the evil in the world. Finally, for the many other goods sometimes said to be produced by evil, such as punishment for sins or aesthetic completion of the whole canvas of creation, if any of these are in fact both good and produced by evil, I welcome them into my account. In (7''') I have singled out one good produced by evil as the good which justifies all the evil in the world, but nothing in this claim rules out the possibility that evil produces various other lesser goods as well which may contribute to the justification of some sorts of evil.

In the brief exposition of this solution in this paper, I cannot hope to have given anything but a sketch and a preliminary defense of it; to do it justice and to consider carefully all the questions and objections it raises would require book-length treatment. What I would like to believe I have done is to have shown that with good will and careful attention to the details of the doctrines specific to a particular monotheism there is hope of a successful solution to the problem of evil along the lines developed here. (1)

Source:
(1) Excerpts from *The Problem of Evil*, by Eleanore Stump, Faith and Philosophy Vol. 2 No. 4 October 1985

Bruce A. Little (1945)

A Creation-Order Theodicy (2005) by Bruce A. Little is an argument against greater-good type theodicies. Little is a strong proponent of the view that gratuitous evil exists concurrently with the sovereignty of God and therefore stands in contrast to greater-good theodicies.

A greater-good theodicy is one in which God allows evil to happen. This evil will be used to bring about a greater-good or to prevent an evil equal to or greater than the evil permitted. A greater-good theodicy claims that the good obtained from an evil justifies that evil. Gratuitous evil is an evil from which God does not obtain a greater-good. Greater-good theodicies are based on the premise that gratuitous evil does not exist.

Little's belief in the existence of gratuitous evil comes as an outworking of his Creation Order theodicy. Foundational to Little's theodicy are a) creation order, b) libertarian freedom, c) the best of all possible worlds and d) middle knowledge (i.e., Molinism). Little combines these elements to construct his theodicy.

a) Creation order is the position that God orders creation. For example, Michael Peterson builds his theodicy on the notion that gratuitous evil does exist and that it does not count against the moral perfection of an Omni-perfect God. That is, Peterson affirms that gratuitous evil exists and explains why the existence of gratuitous evil does not count against God's moral perfection.

Although God did not design man to choose evil, He allows man the libertarian freedom of choice as in Arminianism. This is so, because God is faithful to His creation and His creation order. He will not interfere with the order He has established, even though some of His beings turn against Him.

Within God's creation order, humans can make free choices from the limited choices made available. These limits define the 'moral framework' in which humans can operate. A human operating within this framework has an authentic mind and libertarian freedom, able to influence history.

b) Libertarian freedom means that people can make choices and cause events. A choice may be influenced but not controlled by an antecedent choice or event.

c) Little finds the concept of the best of all possible worlds critical to the development of his theodicy. God is all powerful and all good and therefore can only create that which is good. When choosing to create, God must, by his nature, create that which is the best of all the possible worlds, as proposed by Leibniz.

d) Essential to the concept of the best of all possible worlds is God's middle knowledge, i.e., Molinism. This middle knowledge means that God knows all possible contingents stemming from the free choices of his free moral agents under any set of circumstances.

Knowing all the possible contingents allowed God to select the best combination of contingents, thereby selecting or actualizing the best of all possible worlds. Although middle knowledge is controversial, Little believes there are 'good and sufficient reasons' to accept the concept of middle knowledge.

The Creation Order theodicy does not assert that all evil is gratuitous. There may be some good that results from an evil. However, the argument is that a particular evil was not necessary to obtain a specific good. God may have reversed the intent of the evil to bring about a good despite that evil, not because of the evil.

Concluding his argument, Little asserts that 'the sad fact is that in this present age there is much suffering and a large measure of it is gratuitous, which seems to be exactly what one would expect in a place alienated from God.'

_____

Source:
https://www.researchgate.net/publication/332910326_Creation_Order_Theodicy_The_Argument_for_the_Coexistence_of_Gratuitous_Evil_and_the_Sovereignty_of_God

_____

Part IV

Irenaean
Soul-Making Type Theodicies

Part IV is an aggregation of information from different sources
regarding the history and development of Irenaean
Soul-Making Type Theodicies.

A Biography of Irenaeus (130-202 AD)

Irenaeus was a Greek Bishop born during the first half of the 2nd
century, the exact date is thought to be between the years 120 and
140 AD. He is noted for his role in guiding and expanding Christian
communities in what is now the south of France and, more widely, for
the development of Christian theology by combating heresy and defining
orthodoxy. Originating from Polycarp's hometown of Smyrna in Asia
Minor, now İzmir, Turkey, he had seen and heard the preaching of
Polycarp, the last known living connection with the Apostles, who in
turn was said to have heard John the Evangelist. He was brought up in
a Christian family, unlike many of his contemporaries who converted as
adults.

Irenaeus became the leading representative of the Asiatic Johannean
school in the second half of the second century, the champion of
Catholic orthodoxy against Gnostic heresy, the mediator between the

Eastern and Western Churches, the enemy of all error and schism, and, on the whole, the most orthodox of the Ante-Nicene Fathers. Chosen as bishop of Lugdunum, now Lyon, his best-known work is *Against Heresies*, an attack on Gnosticism. To counter the doctrines of the gnostic sects claiming secret wisdom, he offered three pillars of orthodoxy: the scriptures, the tradition handed down from the apostles, and the teaching of the apostles' successors. Intrinsic to his writing is that the surest source of Christian guidance is the Church of Rome, and he is the earliest surviving witness to regard all four of the now-canonical gospels as essential. He is recognized as a saint in both the Catholic Church and in Eastern Orthodox Churches.

During the persecution of Marcus Aurelius, the Roman Emperor from 161–180, Irenaeus was a priest of the Church of Lyon. The clergy of that city, many of whom were suffering imprisonment for the faith, sent him in 177 to Rome with a letter to Pope Eleutherius concerning the heresy of Montanism, and that occasion bore emphatic testimony to his merits. While Irenaeus was in Rome, a persecution took place in Lyon. Returning to Gaul, Irenaeus succeeded the martyr Saint Pothinus and became the second bishop of Lyon. During the religious peace which followed the persecution of Marcus Aurelius, the new bishop divided his activities between the duties of a pastor and of a missionary (as to which we have but brief data, late, and not very certain). Almost all his writings were directed against Gnosticism. Irenaeus alludes to coming across Gnostic writings, and holding conversations with Gnostics, and this may have taken place in Asia Minor or in Rome. However, it also appears that Gnosticism was present near Lyon as he writes that there were followers of 'Marcus the Magician' living and teaching in the Rhone valley.

Little is known about the career of Irenaeus after he became bishop. The last action reported of him (by Eusebius, 150 years later) is that in 190 or 191, he exerted influence on Pope Victor I not to excommunicate the Christian communities of Asia Minor which persevered in the practice of the Quartodeciman celebration of Easter. Nothing is known of the date of his death, which must have occurred at the end of the second or the beginning of the third century. He is regarded as a martyr by the Catholic Church and by some within the Orthodox Church. He was buried under the Church of Saint John in Lyon, which was later renamed St Irenaeus in his honour. The tomb and his remains were utterly destroyed in 1562 by the Huguenots. (1)

133

Irenaeus – Precursor to Theodicy

Irenaeus did not himself develop a fully formed theodicy. The foundational ideas that he proposed lay dormant until Friedrich Schleiermacher (1768-1834) developed them into a full-fledged theodicy. Later, John Harwood Hick, in his book *Evil and the God of Love* (1966) further developed Scheirermacher's ideas into his own theodicy and labeled it an Irenaean type theodicy in honor of Irenaeus being the 'father' of the main ideas.

Like the Augustinian theodicy, the Irenaean type theodicy is a response to the 'evidential' problem of evil, which raises the problem that, if an Omni-perfect God exists, there should be no evidence of evil in the world. Evidence of evil in the world would make the existence of God improbable. Therefore, the Irenaean theodicy attempts to demonstrate that the existence of God remains probable, despite the preponderance of evidence that evil, even the most horrific evil imaginable also exists.

Of the numerous variations of Irenaean soul-making theodicies that have been proposed, they all assert that the world is the best of all possible worlds because it allows humans to develop toward their full potential of moral perfection of being in the likeness of God. They propose that creation is incomplete, as humans are not yet morally mature, and experiencing evil and suffering is necessary for such moral development. Even though humans brought evil into the world by disobeying God, it is God who is responsible for evil in that He created humans with a morally freewill, and it was inevitable that they would disobey Him.

The Irenaean type theodicy proposes that God ordains both moral and natural evil and uses the consequent pain, suffering, and hardship to further His plans and good purposes of bringing humanity to maturity. Therefore, the sometimes painful consequences of moral and natural evil are not to be viewed as a punishment from God for disobedience to God, but rather as God ordained disciplines necessary to motivate and develop humans into the likeness of God. Therefore God is justified for being responsible for evil. To illustrate the benefits of suffering, Irenaeus cited the Biblical example of Jonah, from the Book of Jonah. His suffering, being swallowed by a whale because of disobedience, both enabled God's plan to be fulfilled and also brought Jonah closer to God: Jonah ended up repenting for his sin, and the people of Nineveh turned to God.

Creation and Human Development

According to the Irenaean tradition, humans are not created in a state of perfection, but rather in a childlike state of moral immaturity. The theodicy teaches that creation has two stages. Humans are first created in this world in the image of God with an immature, childlike moral character. In this way, humans are imperfect, not because there is any flaw in them, but because the second-stage of growth into the likeness of God is incomplete. Humans must be gradually refined and developed in an evolutionary-like process to achieve the likeness of God. And this process must proceed in agreement with the person's morally freewill. Therefore, like Augustine, Irenaeus believed a morally freewill is a great good thing to have. And this maturation process will take place throughout the persons' life in this world and in a life or lifetimes to come. Sometime later, there will be a fiery purge that will purify everyone, culminating in a time where everyone's moral character will be fully and finally matured into the likeness of God.

Irenaeus' eschatology was based on a literal interpretation of the Bible, especially the Book of Revelation. He believed that there would be 6000 years of suffering before the world ends in a fiery purge. This fire would purify believers ahead of a new human community existing in the New Jerusalem. The afterlife, Irenaeus proposed, focuses more on a period of time rather than a physical place. He looked forward to a time and place in which humans are developed to moral perfection and live the life of God. In one sense, this is an optimistic view of humanity in that there is no Hell, and all people will eventually be evolved into the likeness of God. And once the likeness of God is attained, the person will live forever in the New Jerusalem in the presence of Jesus Christ, where there will be no pain, suffering, and hardship, in that evil will have served its purpose.

These ideas are based on the understanding that God's declaration in the Book of Genesis that His creation was very good meant that the world is the best of all possible worlds to mature the moral character of humans, rather than be a world free from suffering. The value of this world is to be judged, not primarily by the quantity of pleasure and pain occurring in it at any particular moment, but by its fitness for its primary purpose, the purpose of soul-making.

Modern Irenaean type theodicies do not take the story of Adam & Eve in the Garden of Eden and their subsequent Fall from Grace seriously. They posit that Adam & Eve were not created as mature adults, but instead, they were created as young children. And as with any child, God fully expected them to misbehave and disobey Him. Also, the idea that all progeny of Adam & Eve are born with Original Sin because they were seminally present in the loins of Adam in the Garden, as the Augustinian tradition posits, is not plausible.

Irenaeus was the first to formulate the Recapitulation Theory of the Atonement clearly. This view is a doctrine in Christian theology related to the meaning and effect of the death of Jesus Christ. The English word 'recapitulate' carries with it the notion of going over something again. Used in this way, it means that Christ has reversed the course of humanity from disobedience to obedience by going over again and undoing the wrong that Adam did. Irenaeus saw Jesus Christ as the new Adam, who succeeds where the first Adam failed. And because of His union with humanity, Jesus leads humankind on to eternal life by way of obedience and the gradual moral perfection of a persons' moral character. For Irenaeus, the ultimate goal of Christ's work of solidarity with humankind is to make humankind divine. Irenaeus said in so many words that 'Jesus became what we are so that we could become what He is.' Further, Irenaeus argued that for humans to have freewill, God must be at an 'intellectual distance' from humans, far enough away that belief in God remains a free choice. That is, if humans were too close to God intellectually, they would have no real choice except to believe in Him, and if too far away, then humans would never be able to believe in Him.(1)

Source:
(1) https://en.wikipedia.org/wiki/Irenaeus
http://www.tentmaker.org/books/Retribution/retribution23.htm
https://en.wikipedia.org/wiki/Polycarp
Evil and the God of Love (1966), by John Harwood Hick

Origen of Alexandria (184–253 AD)

Early Christian theologian Origen also presented suffering as necessary for the development of human beings. Theologian Mark Scott has argued that John Hick's theodicy is more closely aligned with Origen's beliefs than Irenaeus' and ought to be called an "Origenian Theodicy." Origen used two metaphors for the world: it is a school and a hospital for souls, with God as Teacher and Physician, in which suffering plays both an educative and healing role. Through an allegorical or symbolic reading of Exodus and the books of Solomon, Origen casts human development as a progression through a series of stages which take place in this life and after death.

Origen believed that all humans will eventually reach Heaven as the logical conclusion of God being 'all in all.' Hell is a metaphor for the purification of our souls where our sinful nature goes to 'Hell' and our original nature, created by God, goes to Heaven.

Development of the Modern Irenaean Theodicy
Friedrich Schleiermacher (1768-1834)

In the early 19th century, Friedrich Schleiermacher proposed a theodicy which John Harwood Hick later identified as Irenaean in nature. Schleiermacher began his theodicy by asserting that God is Omni-perfect and concluded that, because of this, 'God would create flawlessly.' He proposed that it would be illogical for a morally perfect creation to go wrong, as Augustine suggested, and therefore that evil must have been created by God for a good reason. Schleiermacher conceived a perfect world to be one in which God's purposes can be achieved naturally, and will ultimately lead to dependence on God. This theology led Schleiermacher to propose Universalism, arguing that it is God's will for everyone to be saved and that no person could alter this. If we proceed on this definite assumption that all belonging to the human race are eventually taken up into loving fellowship with Christ, then we have the idea of divine fore-ordination of all people.

John Harwood Hick (1922-2012)

In *Evil and the God of Love* (1966) John Hick further developed Schleiermacher's theodicy which itself was based on the work of

137

Irenaeus. Hick's guiding analogy of God as a kind, wise parent, not a malicious, punitive judge, and the world as a schoolroom, not a playroom, for soul-development, gives us the essential contours of his soul-making theodicy. If there is any analogy between God's purpose for his human creatures, and the purpose of loving and wise parents for their children, we have to recognize that the presence of pleasure and the absence of pain cannot be the supreme and overriding end for which the world exists. Rather, this world must be a place of soul-making. And its value is to be judged, not primarily by the quantity of pleasure and pain occurring in it at any particular moment, but by its fitness for its primary purpose, the purpose of soul-making. Hick interprets suffering as providential, not punitive, as an expression of love, not vengeance. According to Hick, "the long travail of the soul-making process" engenders moral goodness, and goodness that arises from strenuous effort has intrinsic value, and more value than readymade goodness, in the eyes of God. Again, if there is any analogy between God's ways and human ways then God cannot be blamed for human disobedience and its consequences, any more than an auto maker can be blamed for a person misusing the car by disobeying the speed limit and having an accident, damaging the car and injuring themselves in the process.

Hick framed his theodicy as an attempt to respond to the problem of evil in light of scientific development, such as Darwin's theory of evolution, and as an alternative to the traditionally accepted Augustinian theodicy. Hick interpreted the Fall of Man, described in the book of Genesis, as a mythological description of the current state of human affairs. He rejected the Augustinian idea that humans were created as morally mature adults in the Garden and then fell away into moral corruption due to disobedience; instead Hick argued that humans are still in the process of moral development.

Hick used Irenaeus' notion of a two-stage development of moral character from the image of God into the likeness of God. He argued that to be created in the first stage image of God means to have the potential for knowledge of and a relationship with God, and this is fulfilled in the second stage when development into the likeness of God is complete. Humanity currently exists in a childlike moral image of God and is being developed into a morally mature adult, in the likeness of God, which is still a work in progress. Hick proposed that human morality is developed through the experience of evil and argued that it is possible for humans to know God, and be conformed into the likeness of God, but only if they choose to do so out of their own freewill.

Hick acknowledges that some instances of suffering seem to serve no constructive purpose and instead just damages the individual. He justifies this by appealing to the concept of mystery. He argues that, if suffering was always beneficial to humans in some way, then it would be impossible for humans to develop compassion or sympathy for another because they would know that the person who is suffering will certainly benefit from it. However, if there is an element of mystery to suffering, to the effect that some people suffer without benefit, it allows feelings of compassion and sympathy to emerge. Nevertheless, indiscriminate, disproportional suffering, what Hick calls the "mystery of evil," still contributes to the soul-making design of the Universe at a macro level, since it cultivates compassion and elicits sympathy for those who suffer unfairly, and since it causes us to strive for the good for its own sake, without any promise of reward for good behavior.

The value Hick placed on freewill was the result of his belief that it is necessary for genuine love. He believed that love which is not freely chosen is valueless. Therefore a genuinely loving God, he argued, would have created humans with freewill. Hick held that it would be possible for God to create beings that would always freely choose to do good, but argued that a genuine loving relationship requires the possibility of rejection. Irenaeus' notion of humans existing at an intellectual distance from God also influenced Hick, as it would ensure a free choice in belief in God. Hick argued that a world without pain or suffering would prevent moral development; that this would leave humans unable to help or harm one another, allowing them no moral choices and so preventing moral development.

The nature of his theodicy required Hick to propose an eschatology in which humans will eventually become fully morally developed. Therefore, he proposed a Universalist theory, arguing that all humans would eventually reach Heaven. For Hick, belief in the afterlife is "crucial for theodicy," and his theory leans heavily on the future accomplishment of God's soul-making design of the world. "Theodicy cannot be content to look to the past, seeking an explanation of evil in its origins, but must look toward the future, expecting a triumphant resolution in the eventual perfect fulfillment of God's good purpose."

Hick is, by necessity, imprecise in his description of the afterlife and its part in our soul-making. And yet, it plays a crucial role in his theodicy. Without the reality of Heaven, Hick believes, soul-making theodicy would fail, since it would leave evil unredeemed, which would mean the failure of God's benevolent, soul-making plan of the Universe. "Without such an eschatological fulfillment, this theodicy would collapse; Heaven completes the soul-making process and vindicates God."

Hick believed that there would be no benefit or purpose to an eternal Hell, as it would render any moral development inconsequential. The eternal suffering of Hell could not be explained in terms of human development, so Hick rejected it. Despite this, he did not reject the existence of Hell as an 'idea,' since to do so could make living morally in this life irrelevant. Rather, he argued that Hell exists as a mythological concept and as a warning of the importance of this life for moral development.

Fyodor Dostoyevsky (1821-1881)

Russian novelist Fyodor Dostoyevsky presented a similar argument in his novel, *The Brothers Karamazov*. This is however not a final argument, given the nature of Dostoyevsky's work as many-voiced (both for and against). In the novel, the character Ivan Karamazov presents an account of incredible cruelty to innocent people and children to his theist brother, Alyosha. Then Ivan asks his brother if he would, hypothetically, choose to be the architect of the eternal happiness of mankind, which would come into existence, if, and only if he would torture an innocent child, a necessary evil, after which this eternal happiness would come into existence. "Would you consent to be the architect under those conditions? Tell me honestly!" "No, I wouldn't agree," said Alyosha quietly. But Dostoyevsky's work being many-voiced in nature, also states that the love Christ showed to all people and for all people, which is Alyosha's final stance in the novel, is the 'only' good, and in the face of evil, the beauty that will save the world.

Richard Swinburne (1934)

British philosopher Richard Swinburne proposed a version of the Irenaean theodicy based on his libertarian view of freewill, a view that one's free actions are not caused by any outside agent. It is a great good that humans have a libertarian morally freewill, able to make free and responsible moral choices. This is a version of the "greater good morally freewill" theodicy. However, if humans do have such a morally freewill, then necessarily there will be the possibility of moral evil. It is not logically possible that God could give humans such freewill and yet ensure that we always use it in the right way. And having such a freewill is worth the cost of the evil consequences that may result from humans having it. Swinburne also argued that, in order for people to make free moral decisions, they must be aware of the consequences of such decisions. Knowledge of these consequences must be based on experience, Swinburne rejected the idea that God could implant such knowledge, arguing that humans would question its reliability.

Another controversy in the overall discussion of evil considers the role of natural evil. The familiar line of argument is that a world run by natural laws is necessary for the sake of a stable environment for the conduct of our lives, although the regular operation of natural laws also creates pain, suffering, disaster, and other evils. According to Swinburne natural evils are necessary to humans having meaningful freedom to commit morally good or evil actions. Natural processes alone give humans knowledge of the effects of their actions without inhibiting their freedom, and if evil is to be a real possibility for them they must know how to allow it to occur.

Eleonore Stump rejects Swinburne's argument that natural evils are necessary for the knowledge that is connected to moral freedom because the relevant knowledge of how to bring about moral evil is available by other avenues (such as divine revelation or scientific study) rather than by induction from actual natural evils. Others declare that without such natural evils certain kinds of good and meaningful acts of heroism and sacrifice would be absent.

David Ray Griffin (1939)

The development of Process Theology, and the associated Process Theodicy, has presented a challenge to both the Irenaean and Augustinian theodicies. David Ray Griffin, in *God, Power and Evil: A Process Theodicy* (1976), criticized Augustine's reliance on freewill and argued that it is incompatible with divine omniscience and omnipotence as presented by Augustine. In later works Griffin argued that humans cannot have freewill if God is omniscient. He contended that, if God is truly omniscient, then He will know infallibly what people will do, meaning that they cannot be free.

He proposed that original sin as Augustine conceived it must itself be caused by God, rendering any punishment unjust. He also criticized the utility of the Irenaean soul-making theodicy which supposes that God inflicts pain for His own ends, which Griffin regarded as immoral.

The process doctrine proposes that God is benevolent, and feels the pain of the world (both physically and emotionally), but suggests that His power is restricted to persuasion, rather than coercion and so is unable to prevent certain evil events from occurring. That is, God is not omnipotent, and does not limit Himself in some way for the sake of His creation, but that His power is limited in a metaphysical sense. That is, God has all the power it is possible for Him to have.

Process Theology accepts God's indirect responsibility for evil, but maintains that He is blameless, and does everything in His power to bring about good. Process Theology also teaches that, rather than creating the world ex nihilo (as Augustine proposed), God created it out of a pre-existent chaos.

Against David Ray Griffin, Bruce Reichenbach defends a more nuanced theistic view of God's power. In the end, says Reichenbach, the process deity is not even a personal being and therefore does not resemble the God of the Bible as understood by the community of faith.

In his introduction to Process Theology, C. Robert Melse argued that, although suffering does sometimes bring about good, not all suffering is valuable and most does more harm than good.
(See: Addendum 16 Process Theology p.312
Addendum 17 Theodicy in Process Theology p.319
Addendum 18 When Did Sin Begin in Process Theology? p.333)

Dewi Zephaniah Phillips (1934-2006)

Philosopher D. Z. Phillips published *The Problem of Evil and the Problem of God* in 2004, presenting a challenge to the Irenaean theodicy. Phillips maintained throughout his work that humans are incapable of fully understanding God, and presented an understanding of the moral diversity of human existence. With reference to the suffering of the Holocaust, he rejected any theodicy which presents suffering as instrumental or utilitarian, arguing that such suffering cannot be justified, regardless of any good that comes of it.

Michael Tooley (1941)

Michael Tooley rejected the Irenaean theodicy as unsatisfactory. He argued that the magnitude of suffering experienced by some people is excessive, supporting Eleanor Stump's view that the suffering endured by those with terminal illnesses cannot be for moral development, and that such illnesses do not fall more often upon those seemingly immoral or in need of development. He also challenged the suffering both of animals and of young children as neither of these instances of suffering serves any useful purpose, as they cannot lead to moral development.

Finally, he questioned whether the current Universe is the best possible world for the moral development of humans. Citing the examples of those who die young and those who experience too great a pain to learn from it, as well as people who suffer too little to learn anything, he suggested that this world is not ideally suited to human development.

Henri Blocher (1937)

French theologian Henri Blocher criticized the Universalism of John Hick's theory. Blocher argued that Universalism contradicts freewill, which is vital to the Irenaean theodicy, because if everyone will receive salvation, humans cannot choose to reject God. Hick did attempt to address this issue by arguing that a free action is one which reflects that character of a person, and that humans were created with a "Godward bias," so would choose salvation. Blocher proposed that Hick must then accept determinism to some degree.

Note

The Augustinian and Irenaean type theodicies mentioned in Part III and Part IV cover a wide range of Christian theodicies. Not mentioned are other Christian theodicies that emphasize certain aspects of those already mentioned since they do not differ significantly.

For example, Thomas Jay Oord has presented a theodicy positing that God does not have the power to control humans. The God of infinite love not only does not have the power to control humans now, but that God never had that power.

Oord defines this as 'essential kenosis.' This would seem similar to David Ray Griffin's Process Theodicy, where such a limitation of God's power and omniscience is not divine self-limitation but a metaphysical feature of God's nature.

———————————

Part V

Traditional Christian Theodicies

The information in Part V is from the Patheos Library of World Religions and Faith Traditions. https://www.patheos.com/library/

It includes 15 Christian Traditions and their views on Suffering and the Problem of Evil. Written by the world's leading authorities on religion and spirituality, the Patheos Library offers the most accurate and balanced information available on the web.

Adventists

Adventists look to the future with hope but are pessimistic about the present. The present age is hopelessly evil, and Christ sits in judgment, as described in Revelation 14:7. Only God's direct action can bring redemption.

Source:
https://www.patheos.com/library/adventist/beliefs/suffering-and-the-problem-of-evil

Anglican/Episcopalian

The existence, and indeed prevalence, of evil and suffering in the world, raises the question of the source of evil. A monistic answer posits a single ultimate source of both good and evil. A dualistic answer posits a battle between distinct forces of good and evil. Christianity, and Anglicanism within it, has taught neither of these, affirming that there is one God who is both all-powerful and all-good. Thus, the problem of evil has been acute for traditional Anglicans and other Christians, for the very existence of evil seems to indicate a God who is incomplete either in power or in goodness. Would not any parent, the proverbial question asks, prevent the suffering of their beloved child if they could?

There has never been an official Anglican teaching on theodicy, a term of 18th-century origin referring to the justification of God's power and goodness given the presence of evil. Traditionally, though, Anglicans have affirmed western theodical teachings, which hold that God created the world and all creatures, and created them good. God did not create evil. To some creatures, however, God gave the freedom to choose--to choose a relationship with God or, on the other hand, to exalt self over God. To choose self over God is to reject God, and because God is wholly good and the source of all goodness, to reject goodness. Evil, therefore, is merely a corruption of the good, with no positive essence of its own.

This corruption, traditional Anglicanism continues, occurred when the first human beings (who had been made in God's image) rebelled against God, exalting their own desires over God's command. They fell from their created perfection, and evil entered the world--which is to say the complete goodness of the world became corrupted. The nature of things changed.

Humanity's nature changed from being in perfect communion with God (and therefore sharing in God's goodness) to being severed from God and naturally inclined toward evil. All people sin. Consequently, moral corruption will always taint, at times, to the point of obliterating human goodness toward one another. This is why moral evil pervades humanity, why all human relationships suffer, in some cases, with horrific cruelty.

The nature of the rest of creation also changed. The consequence of human corruption was the corruption of nature itself. Nature is no longer whole and good but broken and marred. Therefore disease, drought, flood, famine, lethal storms, and the rest of what are known as natural evils also entered the world through the rebellious exercise of human free choice.

Why it is often asked, would God have permitted the fall, knowing (as an all-knowing God must) the incalculable suffering that would follow? The traditional answer is that to create and to prevent the fall would not adequately have demonstrated God's love and glory. On the other hand, a rebellion and an undeserved redemption, with the ultimate consequences of rebellion borne by God in Jesus Christ instead of by the rebels themselves, demonstrate God's love and glory more fully. For this reason, Christ is said to have been "glorified" in the crucifixion.

There are a few specifically Anglican points that need to be addressed here. First, in its early years, Anglicanism was heavily influenced by Reformed thought, and a prominent theme was that God did not merely permit the fall, but rather decreed it as part of God's own plan fully to show God's glory and mercy. The Reformed stream in Anglicanism continues today. However, many Anglicans stress instead the freedom of human choice in the fall.

Secondly, although there is variety on this subject, most Anglicans reject the belief that a specific natural evil is the manifestation of God's wrath against a certain person or group of people on account of his, her, or their sin. For instance, most Anglicans reject the portrayal of Hurricane Katrina as God's wrath against the people of New Orleans because of their sin. That some suffer a natural evil from which others are spared cannot be explained according to human reason, as the biblical Book of Job attests.

Thirdly, as in other areas of belief, there is tremendous diversity in Anglican theodical thought, and no single perspective (whether or not traditional) can claim to represent Anglicanism generally. Some theologians (not only Anglicans but Christians generally) are open to answers to the problem of evil that tend more toward monism or dualism than the traditional Christian answers. Some see evil as a necessary part of the world for the sake of human spiritual growth. Human nature, on this view, is not fallen from perfection, but rather ascending toward perfection, and evil within creation is not wholly negative but rather has a constructive purpose in the development of human beings into God's likeness. Others attenuate or even set aside the idea of God's omnipotence. In these perspectives, evil is explicable in that God does not control outcomes in the finite world. Still, others doubt the relevance of abstract defenses of God's power and goodness, emphasizing the practical instead, whether present or future. Such thinkers may project their focus forward to the complete manifestation on earth of God's victory over evil on the cross, or look to the present and to God's solidarity with human sufferers as manifested on the cross of Christ.

In spite of this theological diversity, there is within Anglicanism a broad agreement on the need for the Church and its members to seek to alleviate human suffering. Anglicans worldwide are involved in efforts to bring healthy living conditions, freedom, justice, and the Gospel to the impoverished and the oppressed.

Source:
https://www.patheos.com/library/anglican/beliefs/suffering-and-the-problem-of-evil
https://www.patheos.com/library/anglican/beliefs/suffering-and-the-problem-of-evil.aspx?p=2

Baptists

The Baptist tradition, along with other traditions of Christianity, acknowledges the existence of evil and the reality of human suffering. At the same time, however, the Baptist tradition clearly affirms the goodness of the sovereign God. Hence, Baptists wrestle, both intellectually and existentially, with belief in both a good and sovereign God and the reality of evil.

God is the Creator, and all that God created was good (Genesis 1-2). Evil and suffering were not part of God's original creation, and are not an inherent (or necessary) part of creation. They are, rather, a corruption of the creation.

This corruption--that is, evil and suffering--entered the world not through the work of God but through the free choices made by beings God created. An angel rose in rebellion against God, becoming Satan (or the devil) by opposing God's sovereignty. The apostle John cites this opposition in his explanation of Jesus Christ's coming into the world, namely "to destroy the devil's work" (1 John 3:8). Unfortunately, Satan is not the only one who exercised his free choice by rebelling against God's will. Some of the angels followed Satan and his lead, becoming "fallen angels" or demons, agents of evil. And, also under the influence of Satan, human beings fell into rebellion against God, and thereby became corrupted and agents of evil (as well as of goodness).

Because God is perfectly good, God could not let this violation of the created order go unaddressed. So, God responded with holy judgment on both Satan and human beings. Furthermore, reflecting the fact that the created order is an integrated whole, the effects, including suffering, of rebellion against God, extended beyond these free-will agents to the entire created order (Genesis 3:14-19; Romans 8:19-23). Thus, Baptists believe, based on the Bible, that the entire created order has been corrupted by evil.

Human suffering is the most profound, though not the only result of evil's entrance into the world. Evil, and the corresponding human suffering, is sometimes understood under two major headings: suffering resulting from natural evil and suffering as the result of moral evil. The former refers to suffering that results from the corrupted (by evil) functioning of the natural world (which, technically speaking, because of its corruption is no longer purely "natural"). Examples of such evil and suffering are the pain and losses associated with cancer or Alzheimer's disease or the death and destruction that result from a tornado. Moral evil is suffering caused by the actions of moral creatures, namely human beings. Examples of this include the suffering resulting from physical brutality or murder, or the chronic starvation and poverty that result from corrupt business or government policies. (The line of distinction between natural and moral evil is not always easy to draw, and, in reality, some events are the result of a combination of the two.)

The Baptist tradition holds, however, that this is not the end of the story. Baptists believe the biblical teaching that eventually God will triumph over sin, death, and the devil--in short, overall evil. The same passages that speak of the entrance of evil into the world and of the current evil corruption of the created order also contain words of divine hope and promise that God will triumph over evil (Genesis 3:15b; Romans 8:20-21).

This confidence that God will eventually conquer and destroy evil is held in combination with recognizing the existence of evil and suffering in the present. Baptists recognize that the problem of evil is not only an intellectual and theological problem but that it is even more poignantly an existential problem for millions of people. And this recognition is part of the reason why Baptists seek to minister to people in both body and spirit, addressing both physical and spiritual suffering.

Source:
https://www.patheos.com/library/baptist/beliefs/suffering-and-the-problem-of-evil

Christian Science

Suffering is an error produced by sin or fear. Overcoming sin requires repentance and reformation. All human suffering is ultimately resolved by the victory of Love, God, over evil. Every Christian Science healing is a step in this ultimate direction.

Source:
https://www.patheos.com/library/christian-science/beliefs/suffering-and-the-problem-of-evil

Christianity

Christianity believes in a benevolent God who created the Universe and all things in it. The genesis of creation was God's overflowing love, and God's plan for creation is rooted in divine goodness. God created humans to love them as a parent loves their children.

In a Universe such as this, how do Christians understand suffering and evil? Why would God, a benevolent creator who loves all creatures, especially God's human children, allow evil and suffering to exist?

Christians have faith in a good and loving Creator who has a plan for creation that is also good and loving. This tenet of faith has prompted Christians to seek explanations or justifications for suffering. Human suffering takes many forms: emotional, natural, and moral. Loneliness, anxiety, and grief are examples of emotional suffering. Fires, tornados, earthquakes, hurricanes, tsunami, and physical illnesses (e.g., cancer) are examples of natural suffering. Moral suffering is brought on by the deliberate acts of fellow human beings to cause suffering, something Christians call moral evil.

Toward the end of the 2nd century, Irenaeus, Bishop of Lyons, and a Church Father formulated a theodicy, an argument intended to show that evil is necessary for human moral and spiritual development and is part of God's purpose. God created humans in a morally and spiritually imperfect state so that they can strive in response to suffering, to grow into full fellowship with God. This argument continues to influence Christian thought and belief.

Another early argument with strong contemporary resonance was advanced by the influential theologian Augustine, born in 354, who became the Bishop of Hippo in North Africa. Augustine proposed that, since God endowed people with freewill, we were able to choose to do evil as well as good freely. Simply stated, there is evil in the world because humans choose to do evil things. "Free" will is not free if we can only choose the good, so God does not prevent us from choosing evil. Suffering is the price we pay for this freedom to choose.

A third explanation of evil was advanced by the 18th-century philosopher G.W. Leibniz who believed that despite our suffering and the tragic and catastrophic events in our lives, we live in the best of all possible worlds. God is in control, Leibniz believed. When something terrible happens, it is not because God is not involved. God allowed it to prevent an even more terrible event from occurring. God can anticipate and prevent consequences that we cannot see. Since God is good and loving, we can trust that God creates and sustains the best possible world.

There are other Christian responses to evil that do not claim that evil is part of God's divine plan. Some Christians believe that God disciplines us just as a human father might discipline his children. Our suffering, therefore, is God's punishment and is a sign to us that we should repent. Others believe that God uses suffering to test our faith in divine providence and that suffering is an opportunity to make faith stronger and more constant. Another belief is that our suffering in our earthly life is only temporary and will add radiance and joy to our eternal life.

Others might say that evil is nothing but the absence of good, a strong reminder to us that we should work harder to bring good into this world. Still others might argue that God's connection with the created order is so profound that God has bound divine providence and omnipotence to the human experience. God's activity in the affairs of creation, then, is powerful, but not directive or controlling.

More contemporary approaches to evil include the argument that evil is not a problem for Christian faith. In the Old Testament, the Psalms regard creation as a revelation of God's goodness. Evil, also a part of God's creation, must reveal that inherent goodness as well if we know how to look. Recently some Christians have stopped viewing evil as an existential problem and have begun viewing it as a practical problem. Some, like Alyosha Karamazov, the character in Dostoevsky's novel The Brothers Karamazov, believe that the evil in our midst requires that we act to end it. Explanations or justifications of evil's existence are only secondary to this call to action or are not at all meaningful.

Source:
https://www.patheos.com/library/christianity/beliefs/suffering-and-the-problem-of-evil

---

Eastern Orthodox

Eastern Orthodox Christians express the same range of beliefs about suffering and the problem of evil as the majority of other Christian traditions. The Eastern Orthodox tradition interprets the story of Adam and Eve in the characteristic Christian manner, as a story in which God's cherished creatures, Adam and Eve, disobeyed God's one command, thereby imposing their own will in place of God's. As a punishment, God expelled Adam and Eve from Paradise, sending them into the world where they and their descendants would suffer pain, disease, and death. While some Christian traditions interpret this story literally, Eastern Orthodoxy interprets it symbolically, meaning that while it did not literally happen, it is full of religious truth. It describes the human condition, especially the presence of a barrier between God and humanity.

Eastern Orthodox belief shares the western idea of original sin. In the Orthodox view, all of creation, living and dead, visible and invisible, is holistically connected. What affects one creature affects all creatures. Therefore, the suffering and mortality imposed on Adam and Eve as punishment for their sin is shared by all of creation. However, the Orthodox tradition does not share the Augustinian idea of original guilt. While all creation suffers the consequences of the first humans' sin, no other creature is guilty of that sin. All share, however, in the legacy of the fall from Paradise. We all suffer disease and death, and we are all compelled by our own wills and desires, rather than God's. But we don't inherit Adam's guilt. So, for example, the Orthodox tradition does not teach that unbaptized infants will be sent to eternal fire and damnation.

Eastern Orthodoxy teaches that nothing is greater than God, including evil. Evil results from the freewill of God's creation, and the evil one, Satan, was once good. His name was Lucifer or light-bearer, and the Orthodox tradition likens him to the morning star. But he also opposed his own will to God's will and found himself in darkness. Orthodoxy teaches that Satan is not as powerful as God. But Satan's particular talent is falsehood, so he is able to convince people that he is as powerful as God. Eastern Orthodoxy is very optimistic in its outlook, teaching that the triumph of good over evil on the Last Day is a certainty.

Eastern Orthodox Christians wonder why God would allow evil to exist in the first place, and conclude that this is a mystery. Their interpretation of the scriptures supports this conclusion. Still, Orthodoxy rejects quietism, believing that true love expresses itself in action. In the face of great suffering or evil, the Christian is called to help. Like Alyosha Karamazov in Dostoyevsky's novel The Brothers Karamazov, we do not wait for an explanation of great evil or a justification of God's plan. We are called to keep the commandments to love God and our neighbor. Evil is a practical problem for the Christian, who finds ways to alleviate suffering and reinforce God's love and goodness in the world.

Source:
https://www.patheos.com/library/eastern-orthodoxy/beliefs/suffering-and-the-problem-of-evil

Holiness Pentecostal

Pentecostals are in a theological bind. To be consistent about the nature of the God they believe in, God cannot be the source of evil, so when good people suffer, alternative explanations are needed. Pentecostals have a firm belief in the existence of evil and a clear theological picture of the source of evil. Satan is a real entity in Pentecostalism, as are his legion of demons that spend all of their time in active pursuit of trying to undermine all of God's work.

While Pentecostals are loath to blame everything on Satan, there is a difference of opinion among Pentecostals over the nature of suffering. The questions surrounding theodicy (the role God plays or does not play in allowing evil in the world) are never easy to answer, and Pentecostal answers to this most vexing question of why God allows suffering may strike some as too simplistic and unsatisfactory.

These answers often perpetuate stereotypes about Pentecostals: that their penchant for hyper-spiritualizing and overly emotional responses have predisposed them to blame demonic attacks for nearly everything that goes wrong in their lives. This answer is certainly too simple, and it should be noted that belief in an ongoing demonic activity does not necessarily mean that Pentecostals do not struggle with theodicy. However, Pentecostalism also holds that humanity is involved in a cosmic battle, an active struggle between God and Satan.

Pentecostals do not believe that suffering and evil exist only in the mind. Pentecostals accept the reality of suffering, but often differ as to the author of suffering. Many hold that people suffer because God allows such things to build faith and character. The Biblical teachings about trials and tribulations validate their own suffering, which is temporary, a test. Perseverance, Bible reading, prayer, fasting, and other spiritual practices are all a part of recovering from episodes of suffering.

That said, however, there is a sub-group of Pentecostals that does not accept the idea that God has anything to do with suffering at all; this group has a different interpretation of key Biblical passages that suggest that God allows suffering. They point to the example of the thorn in

Paul's side (2 Corinthians 12:7-10), stating that there is no Biblical basis for assuming that God gave that thorn to Paul. The prominent Word of Faith teacher, Charles Capps, believes that a demonic messenger was responsible for this thorn, and that Pentecostals who use this famous passage as a way of blaming God for suffering as a necessary part of one's life are "religious" people: they have been deceived by "worldly" accounts of that passage, rather than just reading that passage by itself.

This alternative view of suffering among Pentecostals is especially pronounced among Word of Faith adherents. E. W. Kenyon (1867-1948), an early influence on the movement, posited the idea that Jesus' redemptive suffering took place largely on a spiritual plane, not a physical one. The result of such theological innovations is a doctrine called "Duel-Death," espoused by Kenyon and later by contemporary Word of Faith healer Kenneth Copeland. The "Duel Death" doctrine holds that upon Jesus' death, Satan seized Him and breathed into Him his own spirit, so that Jesus experienced the same spiritual death that befalls all humanity. Jesus was "born-again" in Hell and then rose to Heaven, thereby securing His exalted status as the resurrected Son of God. The importance of this doctrine is that there can be no evil, no suffering, that emanates from God. Such things are either the fault of people with no faith or demonic activity. For the Word of Faith movement in particular- and Pentecostalism in general, although the "Duel Death" doctrine is not accepted by all Pentecostals-God must be viewed as the person who gives us everything we ask for and is responsible for the abundant goodness of our lives, and never the source of diminished goods or expectations.

The devil exists for Pentecostals, as do his legion of demons. Demons can afflict Christians if they allow certain "doors to the demonic" to be opened. What usually opens the door for such demonic activity is moral laxity, the transgression of strict Pentecostalism standards for piety, and sexual morality. On nearly every deliverance ministry website, there is a section that informs visitors that certain behaviors are more apt to stir the demonic into action-such things as "sexual sin" (usually adultery and homosexuality), occult activity (fortune-telling, palm reading, tarot cards, Ouiji boards), and sometimes even body piercings. Many deliverance ministries offer services for exorcism, while others offer such things as the anointing and consecrating of homes.

Pentecostals focus on exorcising demonic activity, no doubt, because that is one of the Biblical commands (Mark 16:17) that signals that a person has received the Holy Spirit. This focus on the demonic is especially true in global Pentecostalism, where the reality of evil activity is accepted as part of everyday life. Entire denominations in Latin America and Africa, especially, have been built on their ability to "cast out demons."

This specialization can have its own set of problems. The Universal Church of the Kingdom of God in Brazil, for instance, has reduced almost all of its congregational activity to the demons and spirits it will cast out during that particular day. Because the Universal Church is a hierarchy, only its approved pastors can exorcise demons, and the methods they employ have come under scrutiny. Blending popular religion, folk Catholic practices, and Pentecostalism, the Universal Church uses objects such as rose petals, holy water, sanctified oil, bread, and tree branches, among other things, to perform the exorcisms. These practices, among other perceived heterodox ideas, have placed the Universal Church outside the circle of orthodox Pentecostalism. The Universal Church as well as churches in Africa that allow blended worship using African rituals, have been the most prominent groups that are illustrative of such hybridization.

Source:
https://www.patheos.com/library/pentecostal/beliefs/suffering-and-the-problem-of-evil

Jehovah's Witnesses

Jehovah's Witnesses teach that Satan is the source of all evil and is spiritually present among humans, seducing them with such evils as pornography and violence. We can protect ourselves through prayer, Bible study, and associating with good people.

Source:
https://www.patheos.com/library/jehovahs-witnesses/beliefs/suffering-and-the-problem-of-evil

Lutherans

Like all monotheists (those who believe in one God), Lutherans confront a dilemma on the subject of evil and suffering. Does God want to relieve suffering, but is unable? In that case, God is good but not all-powerful. Is God able to relieve suffering but unwilling or too unconcerned? Then God is all-powerful but not good.

Luther agreed with most of the Christian tradition that the Universe was created from nothing by God. This belief emphasizes God's complete omnipotence. It also carries as a consequence the fact that anything wrong with the Universe cannot be attributed to matter or the material of the Universe since this, too, is created by God.

The entrance point for evil and suffering in the world is the work of Satan, which results in human sin. But this simply pushes the problem back to square one. Could not God have created humans in such a way that they would not sin? One option for Christians has been to argue that God created humans with freewill so that there was a possibility that they would not sin. The buck for sin then stops squarely on the desk of humans. But Luther rejected this option. For him, power is a zero-sum game. If humans had the power to decide to sin or not, then that is less power we attribute to God. Similarly, humans do not have the freewill to choose to accept or reject salvation (this is in contrast to John Wesley and Thomas Aquinas). For Luther, the buck for sin and salvation ultimately stops with God.

Why would God set the Universe up in such a way? Some Christians have argued that God sets it up this way because God's power and glory are more clearly shown in allowing and then saving from sin, than if sin had never entered the world. (This is the tradition of O felix culpa! O happy sin!) Luther also rejected this argument.

The work of Satan is the cause of evil, and human sin is the most significant manifestation of this evil. Sin and evil, the causes of suffering, were finally for Luther a mystery. All the possible ways of explaining it or getting God off the hook for it (called in theology "theodicy," literally, "justifying God") are inappropriate speculation. Luther inherited from the medieval nominalists the belief that God is completely hidden from us.

The only exception is what God has chosen to reveal in Scripture. Scripture is not intended to satisfy our curiosity; it tells us only what we need to know to be saved. One thing it tells us (and this, according to Luther, is absolutely necessary to be saved) is that God's ways are not ours. We ought not wonder why God did not set things up differently or try to make sense of the way things are set up. We are born into the middle of the set-up, and our only hope is to cling to the promise of salvation from sin, evil, and suffering through Christ found in the Bible.

Source:
https://www.patheos.com/library/lutheran/beliefs/suffering-and-the-problem-of-evil

Methodists

Like all monotheists (those who believe in one God), Methodists confront a dilemma on the subject of evil and suffering. Does God want to relieve suffering, but is unable? In that case, God is good but not all-powerful. Is God able to relieve suffering but unwilling or too unconcerned? Then God is all-powerful but not good. Though in the end, the intellectual tensions may not be resolvable, there are a couple of well-worn paths from the Christian tradition through this thicket, one of which is taken by John Wesley and after him, the Methodists.

One path is to argue that there is something inherently corruptible about matter that necessarily makes things go bad. John Wesley does not take this path. He believed that God, perfectly good and all-powerful, created the best of all possible Universes. There is no shortcoming in creation that makes suffering and evil necessary. Rather, suffering enters the world because of evil, and evil enters the world because of an act of will, a choice.

The first creature to make a bad choice was Lucifer, one of God's angels. In addition to information revealed in scripture, Wesley was deeply influenced by John Milton's Paradise Lost. Because angels (as humans) are created in the image of God, they are created with freewill. Lucifer, the greatest angelic being, succumbed to pride (he did not want to spend eternity submitting to God), revolted, taking with him some of the angels. Since that time, there has been a cosmic struggle between good and bad angels, the latter group led by Lucifer, most often referred to as Satan. The story is recapitulated in the Garden of Eden, where Adam and Eve (also created in the image of God with freewill) disobeyed God (also out of pride). Adam and Eve were caught in the cosmic angelic crossfire and were pawns in Satan's game. Satan tempted the first humans into sin, but they nonetheless bear responsibility for freely choosing it.

Wesley adopted a traditional Christian distinction between types of suffering: natural, moral, and penal. People suffer because of disease and natural disaster; people suffer because other people harm them, and people suffer because they are punished for wrongdoing. All are the result of freely chosen sin, personal and corporate.

When one surveys the natural world, with nature red in tooth and claw, and natural disasters, disease, and death, one might wonder if a good powerful God could not have designed a better Universe. Wesley argued that God did in fact design a better Universe, and that nature as it is now, which can be a source of great pain, became the way it is as a result of sin. Human sin dragged the entire created order down with it.

As for moral suffering, it is not hard to see that sin, which is self-centered human nature, gives rise to humans who seek their own good above the good of others and do not mind causing pain along the way. As for penal suffering, it is also not hard to see that a just God would mete out punishment for sin (and as an encouragement to do better).

At this point, a Christian might ask, Why did God not create Lucifer and human beings with freewill, but with the good sense (or will or humility) to make better choices? Again, the tradition offers a couple of options. One is to say that without the Fall, Jesus would not have been necessary, and that God's power and glory and love are more greatly manifested through the Fall and salvation than through creation without a Fall. Wesley agreed with this, as did John Calvin. But in the end, there is an important difference between Wesley and Calvin on this matter.

159

Wesley stressed the human will's freedom to sin. And this will dovetail with the freedom of will we have later to accept justifying grace, and the freedom of will once justified not to sin again (sanctification). Calvin, in contrast, while assigning responsibility for sin to humans through Adam and Eve, was also clear that God did not simply allow this to happen, but that it was part of God's eternal plan. Calvin was unwilling even to appear to detract from divine omnipotence by placing any part of the story in human control. And this supported his argument that we are not free to accept or reject justifying grace; if God offers it, we take it. It also supported his belief that humans, after justification, are not free to stop sinning entirely.

Source:
https://www.patheos.com/library/methodist/beliefs/suffering-and-the-problem-of-evil

---

Mormonism
The Church of Jesus Christ of Latter-day Saints

In Mormon thought, the most important moral principle is that of agency. Agency existed as a necessary element of existence even before human beings populated the earth. Drawing from and elaborating on Biblical accounts, Mormon scripture tells of a "war" in heaven in which God's spirit children had to choose between two plans.

The first plan was presented by God Himself and endorsed by His eldest spiritual child, Jesus Christ. It held that once born into mortality, human beings would be free to choose between good and evil. This plan recognized that some of God's children would choose evil and thus be banished eternally from God's presence. Others would choose good and, in so doing, could eventually become gods and goddesses themselves.

The second plan, designed by Lucifer, one of God's most promising and talented children, called for the suspension of moral agency. Lucifer argued that he would force all humans to choose good over evil. In return for his role in exalting and saving the totality of God's offspring, Lucifer demanded God's throne and glory. Lucifer and the one-third of God's spirit children who sided with him were cast out of God's presence and denied the opportunity to inhabit a physical body. Lucifer, who became known as Satan, and his angels actively tempt mortals to choose evil, but Satan is not the founder or source of evil.

The narrative of the war in heaven is based on the idea that evil existed before Satan. The narrative hinges on two concepts: that moral agency is an eternal principle that cannot be abrogated, even by God. That moral agency requires a choice between, and thus the existence of, good and evil. Mortals are placed on earth to experience the forces of good and evil and to choose between them.

The story of Adam and Eve in the Garden of Eden thus takes on a slightly different cast in the Mormon telling. The Fall of Adam and Eve is not seen as the source of moral evil, because the presence of Satan in the Garden as a fallen and rejected angel presupposes a Universe in which agency, with its attendant choices of good and evil, was already operative. In fact, the Mormon view holds that Satan made a mistake by tempting Adam and Eve because the divine plan required that they be cast out of the Garden. A situation in which moral agency operates is one in which good and evil choices comingle. Moral evil is thus understood within Mormonism as a necessary byproduct of agency and an indispensable part of the mortal and divine experience.

The Book of Mormon expands on this idea and explains that existence itself is defined by the presence of two contrasting and competing choices that may broadly be categorized as good and evil, or light and darkness. The absence of either good or evil as options from which to choose is, according to The Book of Mormon, the absence of being.

Another Mormon text, the Book of Moses, provides a poignant demonstration of the power of misused moral agency to cause pain even to God. Enoch, a mysterious figure mentioned in the Hebrew Bible (Genesis 5:21-24), is, in this Mormon text, a witness to the weeping of God. When Enoch, utterly shocked by this sight, asks God why He weeps, God explains that the wicked choices of his children will result in their damnation and will thus deprive God of their company. The weeping God of Mormonism is thus a potent symbol of the unbreakable bond between being, evil, and suffering. As long as something is, then evil is a possibility.

In contrast to moral evils, natural evils such as death, disease, and natural disasters are understood in the Mormon context in much the same way as they are in other Christian traditions: as a result of the Fall of Adam and Eve. When they were cast out of the Garden of Eden, Adam, Eve, and all of their human posterity became subject to entropy. Their bodies, now mortal, began to decay with age and suffer from disease and the effects of natural forces. Mormons believe that the physical body is a blessing and that every person born on earth will one day be resurrected to live forever with a physical body. The suffering that accompanies the mortal physical body is explained as a necessary part of human experience, and death is as important to the ultimate destiny of each soul as is birth.

Source:
https://www.patheos.com/library/mormonism/beliefs/suffering-and-the-problem-of-evil

---

Presbyterian Reformed

Like all monotheists (those who believe in one God), Reformed Christians confront a dilemma on the subject of evil and suffering. Does God want to relieve suffering, but is unable? In that case, God is good but not all-powerful. Is God able to relieve suffering but unwilling or too unconcerned? Then God is all-powerful but not good. Zwingli and Calvin agreed with most of the Christian tradition that the Universe was created from nothing by God. This is the doctrine of creation ex nihilo. This belief emphasizes God's complete sovereignty. It also carries as a consequence the fact that anything wrong with the Universe cannot be attributed to matter or the material of the Universe since this, too, was created by God, and it was created good. The entrance point for evil and suffering in the world, then, is sin. Zwingli and Calvin agreed that sin is an act of human disobedience against God's command and that this disobedience is entirely humans' responsibility. For Calvin, since the time of the Fall (Adam's original sin), one could not say that humans sin necessarily, by compulsion, because that would make God the author of sin. But one could say that humans sin inevitably. We love it.

But on the question of human responsibility for sin and the role played by God, this claim of human responsibility simply pushes the problem back one square. Could not God have created humans in such a way that they would not sin? Again, Calvin was a thorough systematic theologian. In the end, he had to maintain that we are not privy to God's plans and that it is inappropriate for us to question them or speculate about them. Our task is to trust that God knows what God is doing. But before Calvin got to this point, he spelled out exactly all the things that God did for Adam that delayed the need to appeal to the mystery of God's plan. Adam had an uncorrupted reason, Adam had freewill, Adam lived harmoniously in the presence of God. The one and only positive quality not bestowed on Adam by God was the gift of perseverance. But again, while these theological moves seem to delay assigning responsibility to God for sin, in the end, many people think that Calvin cannot avoid this claim. This is the root of the Arminian controversy and was what eventually would separate Reformed Christians from Methodists. In the end, while continuing to assert that sin was a human responsibility, Calvin's strong emphasis on God's sovereignty meant that the answer to the question of why God allowed sin to occur, or why God set up the Universe in such a way that it could occur, is simply a mystery.

Here, again, we see the influence of the medieval nominalists and their arguments that we cannot reason or speculate our way to knowledge of God, and we cannot draw analogies from human experience and from nature to God. All we know about God is what we learn in scripture. Calvin did not ask the question, "Why is creation the way it is?" He observed the fact of evil and suffering in the world, and the Biblical account in Genesis of the Fall. The elect are given the gift of faith, which brings, along with the assurance that our sins are forgiven, the confidence that while we may not know why God does what God does, God surely does know. Calvin could identify one positive outcome of the divine plan for history that includes the Fall: the elect enjoy the one benefit from God denied to Adam. They are given the gift of perseverance. For Calvin (as for Zwingli and Luther), once you are saved you cannot lose your salvation. Humans do not have it in their power to damn themselves, just as they do not have it in their power to save themselves. Again, this will distinguish Reformed theologies from Catholic and Methodist theologies. Calvin and Zwingli are willing to pay any theological price to protect the doctrine of God's absolute and fatherly sovereignty.

Source:

163

https://www.patheos.com/library/presbyterian/beliefs/suffering-and-the-problem-of-evil

---

Protestantism

Like all monotheists (those who believe in one God), Protestants confront a dilemma on the subject of evil and suffering. Does God want to relieve suffering, but is unable? In that case, God is good but not all-powerful. Is God able to relieve suffering but unwilling or too unconcerned? Then God is all-powerful but not good.

Protestants agree that the Universe was created from nothing by God, and it was created good. This is the doctrine of creation ex nihilo. God is omnipotent and, prior to the effects of evil, Creator of all that is. There is no property of matter that in and of itself could account for evil—creation was good. Therefore evil and suffering entered the world through something other than God's original acts of creation. God is not the creator of evil. (For many modern Protestants, this belief is not incompatible with evolution; God created the Universe in such a way that creation unfolds through the mechanism of evolution.)

The entrance point for evil and moral suffering in the world, then, is the Fall and work of Satan and human rebellion against God (that is, sin). Protestants do not always agree on why sin entered the world. Those who believe that the story of the Fall recounts a historical event agree that the devil tempted Adam. But why did Adam, created without sin, succumb to temptation? One set believes that Adam could have chosen not to sin. In order to create a genuinely free being with whom God could enter into a relationship, God gave Adam freewill. Adam made a bad choice. This belief dovetails with the belief that salvation, in part, requires the individual's free choice to ask for forgiveness and for help in following God's law.

Other Protestants argue that this places too much control over the course of history into the hands of humans rather than God. They argue that Adam sinned necessarily, though not by compulsion; this makes God at least indirectly the author of sin. This second group splits on why creation was set up this way. Some believe that God's mercy and glory are more fully demonstrated in a world in which sin enters, and is then forgiven and defeated. Others believe that scripture simply does not answer this question, that God's ways are not human, and that it is not the place of human beings to interrogate God on why sin entered the world. Zwingli and Calvin belong here. They agree that sin is an act of human disobedience against God's command and that this disobedience is entirely humans' responsibility.

For Calvin, since the Fall (Adam's original sin), one cannot say that humans sin by compulsion, because that would indirectly make God the author of sin. But one can say that humans sin inevitably. When they sin, they are doing what they want to do. But on the question of human responsibility for sin and the role played by God, this claim of human responsibility simply pushes the problem back to square one. Could not God have created humans in such a way that they would not sin? In the end, Calvin, and many other Christians with him, says that humans are not privy to God's plans and that it is inappropriate to question them or speculate about them.

While these theological moves seem to delay assigning responsibility to God for sin, in the end, many people think that Calvin cannot avoid this claim. This is a root of the Arminian controversy. It is this dispute that, perhaps more than any other, separates Reformed Christians from Methodists and other Arminian (or Arminian-like) traditions. In the end, while continuing to assert that sin is a human responsibility, Calvin's strong emphasis on God's omnipotence means that the answer to the question of why God allowed sin to occur, or why God set up the Universe in such a way that it could occur, is simply a mystery. Methodists have a foot in both camps here, wanting both to emphasize God's omnipotence with the Calvinists, and to maintain a degree of freewill in choosing to accept God's grace.

Though sin in the world is the source of human-caused suffering—evidenced in war, violence, poverty, hatred, anger, and so forth—some of the suffering is perceived to be a direct outcome of individual and social behavior and thus a natural consequence, and some of it is perceived to be divine punishment. There is much diversity of belief around the meaning of suffering.

Most Protestants differentiate between suffering caused by sin and evil, as discussed above, and physical or natural suffering—evidenced in earthquakes, tsunamis, tornados, and the like. While all suffering enters the created order because of the original break in Adam and Eve's relationship with God, not all suffering today has a moral source. That is, the natural order of creation is also broken, and thus tragic events occur in the world that display that brokenness but are not directly caused by some moral breach. Not all suffering is caused by sin. God sometimes permits suffering, even though God could have prevented it, for purposes that are beyond human understanding. The story of Job is a good example of this.

Whatever the cause of suffering, Protestants believe that God is greater than sorrow and pain and death, and therefore, Protestants have hope. God can redeem every grief and pain, no matter the source, and use it for divine glory and human good. God weaves good out of evil, and God's ultimate purposes will never be defeated. Suffering is destined to end, and all tears to be wiped away by God's hand. God intends joy to be believers' present reality through faith and their future reality in fullness.

Source:
https://www.patheos.com/library/protestantism/beliefs/suffering-and-the-problem-of-evil
https://www.patheos.com/library/protestantism/beliefs/suffering-and-the-problem-of-evil.aspx?p=2

Roman Catholicism

Suffering and evil are distinct and yet interrelated concepts in Catholic thinking. Ultimately, the Fall of humanity is the cause of all suffering. Humans were created to exist in harmony with God, but instead, they chose the path of disobedience, which brought suffering and death into the world. Catholics believe that while humans have the free choice to disobey, they can never find true joy and peace except in harmony with and obedience to God. As St. Augustine says so eloquently in his *Confessions*, "Our hearts find no rest until they rest in You."

In the Catholic view, human action is not the only cause of suffering: while God, as the source of all goodness, can never act in an evil manner, God may send suffering to open the hearts of those who have refused to hear God's call. In their pride and complacency, humans think that they need neither God nor the grace God offers, but tragedy, sorrow, and suffering can lead to transformation. Because this world is prelude and preparation for the afterlife, even a life filled with suffering is useful if it causes the person to turn to God and accept divine grace. This, Catholics believe, is a central fact of existence: God uses everything, even suffering, to call people back to God.

The Catholic Church teaches that with their limited vision, humans cannot see all the consequences of actions and events, and something they recognize as evil may also be the impetus for great good to occur: God can bring good even out of the evil that humans commit. When Catholics look at a troubled history that eventually led to a better situation, they recognize the hand of God, drawing the whole process to a happy conclusion.

This is the lesson of the felix culpa, the happy fault: human sin brought suffering into the world, but it also paved the way for God's incarnation to occur. The evil remains evil, but the good that God causes to flow from it is greater still. According to St. Augustine, even this perception of good coming from evil results from a limited view: from the cosmic, eternal perspective of God, everything is ultimately good because God uses everything in the service of goodness.

Catholics distinguish between physical evil and moral evil. Physical evil is simply a lack of perfection: all of creation moves toward ultimate perfection in the coming kingdom of God, but nothing on earth yet achieves it. Moral evil is the greater issue, one that is all-pervasive in this world. It is moral evil to which the Church's Catechism refers when it says, "There is not a single aspect of the Christian message that is not in part an answer to the question of evil." Yet moral evil, too, is simply a lack of perfection, in this case, the perfection of the human will.

Just as God has not created a world of physical perfection, saving that for the coming kingdom, so too, God has not created a world of moral perfection in which people cannot sin. St. Augustine explained that God is the source of everything that exists, and everything God created is good. Evil is the absence of good, so, therefore, it must not have real existence. It is instead a lack, the absence of good. God created humanity, Lucifer, and the rebellious angels as beings of goodness and endowed them with the freedom to choose their paths. They chose to turn away from the good, and in doing so, their capacity for goodness was diminished. It is this lack, this diminishment, that is evil. Augustine's formulation has proven to be the most influential understanding of evil in the western Christian tradition.

When they speak of evil, Catholics often refer to Lucifer, or the devil, who is called the Father of Lies. Lucifer's power lies solely in his ability to persuade humans to do his will, just as he persuaded the rebellious angels to follow him, and the result is just as disastrous. Lucifer is mirage and subterfuge, creating the illusion that following him will lead to happiness and light when all that will result is chaos and evil. He, therefore, causes evil, but only with the willing participation of humans utilizing their freewill to choose diminishment of the good. He may be called the Evil One, but Catholic belief does not grant him the power to execute the evil he envisions. His power is very limited, his bid for predominance in heaven already thwarted, his final defeat already destined, just as the end of suffering and evil in the world to come is already destined.

Source:
https://www.patheos.com/library/roman-catholicism/beliefs/suffering-and-the-problem-of-evil

Unitarian Universalism

Unitarian Universalism has no single theology of pain, evil, or suffering, and the religion's liberal optimism creates a focus on the alleviation of suffering rather than the illumination of its cause.

Source:
https://www.patheos.com/library/unitarian-universalism/beliefs/suffering-and-the-problem-of-evil

Part VI

Non-Christian Theodicies

Part VI is an aggregation of information from different sources
regarding the views of Non-Christian religions on
Suffering and the Problem of Evil.

Atheism

(Much of what is written in this section on Atheism is written in the first
person, but this person is not the author of this theodicy; the first person
is the person in the sources.)

The problem of evil is probably the most enduring and the most
potent argument atheism has to offer against theism. Christian
apologist William Lane Craig aptly styled it atheism's killer
argument. Since atheists do not believe in the existence of God, then the
concept of theodicy does not strictly apply to atheism. However, atheism
does address the problem of evil, and that is what follows here.

Atheism is, in the broadest sense, the absence of belief in the existence
of deities. Atheism is contrasted with theism, which, in its most general
form, is the belief that at least one deity exists. In antiquity, it had
multiple uses as a pejorative term applied to those thought to reject the
gods worshiped by the larger society, those who were forsaken by the
gods, or those who had no commitment to belief in the gods. The term

denoted a social category created by orthodox religionists into which those who did not share their religious beliefs were placed. The first individuals to identify themselves using the word atheist lived in the 18th century during the Age of Enlightenment. The French Revolution, noted for its "unprecedented atheism," witnessed the first major political movement in history to advocate for the supremacy of human reason.

Arguments for atheism range from philosophical to social and historical approaches. Rationales for not believing in deities include arguments that there is a lack of empirical evidence for the existence of deities, the problem of evil, the argument from inconsistent revelations, the rejection of concepts that cannot be falsified, and the argument from nonbelief. Atheists contend that the burden of proof lies not on the atheist to disprove the existence of gods but on the theist to provide a rationale for theism. Although some atheists have adopted secular philosophies (e.g. secular humanism), there is no one ideology or code of conduct to which all atheists adhere.

Atheisms Response to Common Christian Arguments

The Hypothetical God Fallacy

Christians say that God can have good reasons for allowing evil, even if we don't know what those reasons are. That is, just because something might seem pointless to us, doesn't mean God can't have a morally justified reason for it. This error is so common that it needs a name: The Hypothetical God Fallacy. This gets us out of every possible jam in which God looks bad. Yes, bad things in the world don't force the conclusion that God can't exist. Fortunately, I don't draw such a conclusion. And yes, if God exists, He could have his reasons for things that we don't understand.

The Hypothetical God Fallacy is a fallacy because no one interested in the truth starts with a conclusion (God exists) and then arranges the facts to support that conclusion. That's backward; it's circular reasoning. Rather, the truth seeker starts with the facts and then follows them to their conclusion. If God exists, He could have terrific reasons for why there's so much gratuitous evil in the world. Therefore, I do not conclude that there is no God, but that is where the evidence points and that is enough.

No God, No Objective Moral Values and Duties

Sounds right, but why imagine that objective moral values exist? What many apologists perceive as objective moral values are actually just shared moral values. That we share moral values isn't too surprising since we're all the same species. Nothing supernatural is required. It is up to the Christian to defend the claim that objective morality exists and that everyone can access it. As for the ordinary, everyday sort of moral grounding, the kind that both Christians and atheists use, you'll find that in the dictionary. Look up "morality," and you'll read nothing about objective grounding.

The Problem of Good

The atheist position's got another problem to deal with: The Problem of Good. In other words, naturalism has the challenge of providing a sufficient moral grounding for goodness itself, in addition to making sense of evil in the world. And that's a pretty tall order for a philosophy with absolutely no room for God.

What's difficult? We're good because of evolution. We're social animals, like wolves and chimpanzees, so we have cooperative traits like honesty, cooperation, sympathy, trustworthiness, and so on. The God hypothesis adds nothing to the conversation, and we must watch out for it being smuggled in as a presupposition, i.e., The Hypothetical God Fallacy. You don't need religion to have morals. If you can't determine right from wrong, then you lack empathy, not religion.

An Atheists view of the Problem of Evil

Here's the actual good news: God doesn't exist. There is no tyrannical psychopath ruling the Universe. No one's going to end up in heaven, but this also means billions more people will escape the unimaginable horror of being tormented in hell. We can look at our situation and be pessimistic. We can develop a keen sense of universal angst. Or, we can rise to the challenge of existence and laugh at the absurdity of it all. Reality is unimaginably complex.

I won't even try to describe how incredibly beautiful, mysterious, and awe-inspiring the Universe is. That's a job a poet would be better suited for. We may not have been put here for some divine purpose, but the fact that we're here at all, despite seemingly insurmountable odds, is nothing short of amazing. We've happened upon an extraordinarily unique opportunity here. The opportunity to exist, to embody the wonder of consciousness, to attempt to understand reality, and to marvel at the mystery of anything even being here in the first place. As far as I'm concerned, you don't need a God telling you that you're special to make this ride worthwhile. The privilege of existing is enough. God isn't real, and that's okay.

Atheism and the Sacred Natural Creative Power

Natura naturans is a Latin tag coined during the Middle Ages, meaning "nature doing what nature does," and is commonly associated with the philosophy of Baruch Spinoza. To Spinoza, Nature and God were the same. The concept of natura naturans has a long history in philosophy, and especially in atheistic metaphysics. Natura naturans is natural creative power, and from now on I'll use that phrase.

Natural creative power is a universal; as such, it is an abstract object. Nominalists deny the existence of abstract objects. So, nominalists are likely to deny the existence of natural creative power. Some atheists are nominalists; however, atheism does not entail nominalism. You can be an atheist and affirm all sorts of abstract objects. The thesis that there exists some natural creative power is entirely consistent with atheism. This power is natural, immanent, ultimate, and thus at work in every natural thing, and this concept is found in atheistic philosophers like Spinoza, Schopenhauer, Nietzsche, and Donald Crosby.

For religious naturalists like Crosby, it is an atheistic concept of the divine; it is an atheistic concept of the sacred or holy. Natural creative power is not the theistic deity, and certainly not the Christian or Abrahamic God. After all, any theistic deity is a thing, a particular, while natural creative power is a universal. An atheist is entirely free to recognize the existence of natural creative power. Schellenberg describes a "reality unsurpassably deep in the nature of things." On my interpretation, this unsurpassably deep reality is natural creative power. For Shellenberg, affirmation of this unsurpassably deep reality is ultimism. He writes: "Ultimism is my label for the general religious view that there is a reality unsurpassably deep in the nature of things and unsurpassably great in relation to which an ultimate good for us and the world can be attained."

The idea of a caring God concerned to enter into personal relationship with us represents one way of trying to give more specific content to this view; . . . But there are other attempts to fill out this notion in existing nontheistic religions; consider monistic Hinduism or Buddhism or Taoism, and it may well be filled out in many completely new ways in the future. Atheistic religious naturalism and atheistic nature-religions are examples of this ultimism. To cite Schellenberg, they are some of the "completely new ways" that "more specific content" can be given to "a reality unsurpassably deep in the nature of things."

Natural creative power is a universal; it is not a thing, it is not a particular. It is a power of being that is active in every existing thing. It is the power of natural existence itself. For naturalists, this means that it is the power of being in every existing thing. It is at work in every creatively active thing in nature. It is at work in the quantum fields; in the cores of stars fusing lighter nuclei into heavier nuclei; in chemical and biological evolution. It drives the complexification of nature.

As the ultimate immanent power of being, natural creative power is being-itself. It is being-as-being, the power of existence itself, the power to be rather than to not be. It's obviously not supernatural and it fits perfectly well into the scientific study of the nature of reality. The existence of being-itself is certainly consistent with natural science. The same line of reasoning that justifies the existence of scientific universals, like mass, spin, and charge, can be extended to justify the existence of an abstract power like being-itself.

The existence of natural creative power is hardly a radical idea. Being-itself is simply what all beings have in common. If you affirm that many distinct beings exist, then you also affirm that they have existence in common; they all share being-itself as their ultimate universal or power of being. And surely your affirmation is based on the observation of things: the existence of being-itself is empirically justified just as much as the existence of properties like mass or charge.

Natural creative power participates in explanatory relations: Why is there something rather than nothing? Because the natural creative power of being must be; it cannot fail to create; it necessarily generates. Religious naturalists have reverence and admiration for natural creative power, especially as it is manifest in the myriad forms of life on earth. Natural creative power is not a thing; therefore, it is not a god. But it is holy, sacred, and divine. Atheists are not prohibited from affirming the existence of holy, sacred, or divine powers. Nominalists and positivists might be prohibited; but there's no reason atheists have to listen to them.

Source

https://en.wikipedia.org/wiki/Atheism

https://www.patheos.com/blogs/daylightatheism/essays/all-possible-worlds/

https://patheos.com/blogs/camelswithhammers/2011/12/atheism-and-the-sacred-natural-creative-power

https://www.patheos.com/blogs/secularvoices/2018/11/07/the-problem-of-evil-atheist/

http://en.wikipedia.org/wiki/Natura_naturans

https://www.patheos.com/blogs/crossexamined/2018/05/the-hypothetical-god-fallacy/

Baha'i

The Baha'i Faith is a religion teaching the essential worth of all religions, and the unity and equality of all people. The Bahá'í teachings state that there is no such physical place as heaven or hell, and emphasize the eternal journey of the soul towards perfection. The world beyond, is as different from this world as this world is different from that of the child while still in the womb of its mother.

Baha'I teaches that the life of the individual begins at conception, when the soul associates itself with the embryo. When death occurs, the soul's association with the body draws to a close. At that point the body returns to the world of dust, while the soul continues to progress in the spiritual worlds of God, in an eternal journey towards perfection. An illumined soul continues to have an influence on progress in this world and the advancement of its peoples. It acts as the leaven of the world.

Bahá'í teachings are in some ways similar to other monotheistic faiths, in that God is considered single and all-powerful. However, Baha'i teaches that religion is revealed by this single and all-powerful God through individual manifestations of God.

These individual manifestations of God are the founders of major world religions throughout history, whose purpose is to transform the character of humankind and to develop, within those who respond, moral and spiritual qualities; Buddha, Jesus, and Muhammad being the most recent. Religion is thus seen as orderly, unified, and progressive from age to age.

Baha'ís regard the major religions as fundamentally unified in purpose, though varied in social practices and interpretations. At the heart of Bahá'í teachings is the goal of a unified world order that ensures the prosperity of all nations, races, creeds, and classes. Three principles are central to Baha'i faith: the unity of God, the unity of religion, and the unity of humanity.

Defining evil, "...lead us not into temptation, but deliver us from evil." From the Lord's Prayer. Every Christian is very familiar with these words. But in the Baha'i writings its meaning can be found. To find that meaning, first one needs to realize that suffering in this physical world has two origins: natural causes and human causes. The first occurs as a result of natural laws, which we will simply call suffering, and the latter results from the freewill of human beings, and human-caused suffering is called evil.

According to Baha'i teachings evil is understood to be an absence rather than a presence: "Briefly, the intellectual realities, such as all the qualities and admirable perfections of man, are purely good, and exist. Evil is simply their nonexistence... In the same way, the sensible realities are absolutely good, and evil is due to their nonexistence; that is to say, blindness is the want of sight, deafness is the want of hearing, poverty is the want of wealth...". "...all that God created He created good. This evil is nothingness; so death is the absence of life... all evils return to nonexistence. Good exists; evil is nonexistent." Does this mean that evil does not exist? No, it means evil has no existence of its own, i.e., it derives its existence from something else that does exist. For example, a shadow is a dark area or shape produced by an object that does exist coming between rays of light and a surface.

The definition of evil has also been presented from a more empirical and symbolic viewpoint: "Evil is imperfection. Sin is the state of man in the world of the baser nature, for in nature exist defects such as injustice, tyranny, hatred, hostility, strife... Through education we must free ourselves from these imperfections." "The reality is that the evil spirit, Satan, or whatever is interpreted as evil, refers to the lower nature in man. This baser nature is symbolized in various ways... God has never created an evil spirit; all such ideas and nomenclature are symbols expressing the mere human or earthly nature of man. It is an essential condition of the soil of earth that thorns, weeds and fruitless trees may grow from it. Relatively speaking, this is evil; it is simply the lower state and baser product of nature."

The Baha'i approach teaches a new way to think about the problem of evil. Christ admonished his followers to ask God not to let them fall into the temptation of reducing themselves to their lower nature. If we understand evil as our lower nature; e.g., revenge, violence, hatred and the like, then we know those characteristics could eventually reduce us to nothingness.

According to Baha'i scripture, there are many aspects to the question of suffering and evil. Those in the Baha'i faith believe that God created the Universe and since God is the source of all good, there cannot be any evil force in it, such as Satan or the Devil or evil spirits. The human being has a physical and a spiritual aspect. If the spiritual side of a human being is underdeveloped, then it cannot control the physical side. Thus for example, while food is a necessity, if the spiritual side is underdeveloped and fails to control the animal aspect of the human being, the result is gluttony; if the impulse for sex is not controlled, the result is lust and promiscuity; if the natural desire to acquire sufficient wealth to provide for oneself and one's family is not controlled, the result is greed and avarice.

Any human in whom the lower nature is not balanced and controlled by the spiritual nature becomes the embodiment of evil. It is this, Baha'is believe, that the scriptures of other religions have referred to as the Devil or Satan. The problem of suffering is more complex and has several aspects. If humans allow their physical nature to dominate their spiritual nature, while the short-term result may seem pleasurable, the ultimate consequence is suffering. Physical pleasures never give lasting satisfaction and the effect fades so that each time a greater stimulus is required just to get the same level of pleasure. Thus these desires are insatiable. Ultimately this leads to such a distortion of human nature that mental and physical suffering are inevitable.

Excesses of gluttony, lust, and greed often lead to antisocial or criminal activities, the consequences of which add to the unhappiness and suffering caused by the inability to satiate these desires. Individuals in this state cause great suffering, both to themselves and to those around them. Sometimes suffering is the result of unwise human actions. If one does not live one's life with due regard for the physical laws, one is likely to be hurt; for example, if one jumps out of a second-story window. Similarly, if human beings go against the spiritual laws that God has given, then they are likely to suffer because these spiritual laws are in accordance with the reality of things and so following them protects one from suffering.

Baha'is also believe that it is through suffering that human beings are encouraged to perfect themselves and to travel along the spiritual path. If human beings did not experience suffering, they could not fully develop virtues such as patience and fortitude. And if human beings did not witness suffering in the world, then they could not manifest the virtues of kindness and compassion. Tests and tribulations test the qualities that human beings are acquiring. It is easy to be loving and beneficent toward people who are pleasant. These virtues are only truly put to the test when confronted by unpleasant people who make others suffer. Thus, overcoming or transcending tests, difficulties, and suffering are ways of both progressing spiritually and measures of how much spiritual progress has been made. The Baha'i scriptures see the world as a giant classroom in which everything is laid out to help human beings to grow and develop spiritually.

One area that is frequently debated when the problem of suffering arises is the question of why, if God is a loving God, He allows large-scale suffering such as the Holocaust to occur. There are several possible answers to this question. Since Baha'i theology maintains that God has created human beings in order that they might know Him, and since it is necessary for human beings to have the divine attributes (potentially at least) in order to know them in Him, then clearly, human beings must be given the attribute of freewill. Otherwise they could not know the freewill of God.

God cannot give human beings freewill and then prevent them from exercising it every time they choose badly. God did not create the Holocaust; human beings created the Holocaust by exercising their freewill and going against the teachings of God. Human beings cannot call on God to prevent such episodes unless they call on Him to remove human freewill, and if He did this, they would no longer be human. According to the Baha'i view of history, episodes such as the Holocaust are the direct result of human perversity, which is largely the outcome of humanity's rejection of God's message for each era.

Natural Disasters and the Problem of Evil

Two kinds of disaster imperil us, natural and man-made. Our wars and genocides have harmed and killed many times the number of people ever hurt by natural disasters, so promoting peace should be our priority. But with humanity's remarkable scientific advances in the past several decades, we have learned that we can find ways to mitigate or avoid even the worst natural disasters by turning society's resources toward protecting the sanctity of human life.

In May of 1803, the Lewis and Clark expedition set off across the uncharted western part of the North American continent, and lived through multiple natural disasters, including floods and large earthquakes. How did they do it? A member of their expedition kept a diary, and he said the earth shook violently one night, making the earth move, the mountains groan and the trees sway violently and crash to the earth. But the earthquake did not hurt any of members of the expedition, because they all slept on the ground under the sky. His story reminds us that many so-called "natural" disasters tend to be man-made, instead of some act of vengeance or retribution perpetrated by an angry God.

Which brings up the eternal questions: If a loving and merciful God exists, why would He let us suffer? Why would God allow natural disasters to affect so many innocent people? How could a just, all-powerful God permit the existence of evil? This fundamental question, usually called theodicy or "the problem of evil," has plagued humanity since the beginning of time. The Baha'i teachings resolve the problem of evil in a unique and very modern way: "...the evil spirit, Satan or whatever is interpreted as evil, refers to the lower nature in man. This baser nature is symbolized in various ways. In man there are two expressions, one is the expression of nature, the other the expression of the spiritual realm. The world of nature is defective.... God has never created an evil spirit; all such ideas and nomenclature are symbols expressing the mere human or earthly nature of man. It is an essential condition of the soil of earth that thorns, weeds and fruitless trees may grow from it. Relatively speaking, this is evil; it is simply the lower state and baser product of nature."

Complete evil, according to the Baha'i teaching, does not exist, but instead see evil as simply the absence of good: "Evil is imperfection. Sin is the state of man in the world of the baser nature, for in nature exist defects such as injustice, tyranny, hatred, hostility, strife: these are characteristics of the lower plane of nature.... Through education we must free ourselves from these imperfections."

This theory of the relativity of evil, which has serious implications for how we treat each other, makes all people our relatives, relegates the very idea of an evil person to the past, and gives us each the ability to look for the good in others, and to avoid even thinking of another human being as evil. The three "spiritual prerequisites for success" which "stand out as preeminent and vital" are, "a high sense of moral rectitude" in social and administrative activities, "absolute chastity", and "complete freedom from prejudice" in dealings with peoples of a different race, class, creed, or color.

Source
https://www.patheos.com/library/baha'i/beliefs/suffering-and-the-problem-of-evil
https://www.patheos.com/library/baha'i/beliefs/suffering-and-the-problem-of-evil.aspx?p=2
https://bahaiteachings.org/natural-disasters-and-the-problem-of-evil
https://bahaiteachings.org/how-do-you-define-evil
https://en.wikipedia.org/wiki/Bah%C3%A1%27%C3%AD_Faith
https://www.bahai.org/beliefs/life-spirit/character-conduct/articles-resources/extract-writings-shoghi-effendi-character-conduct

https://www.bahai.org/beliefs/life-spirit/human-soul/life-death
https://www.bahai.org/beliefs/life-spirit/human-soul/heaven-hell

---

Buddhism

Scholars of religion have argued that the teachings of Buddhism challenge Augustine's view of good and evil, proposing a dualism in which good and evil have equal value instead of casting good over evil, as Augustine did. This is similar to the Manicheist account of good and evil – that the two are equal and in conflict – though Buddhism teaches that the two will come to a final conclusion and transcend the conflict.

Regarding the Problem of Evil, Buddha questioned the Hindu god Brahma, who created the world and all creatures. "If Brahma is lord of the whole world and creator of the multitude of beings, then why (i) has he ordained misfortune in the world without making the whole world happy, or (ii) for what purpose has he made the world full of injustice, deceit, falsehood and conceit, or (iii) the lord of beings is evil in that he ordained injustice when there could have been justice."

Understanding Buddhism begins with its historical context. Buddhism developed as a response to the social evils of Buddha's day against the prevailing corruptions of Hinduism, similar in type to the protestant reformation of Catholicism. For Buddha, it was the corruption and abuse of the Brahmins hold on religious teachings, and a challenge to the individual to think clearly about his or her own religious values. Buddha's enlightenment and message was aimed in part at the power structures of his day. He argues logically for a belief without authority, and without ritual, speculation, and tradition as a response to the religious and social cast of his day. Instead, he preaches a religion of self-effort, lacking grace which calls the individual to action. As self-effort, Buddhism is a religion of discipline that diminishes personal ego. This leads to an awakening through the Eightfold Path, to a state of Nirvana or the extinguishing of desire, and shapes the Buddha preaching to transform the social evils of his time; vaguely and remotely similar to Jesus' Sermon on the Mount.

A valid question to begin with is why should Buddhism even be concerned with the problem of evil in the first place? After all, the problem of evil is the problem of how to reconcile the existence of an omnipotent, omniscient, and perfectly good God with the presence of evil in the world. But such a problem simply does not exist in Buddhism. The reason why there is no such problem is that Buddhism denies the existence of a being comparable to the Christian God. Now, to be sure, Buddhism is not really an atheist religion. The traditional Indian Buddhist conception of the Universe comprises six realms of being, one of which is the realm of gods. But though these gods enjoy an exceptionally happy life and will live for a very long time (millions of years), they are not immortal and are still part of the cycle of rebirths. Their happiness results from good karma accumulated in earlier lives, but once these karmic benefits are consumed, these gods will die and be reborn like everyone else.

Although there are gods in Buddhism (or at least in most Buddhist traditions), these gods are part of the world (in the broadest sense of the word). They do not transcend it; i.e., they are still subject to its laws. And, most importantly, they are not creators of this world. They cannot be held responsible for the existence of evil in the world, because the world is not their creation. So there cannot be something like the problem of evil in Buddhism, just because nobody is ultimately responsible for its existence. But then what has Buddhism got to do with the problem of evil? The answer is that both Buddhism and Christianity are concerned with the problem of suffering, both try to explain why there is suffering in the world, although their explanations are quite different.

In Buddhism, while life may be full of suffering, suffering is not evil, nor are there evil entities in the world tempting people to sin and self-destruction. If there is evil in Buddhism, it is the greed, anger, and delusion that give rise to cycle of death and rebirth to which life in the material world is bound. The cycle of death and rebirth that binds us to the world is called 'samsara' in Sanskrit.

The goal of the Buddha's teaching is not to eliminate all suffering or to create a perfect life or world, but to learn how best to deal with the suffering that is a normal part of human life. What the Buddha had been seeking when he became enlightened was a way out of samsara, a way out of the endless cycle of death and rebirth binding us to this world. The Hindu texts, the Upanishads, which were written at around the same time, had argued that the way out of the endless cycle of death and rebirth was to realize that one's individual self or soul (atman) is a part

181

of the world soul (Brahman). Some scholars argue that the Buddha's solution to end this cycle was to realize that there is no self, no atman. If there is no self, there is nothing to reincarnate, nothing to endure this endless cycle of death and rebirth. One of the core contentions of Buddhism is that all life involves suffering. The basic idea is this: if it is true that all life necessarily involves suffering (as Buddhist philosophers claim), then it is not possible that God could have created a world in which there is life but no suffering.

Shortly after his enlightenment and after deciding to teach his insights, the Buddha gave his first sermon to a small group of ascetics. This sermon contains the core of all Buddhist teachings. According to the texts, the Buddha began his sermon by saying that one should follow a middle path between asceticism and hedonism, and then he listed the elements of the Eightfold Path, one meaning of which is that extreme approaches to seeking enlightenment are not necessary. Most notably his teaching describes the Four Noble Truths which are four statements expressing the insight into the fundamental nature of the Universe the Buddha had gained. They might more accurately be called the four realities of life known to those who are more spiritually noble and aware. The first of these noble truths is that all things are tainted with suffering. The remaining three truths are: the truth of the origin of suffering, the truth of the cessation of suffering, and the truth of the path to the cessation of suffering.

The importance of the Buddhist approach to the problem of evil lies in opening up the possibility of changing ones perspective of the problem rather than finding a solution to the problem of evil. This change in perspective means abandoning the question of what the point of evil is, because there need not be an answer to it. Higher-order goods defenses regard evils as conditionally necessary, i.e. necessary under the condition that a higher good shall be achieved through evil. If you want higher goods like bravery and compassion, then you have to accept the suffering that is necessary to achieve them. So in this way evil is justified. But the Buddhist defense goes further in that it regards evils as necessary without any qualification or condition, i.e., without any compensating good. Therefore, we don't have to look for reasons for a particular instance of evil; there is no need to justify it. Evil is inevitable — it is necessary, but not necessary for something good to come from it.

Given the metaphysical structure of the world, there cannot be no evils. Evil is just there and it cannot not be there. It's nobody's fault – not even God's. If we accept this, we can go one step further and admit that even the existence of pointless evil is compatible with the existence of God. When we try to justify the existence of evil, we try to find the point of it. But this approach is never really satisfying, for even if we can convince ourselves that God has a reason to allow evil to occur, the problem remains that someone, anyone, even God, who inflicts evil on others even for a good reason stands in need of atonement and forgiveness (as D. Z. Phillips famously said). But if we accept the inevitability of evil following the Buddhist defense, then we can accept that some evil is pointless. Even if there is a God, there can be pointless evils. And even if each and every instance of evil in the world were completely pointless, this would still not be a disproof of the existence of God. This acceptance of the pointlessness of evil is what can be gained from the Buddhist solution to the problem of evil, and what might possibly open up new ways of approaching it.

Source:

https://philpapers.org/rec/GBWDW

https://pluralism.wordpress.com/2008/02/28/how-do-buddhists-do-the-problem-of-evil/

https://en.wikipedia.org/wiki/Augustinian_theodicy

https://www.patheos.com/library/buddhism/beliefs/suffering-and-the-problem-of-evil

---

Confucianism

The Chinese philosopher Confucius (551– 479 BC), considered himself a re-codifier and re-transmitter of the theology and values inherited from the Shang (1600–1046 BC) and Zhou dynasties (1046–256 BC). He developed and formalized an ethical and philosophical system that includes moral, social, political, philosophical, and quasi-religious thought. While his neighbors in India were obsessed with metaphysical debates, Confucius was solely focused on everyday concerns. He was indifferent to the big mysteries of existence such as the origin or the Universe, god or the afterlife. In its original form, therefore, the problem of evil does not seem to exist in Chinese philosophy because theodicy is closely linked to the existence and ultimate goodness of God, which classical Chinese philosophers do not assume or explicitly endorse.

Yet, the observation and reflection that virtuous people, despite their effort and hard work, often suffer from random misfortune, and that their goodness is not rewarded, are clearly recorded and discussed in classical Chinese texts. And according to some interpretations of Confucianism, suffering and evil are inevitable in human life, and can promote learning and growth. A mistake is not a "sin," but an opportunity to learn and do better next time. Empathy for the suffering of others also provides motivation to grow morally, but not all humans are capable of empathy. The most influential Confucian reflections on suffering and the problem of evil come from Mengzi (372 – 289 BC) and those who sustained Mengzi's tradition.

While the problem of evil, as it is originally defined, is a problem of Western philosophy and theology, its broad philosophical significance can be shared by any philosophical tradition. Particularly, early Chinese philosophy is a great intellectual environment where the tension between moral efficacy (human effort) and the uncontrollable contingencies (luck) of life are intensely discussed and debated in relation to the power and presence of Tian or Heaven in human life. In indigenous Chinese religion, Tian or Heaven is the supreme power reigning over lesser gods and human beings. The term may refer to a deity, to impersonal nature, or to both. Tian seems to participate in functions of "fate" and "nature" as well as those of "deity."

Confucius seems to be of two minds about Tian. At times, he is convinced that he enjoys the personal protection and sanction of Tian, and thus defies his mortal opponents as he wages his campaign of moral instruction and reform. At other moments, however, he seems caught in the throes of existential despair, wondering if he has lost his divine backer at last. What remains consistent throughout Confucius' discourses on Tian is his threefold assumption about this extra-human, absolute power in the Universe: (1) its alignment with moral goodness, (2) its dependence on human agents to actualize its will, and (3) the variable, unpredictable nature of its associations with mortal actors. Thus, to the extent that the Confucius is concerned with justifying the ways of Tian to humanity, he tends to do so without questioning these three assumptions about the nature of Tian, which are rooted deeply in the Chinese past.

Confucianism and Humanism

Confucianism, also known as Ruism, is described as tradition, a philosophy, a religion, a humanistic or rationalistic religion, a way of governing, or simply a way of life with particular emphasis on the importance of the family and social harmony, rather than on an otherworldly source of spiritual values and guidance, and therefore the core of Confucianism is humanistic. Humanism is the central feature of Confucianism, which revolves almost entirely around issues related to the family, morals, and the role of the good ruler. It stresses the need for benevolent and frugal rulers, the importance of inner moral harmony and its direct connection with harmony in the physical world. Rulers and teachers, according to this view, are important models for society: a good government should rule by virtue and moral example rather than by punishment or force. Filial piety and ancestor worship, which are old traditional Chinese values, are also part of the key components of Confucian doctrine.

Humanist philosophies such as Confucianism, do not share a belief in divine law and do not exalt faithfulness to a higher law as a manifestation of divine will. Those familiar with Enlightenment-influenced presentations of Confucius depict him as an austere humanist who did not discuss the supernatural, but that may not be entirely accurate. Some conceptualize Confucianism as a religion which regards "the secular as sacred." Confucianism transcends the dichotomy between religion and humanism, considering the ordinary activities of human life, and especially human relationships, as a manifestation of the sacred, because they are the expression of humanity's moral nature, which has a transcendent anchorage in Heaven or Tian, and unfolds through an appropriate respect for the spirits or gods of the world. While Tiān has some characteristics that overlap the category of godhead, it is primarily an impersonal absolute principle, like the Dào or the Brahman.

The worldly concern of Confucianism rests upon the belief that human beings are fundamentally good, and teachable, improvable, and perfectible through personal and communal endeavor, especially self-cultivation and self-creation. Confucian thought focuses on the cultivation of virtue in a morally organized world. Some of the basic Confucian ethical concepts and practices include 'benevolence' or 'humaneness' as the essence of the human being which manifests as 'compassion.' Confucianism is the virtue-form of Heaven. It is the upholding of righteousness and the moral disposition to do good. It is a system of ritual norms and propriety that determines how a person should properly act in everyday life in harmony with the law of Heaven. It is the ability to see what is right and fair, or the converse, in the behaviors exhibited by others. Confucianism holds one in contempt, either passively or actively, for failure to uphold the cardinal moral value of compassion.

Source
https://www.patheos.com/library/confucianism/beliefs/suffering-and-the-problem-of-evil
https://www.ancient.eu/Confucianism/
https://muse.jhu.edu/article/633068/summary
https://www.iep.utm.edu/confuciu/
https://muse.jhu.edu/article/633068/summary
https://en.wikipedia.org/wiki/Confucianism
http://worldreligions.weebly.com/confucianism.html

Hinduism

The problem of evil is a touchstone of any religion. It is from our direct confrontation with evil that suffering results, and then endless questions about the meaning of life follow. That is why all religions have to give a proper answer regarding the origin, nature and end of evil and suffering. There are three major religious alternatives in explaining evil, stated by the pantheistic, dualistic and monotheistic religions.

Pantheistic religions regard evil as ultimately unreal. Human suffering is a product of spiritual ignorance gathered in previous lives and distributed in the present one according to the dictates of karma. In the dualistic religions, good and evil are two eternal and rival principles. Neither has created the other one and each acts according to its own nature. In the monotheistic religions, evil has a personal identity. Its source is a being that has fallen from an initial good status as a result of misusing their God-given freedom of will. Hinduism is a complex mixture of pantheistic religious trends. Concerning the relation between Ultimate Reality and evil, there are at least three major perspectives, given by the Vedas, the Upanishads, and the Epics and Puranas.

Unlike Christianity, Hinduism does not dichotomize good against evil. Hindu theology depicts evil as being created alongside the rest of the Universe. Thus, there is not the perspective that evil is unnatural and must be vanquished or conquered as there is in Christian theology, especially surrounding the figure of Jesus Christ. Even though Hinduism predominantly treats evil as a natural force of the Universe, it still holds that people should strive to live their lives in a good way as opposed to an evil way.

Much of Hindu theology, in fact, focuses on the idea of the gods maintaining balance between order and chaos, creation and destruction. The trio of major Hindu gods called the "trimurti" includes Brahma, Vishnu, and Shiva. Vishnu is the preserver of the Universe, while Shiva's role is to destroy it in order to re-create. Brahma's job was creation of the world and all creatures. The whole world derived from Brahma by way of the process of evolution. The god Brahma should not be confused with the god Brahman, who is the supreme god force present within all things.

Even so, the roles that gods play are somewhat ambiguous in their moral classification. Hindu mythology does not clearly define whether or not Hindu deities are purely good. In fact, the lack of a dichotomy between good and evil in Hinduism extends down to gods and demons in Hindu mythology. While gods are popularly depicted to be good and demons depicted to be evil, one's interpretations could vary depending on the specific myths one believes.

Karma

In the Indian tradition, karma refers to action driven by intention which leads to future consequences. Those intentions are considered to be the determining factor in the cycle of death and rebirth to which life in the material world is bound. According to the theory of karma, a person is responsible for their own life, i.e., what happens to a person happens because they caused it with their previous intentional actions, therefore people get what they deserve. The theory of karma can be thought to be an extension to Newton's third law of action and reaction where every action of any kind including words, thoughts feelings, the totality of our existence, will eventually have a reaction, i.e., same type of energy coming back to the one who caused it.

One way some Christians understand karma, from a spiritual perspective, is that by the perfect life and obedient death of Jesus Christ, He took or canceled the bad karma of all people so that we can avoid the consequence of eternal death that our intentional bad actions deserve. That is, God has extended Grace, or unmerited favor to everyone based on the meritorious life, death, and finished work of Jesus Christ.

Even though karma answers theodical questions fairly well, it does so by omitting divinity from its consideration. This causes problems for some Hindus, and while karma has been hailed by Western scholars as a wonderful doctrine for its explanatory logic, ironically, it is not held in the same high regard by all Hindus. Max Weber, wrote sweeping adulations about karma, saying, "The most complete formal solution of the problem of theodicy is the special achievement of the Indian doctrine of karma." Peter Berger has said that karma is the most logical answer devised to the question of theodicy, so perhaps this is why karma has become popular outside of India and Hinduism. The doctrine or theory of karma basically states that the moral implications of one's past actions dictate what sort of events will happen to one's future self.

For hundreds of years, philosophers, scholars and theologians have wrestled with questions of theodicy: "Why do bad things happen to good people?" and "Why do good things happen to bad people?" Within the study of theology, these questions also include questions about the role of divine beings, specifically, "If there is a benevolent god, why does he/she/it allow for the existence of evil and suffering?"

Even Buddha questioned the Hindu god Brahma, who created the world. "If Brahma is lord of the whole world and creator of the multitude of beings, then why (i) has he ordained misfortune in the world without making the whole world happy, or (ii) for what purpose has he made the world full of injustice, deceit, falsehood and conceit, or (iii) the lord of beings is evil in that he ordained injustice when there could have been justice." Hinduism treats these questions in unique ways. First, it provides an answer to the first two questions with the doctrine of karma. Through a combination of the principle of cause-and-effect and the unique, South Asian conception of rebirth and reincarnation, karma gives an explanation for why both good and bad things befall people. Second, it possesses a unique mythology which contains at least two distinct explanations for why gods would allow evil to exist in the world.

While a religious scholar coming from a Christian background might be seeking to find a specific Hindu answer to theodicy and how it treats evil, the reality is that, within Hinduism, there rarely is a single, universal answer to any given question. For instance, while karma is a very rational answer to theodicy, if one is a believer of bhakti mythology, then he or she would probably relegate the importance of karma in comparison to the benevolence and power of his or her Supreme Lord or Lady. Unlike Christianity, within Hindu theology, there are no absolute universals. Therefore, in order to better understand how Hinduism treats evil and theodicy, one must examine multiple perspectives and the contexts in which they are applicable.

Source:
http://comparativereligion.com/evil.html
Evil and theodicy in Hinduism PDF by Sunder Willett

Islam

The monotheistic faiths must consider the problems of suffering and evil within the context of God's omnipotence, omniscience, justice, and mercy. Muslim theologians do not address the problem of evil directly as such, but ask questions about good and evil, what to do about them, who created them, and who is responsible for them. From an Islamic perspective, these questions are related to fundamental inquiries into the nature of good and evil and the nature of God. That is, why would a merciful God create a world in which evil exists?

Muslims believe that only God has the power to create, and that He is omnipotent, omniscient, merciful and just. Thus, from an Islamic perspective, a perspective which includes the concept of a judgment day as well as a day of accountability in an afterlife, a particularly important question arises as to how people could be punished if God is responsible for everything, including human actions. This is tied in to the question of why it is that bad things can happen to good people, and why good things happen to bad people. That is, shouldn't a 'just' God reward good deeds and punish bad deeds appropriately?

One way to answer the question of why evil exists is to claim that it is not God who commits bad actions, it is people that do. This answer hinges on a conception of freewill, on the notion that humans are, to a degree, free to make independent choices for which they are accountable. The first great theological controversy in the Islamic world occurred over the question of why evil exists, because it seems to run counter to other prevailing notions about God, e.g., the omniscience and omnipotence of God.

In Islam, there are two views of suffering, both of which in some ways resemble views held by its sister monotheistic faiths, Judaism and Christianity. Suffering is either the painful result of a person's sin, or it is a test of a person's faith. In the latter view, suffering tests belief, in that a true Muslim will remain faithful through the trials of life. But suffering also reveals the hidden, inner most self to God. Suffering is built into the fabric of existence so that God may see who is truly righteous, and who is not. In other words, God not only allows or permits the various agonies and struggles of life to exist, but He has a purpose for them as well. Suffering opens up the soul and reveals it to God. God uses suffering to look within the lives of believers and test their character, as well as correct unbelievers.

Suffering is also a painful result of sin, and in Islam, sin is associated with unbelief. Muslims surrender to God's will, and find peace in that surrender. Sometimes people forget to listen to the prophets, and fail to serve God in all that they do. This leads to a state of unbelief called kufr, which literally means to forget by way of intentionally hiding from the truth. Therefore a kafir is someone who has purposefully forgotten the Lord. They become preoccupied with their own particular needs and their own particular passions. Islam does not condemn human passions or human needs, seeing them as a necessary part of a full and useful life. But when people forget to serve God, these needs and passions can enslave them, and they begin to misuse their divine gifts of intelligence, will, and speech. Enslaved by lust, and by cravings for wealth and pleasure, people do evil things. Such moments of unbelief can happen to anyone, and people suffer when they occur. Seen in this light, suffering is not only painful, but is also a lesson. It reminds humans of the truth of God's revelation and directs them back to God.

Although all people are imperfect and vulnerable to sin, Islam does not teach that people are essentially evil. When people realize their sin and make amends with true remorse, God forgives them their sin. Genuine repentance is all that is needed to restore a person to a sinless state. However, individuals are always vulnerable to unbelief, and sin and suffering are serious matters. The great struggle, or jihad, of human life is the struggle to perfect one's heart, and to live a sinless life in total submission to God. Muslims believe that it is possible to be a perfect Muslim, since God does not ask anyone to do anything that is beyond his or her ability. But perfect Muslims, like prophets, are very rare individuals. Most individuals must be vigilant and always begin to do something with the intention of doing good.

While there is no concept of original sin in Islamic thought, the common assumption is that the human condition turns people into sinners and therefore in need of divine assistance to achieve salvation. However, ordinary human beings can contribute to their salvation if they sacrifice their life through martyrdom. However, Islam also teaches the faithful to work actively to alleviate the suffering of others. In the Islamic view, righteous individuals are revealed not only through patient acceptance of their own suffering, but through their good works to help relieve the pain and suffering of others. Islam teaches the endurance of suffering with hope and faith. The faithful are not counseled to resist suffering, or to ask why they are suffering. Instead, they are to accept it as God's will and live through it with the understanding that God never asks more of them than they can endure.

The problem of how to reconcile God's omnipotence and justice with the existence of evil in this world has occupied Muslim theologians since the formative period, and freewill and predestination are at the heart of the matter. Sunni theologians emphasize God's transcendence when explaining God's predestination of some people to hell. Shia theologians emphasize God's justice when explaining that people with divinely bestowed freewill determine their own fate, whether it be heaven or hell. Shia scholars believe that it is simply in the nature of the created world, which is at the bottom of the hierarchy of being, that it contains certain imperfections or evil. Some of these deficiencies are furthermore only apparent and ultimately serve a higher purpose.

Therefore, while the world as it is presently may not actually be the best of all possible worlds, it preserves that potential. The current picture of the world simply reflects human nature, and forms part of a larger divine plan for human salvation. Regarding predestination, Sunni Islam resembles Christian Calvinism and Reformed theology, and Shia Islam resembles Christian Arminianism when it comes to freewill.

Shia Islam

Shia belief in freewill stems from their desire to hold people accountable for their actions, which they have to be if God is just, then each person deserves the reward or punishment they receive. Therefore, in order to preserve the notion of a just God Shia insist on human freewill. Also, Shia refuse to believe that God would predestine anyone to hell. This view against predestination creates great discomfort for Sunni orthodox theologians. Shia belief centers on the concepts of divine justice. They attempt to resolve the theological problem of evil, which is how to reconcile the justice of an all-powerful God with the reality of evil in the world, and attempt to do so in accordance with the teaching of the Quran. Shia believe that humans can discern the difference between good and evil and choose freely between them. And that a just God would be compelled to reward good deeds and punish bad ones, as this is the essential character of the relationship between humans and God. Shia reason that since God is believed to be just and wise, and since He cannot command what is contrary to reason or act with disregard for the welfare of His creatures, evil must be regarded as something that stems from errors in human acts, arising from the abuse of divinely bestowed freewill.

Sunni Islam

Sunnis do not accept that God, who is above human rules and rationality, could be compelled to do anything, even to be bound by his own nature. To preserve the Sunni tenet of God's complete and utter transcendence and superiority over humans, they posit that God alone determines what is just and unjust, and that God alone determines what was good and what was evil, and therefore human perception of justice and goodness is in every way inferior to God's. Most Sunni theologians argue that ordinary human moral judgments stem from human emotion and social convention, which are inadequate to either condemn or justify divine actions.

Sunni theology insists that human knowledge is limited to what has been revealed through the prophets. And what has been revealed regarding God's creation of evil has to be accepted without asking how. That is, it is God's prerogative to have bad things happen to good people, for reasons He alone possesses, and it is humankind's responsibility to accept and submit to His will. Though Sunnis believe in a merciful and compassionate God, they did not want to subject God to human processes of judgment and reason. This understanding of God's prerogatives resembles Christian Skeptical Theism. Sunni theologians also hold that God creates everything, including human actions, but distinguish creation from acquisition of actions. They allow individuals the latter ability, though they do not posit the existence of freewill in a fuller sense of the term as do the Shia. In their words, "God creates, in man, the power, ability, choice, and will to perform an act, and man, endowed with this derived power, chooses freely one of the alternatives and intends or wills to do the action, and, corresponding to this intention, God creates and completes the action." Shia and Sunni disagree over a number of Islamic doctrinal points. But the fundamental issue between the two is who has responsibility for human actions. That is, are people responsible for their own actions or is God responsible, and what that means for predestination and freewill.

Source

https://www.patheos.com/library/islam/beliefs/suffering-and-the-problem-of-evil

https:// https://en.wikipedia.org/wiki/Theodicy#Islamic_world

https://www.patheos.com/library/sunni-islam/beliefs/suffering-and-the-problem-of-evil

https://medium.com/@mustaphahitani/mutazila-between-reason-and-faith-3c5df65fe481

https://en.wikipedia.org/wiki/Mu%CA%BFtazila

https://en.wikipedia.org/wiki/Mutazila

https://www.patheos.com/library/shia-islam/beliefs/suffering-and-the-problem-of-evil

---

Jainism

All sentient beings do harm by simply existing. The harmful action of existing and the karma it generates are at the root of all evil and suffering. The evil and violence inherent in existence prove to Jains that there is no omnipotent, wholly good creator God or god. Therefore, Jains do not believe in a God or gods in the way that many other religions do, but they do believe in divine beings, or at least perfect beings who are worthy of devotion. The Jain view of God enables Jainism to explain the evil and suffering that exists in the world without the intellectual difficulties faced by religions that have an omnipotent, wholly good creator God at their heart, as do the Abrahamic monotheistic religions. Where religions such as Christianity find the problem of evil one of their most difficult problems, Jains use the problem of suffering and evil as a reason for denying the existence of an omnipotent, wholly good Creator. In many ways the Jain attitude toward perfect beings is both intelligible and satisfying, and sufficient to deny the claim that Jainism is an atheistic religion. If one wants to argue that Jainism is atheistic then one must do so from a specific, limited, idea of what it means to be divine.

Furthermore, Jainism is dismissive of the very idea of the existence of an omnipotent, wholly good Creator or creative spirit. If God created the world, where was He before creation? If you say He was transcendent then, and needed no support, where is He now? The perfect beings that Jains worship are beyond human contact, cannot intervene in the world, and have no interest in human beings. And Jains believe that karma is a physical process, and has nothing to do with spiritual beings.

The supreme principle of Jain living is non-violence. And the three guiding principles of Jainism, are right belief, right knowledge, and right conduct. And at the heart of right conduct lie the five great vows:

Nonviolence - Not to cause harm to any living beings
Truthfulness - Speak the harmless truth only
Non-stealing - Not to take anything not properly given
Chastity - Not to indulge in sensual pleasure
Non-possession/Non-attachment - Complete detachment from people, places, and material things

Along with Hinduism and Buddhism, Jainism is one of the three most ancient Indian religious traditions still in existence and an integral part of South Asian religious belief and practice. Scholars of religion generally hold that Jainism originated in the 7th–5th century BC in the Ganges basin of eastern India, the scene of intense religious speculation and activity at that time. Buddhism also appeared in this region, as did other belief systems that renounced the world and opposed the ritualistic Brahman schools whose prestige derived from their claim of purity and their ability to perform the traditional rituals and sacrifices and to interpret their meaning. These new religious perspectives promoted asceticism, the abandonment of ritual, domestic and social action, and the attainment of spiritual illumination in an attempt to win, through one's own efforts, freedom from repeated rebirth.

Followers of Jainism are called Jains, a word derived from the word Jina, which refers to a human being who has conquered all inner passions like anger, attachment, greed and pride, and who possesses pure infinite knowledge. Followers of the path shown by the Jina's are called Jains. The origins of Jainism are obscure. Jains believe that their tradition does not have a historical founder. They claim their religion to be eternal and consider Rishabhanatha to be the founder in the present time cycle, the first of 24 Jain saviors and spiritual teachers. The first Jain figure for whom there is reasonable historical evidence is Parshvanatha (or Parshva), a renunciant teacher who may have lived in the 7th century BC and founded a community based upon the abandonment of worldly concerns.

Jain scriptures are called Agamas. They are believed to have been verbally transmitted by oral tradition from one generation to the next, much like the ancient Buddhist and Hindu texts. The Jain tradition believes that their religion is eternal, and that the teachings of their first savior and spiritual teacher Rishabhanatha have been verbally transmitted by oral tradition from one generation to the next, much like the ancient Buddhist and Hindu texts. Jain texts reject the idea of a creator, ruler or destroyer god and postulate an eternal Universe. According to Jainism, the Universe was never created, nor will it ever cease to exist. It is independent and self-sufficient, does not require a creator or any superior power to govern it, nor a judge nor a destroyer. In this belief, it is distinct from the monotheistic Abrahamic religions.

All three religions, Jainism, Buddhism, and Hinduism share concepts and doctrines such as karma and rebirth, and have similar mythologies and monastic traditions. And they do not believe in an eternal heaven or hell or day of judgment. Jainism, like Buddhism and Hinduism, grants the freedom to choose beliefs such as in gods or no-gods, agree or disagree with core teachings, participate or not participate in prayers, rituals and festivals. They all consider ethical values such as non-violence to be important, and link suffering to individual cravings, actions, intents and karma, and believe spirituality is a means to enlightened peace, bliss and eternal liberation from the cycle of rebirth.

Jainism differs from both Buddhism and Hinduism in its understanding of the nature of reality. All three believe in impermanence, but Buddhism incorporates the premise of no eternal self or soul. Hinduism incorporates the premise of an eternal unchanging self or soul, while Jainism incorporates the premise of a self or soul that is both changing and eternal.

Source
https://sites.fas.harvard.edu/~pluralsm/affiliates/jainism/jainedu/ma havir.htm
https://en.wikipedia.org/wiki/Jainism
https://patheos.com/library/jainism/beliefs/suffering-and-the-problem-of-evil
https://bbc.co.uk/religion/religions/jainism/beliefs/god.shtml
https://britannica.com/topic/Jainism/Early-medieval-developments-500-1100

Judaism

The Judaic view, while acknowledging the difference between the human and divine perspective of evil, is rooted in the nature of creation itself and the limitation inherent in matter's capacity to be perfected; the action of freewill includes the potential for perfection from individual effort and leaves the responsibility for evil in human hands. Throughout history, Jews have addressed the relation between God, evil, and human suffering by demonstrating a spectrum between those who defend, justify, or accept God's relationship to evil and those who refuse to ascribe any positive meaning for the presence of evil in the world, even reaching the extreme of protesting against God on behalf of their respective communities. Yet in between those extremes exist the bulk of Jewish responses to evil. Here visions of God's omnipotence, omnipresence, and goodness are radically compromised and God's relationship to evil is blurred in the face of unjustified suffering, illustrating the continually swinging pendulum between theodicy and anti-theodicy throughout history.

In the Biblical and First Temple periods, evil was not even discussed, based on the assumption that God is just. There was a sense of collective Judaic responsibility for evil as sin, expressed most clearly in Deuteronomy 30:15-20. "See, I have set before you today life and prosperity, and death and adversity; in that I command you today to love the Lord your God, to walk in His ways and to keep His commandments and His statutes and His judgments, that you may live and multiply, and that the Lord your God may bless you in the land where you are entering to possess it.

"But if your heart turns away and you will not obey, but are drawn away and worship other gods and serve them, I declare to you today that you shall surely perish. You will not prolong your days in the land where you are crossing the Jordan to enter and possess it. I call heaven and earth to witness against you today, that I have set before you life and death, the blessing and the curse. So choose life in order that you may live, you and your descendants, by loving the Lord your God, by obeying His voice, and by holding fast to Him; for this is your life and the length of your days, that you may live in the land which the Lord swore to your fathers, to Abraham, Isaac, and Jacob, to give them."

Influenced indirectly by Hellenistic thought and literature during the Second Temple period, the Book of Job was the first individual, critical response to the doctrine of retribution in the Torah. The author clearly expresses a tension between theodicy, an undying faith in God's justice despite terrible personal tragedy, and an active protest in which God is put on trial. Job becomes the plaintiff and prosecutor with his friends serving as witnesses, co-defendants, and judges. God is forced to be the defendant in the case, yet remains the ultimate judge against Job and his friends. The author indicts God for not holding up the covenant, by censuring and silencing God throughout the text to uphold Job's innocence. Ultimately, the text does appear to turn the authority back to

God at the end with a divine speech, undermining Job's defense and even swinging the pendulum back to intensified faith in God, creation, and providence. Yet God's response does not necessarily satisfy the reader, because it never addresses Job's complaint, and instead shifts the blame back on Job for his ignorance of divine providence.

In the Rabbinic period between 70-500 C.E., the rabbis constructed a theodicy by arguing that God created every human being with a "good urge," and a "bad urge." They asserted that both urges were necessary because the bad urge provided individuals with the libido or energy that they needed to use for productive purposes like building houses, marriage, having children, and conducting business. However, if not channeled in the appropriate way, the bad urge could become the source of evil. The rabbis also tried to explain why the righteous suffer by arguing that if a righteous person suffers in this world, he or she will be rewarded in olam ha-bah, the "World to Come," when all the righteous souls will be reunited with their bodies after the Messiah comes.

However, the rabbis also demonstrated a tension between theodicy and anti-theodicy by constructing a counter-lawsuit similar to that of Job in Lamentations Rabbah, a commentary to the Biblical Book of Lamentations, that laments the destruction of the First and Second Temples. In their commentary on Lamentations, the rabbis interspersed examples of Israel's guilt for the destruction of both Temples, based on a rejection of God, failure to study Torah, and ethical and cultic violations.

There is a heavenly trial scene in which Israel's advocates—Abraham, Jacob, Moses, and Rachel—actually turn the trial on its head by moving from divine judgment to solidarity with Israel in its suffering over against a defensive God. Abraham reaffirms Israel's zealous observance of the Torah, and the trial reaches a climax with Moses' appeal to the absence of divine justice, using the Leviticus law on slaughtering of animals against its supposed author. Finally, Rachel cites an absence of divine mercy, with the conclusion of the story faulting God and forcing the withdrawal of God's complaint against Israel.

During the medieval period, three different types of theodicies emerged to cope with persecution and suffering. In response to the Crusades in 1096, the Ashkenazic Jews of the Rhineland advocated a martyr logical theodicy by advocating dying for "the sanctification of God's name," rather than converting to Christianity. The 11th-century rabbinic commentator Rashi provided the soteriological theodicy by arguing that it wasn't Christ who suffered for the sins of the world, but rather the Jewish people as a whole. Finally, the 12th-century philosopher Yehuda Halevi constructed a missionary theodicy by arguing that Jewish suffering in exile was justified in the sense that through their dispersion, they could fulfill their mission of spreading the knowledge of God to the non-Jewish world.

The tension between theodicy and anti-theodicy reached its extremes following the Holocaust when Jewish theologians were faced with the tremendously difficult task of affirming their covenant with God while recognizing that the same God of Sinai is also the God of Auschwitz. Their responses span the spectrum of theodicy to anti-theodicy. In *Faith After the Holocaust* (1974), Eliezer Berkovits rejected the Deuteronomic notion that the Holocaust could be interpreted as a punishment for sin, but constructed a post-Holocaust theology with a strong theodic thrust by transferring much of the blame for the Holocaust from God to humanity, and more specifically Christian culture.

In *To Mend the World* (1982), Emil Fackenheim viewed the Holocaust as historically unique and rejected traditional theodicies. Instead, he created his own fragmented theology by arguing that the Holocaust represents a cosmic rupture that can never be fully repaired theologically.

In *After Auschwitz* (First and Second Editions, 1966, 1992), Richard Rubenstein constructed a complete anti-theodicy by rejecting what he considered to be the traditional Jewish portrayal of an omnipotent and transcendent Biblical God for whom the Holocaust would be a punishment for Jewish sins, concluding that we now live in the age of the death of the historical God. (1)

Orthodox Judaism

Orthodox Judaic theology adheres to the ancient Jewish teachings, going back to the Biblical prophets, which teach that suffering is a sign of divine displeasure with humankind, and that, in the words of the Talmud, "there is no suffering without sin." However, in the wake of the Holocaust's unprecedented challenge to this traditional theodicy, a number of Orthodox thinkers have developed more complex theories about suffering and evil. (2)

Source:
(1) https://www.patheos.com/library/judaism/beliefs/suffering-and-the-problem-of-evil
https://en.m.wikipedia.org/wiki/Theodicy
(2) https://www.patheos.com/library/orthodox-judaism/beliefs/suffering-and-the-problem-of-evil

---

New Age Beliefs

New Age beliefs tend to deny or at least minimize the fundamental existence of evil. In this regard, the New Age parallels both its theological forerunner, the 19th century New Thought movement, and its culture of origin, the progressive, optimistic mindset of postwar America. The New Age partially derived from New Thought, which is itself a derivative of Christian Science, inherited the latter's position on the ultimate illusionary nature of evil. New Thought declared that evil, illness, and sin only exist because the human mind wills it so, and that one can overcome all these positions through the power of the mind. The New Age accepts this basic premise as well. Most New Age healing techniques seek to use the power of the mind to overcome the physical taints of evil and suffering.

Yet American culture, specifically the optimism and can-do spirit of the postwar era, also influenced the New Age's perspective on suffering and evil. The New Age's overall sense of optimism clearly follows in a long line of American progressivist thinking, most specifically the school of thought founded by Norman Vincent Peale called "positive thinking." This approach declares that suffering is merely a state of mind and that one can overcome all obstacles through optimism and perseverance. The New Age movement draws upon this approach and declares that evil or suffering exists only because human beings let them exist. Ideally, human beings will develop themselves so as to overcome both suffering and evil, and thereby achieve a higher consciousness.

Groups and subcultures within the New Age exhibit the belief differently that evil exists only as an illusion propagated by unthinking minds. *A*

Course in Miracles, one of the most popular channeled texts of the New Age, insists that the physical world itself represents merely a shadowy projection of the power of thought. Evil, good, suffering, and pleasure do not really exist in this worldview, at least not in the bodily physical way that most people assume. In this regard, *A Course in Miracles* clearly follows a long line of philosophical thinking that similarly denies the reality of this world. Other groups and texts within the New Age take a different approach. Those who focus on oracle traditions, such as tarot, astrology, or the *I Ching*, generally understand suffering as derived from failure to follow the appropriate path as described by the oracles, and evil as a general lack of balance as well as broader social failure to follow its proper path. Again, evil exists because the human mind has caused it to be so.

Since New Agers generally believe that the human mind can overcome evil just as it produces it, they look to various practices to accomplish that goal. Most New Agers understand meditation as the most effective means of overcoming evil. Here New Age practitioners draw upon a rich tradition of meditation within Asian religions that also looks to the practice to overcome illusion. Many strands of Hinduism and Buddhism teach that the world is filled with Maya or illusion, and that the human mind can overcome this illusion through meditation. New Agers have utilized these Asian religious practices to similarly free their minds of the illusions of evil and suffering.

There is, one must admit, very little sustained attention to evil and the problem of evil in the New Age movement and rather far more focus on suffering and its causes. Though New Age practitioners disagree on the precise nature of suffering, the common bond that unites them is the concept of Karma. Here the New Age again draws on the reservoir of Asian religion, albeit as transmitted through the 19th-century new religion Theosophy, which introduced the concept of Karma to the American religious community. New Agers believe that Karma explains why individuals suffer and that achieving a proper understanding of Karma and mastering the sort of Karma that one accumulates leads to the end of suffering.

In keeping with the overall approach that humans create their own realities, the New Age worldview looks to Karma to explain the nature of the human experience of the world. Though New Age understandings of Karma vary, all agree that negative actions and thoughts lead to bad Karma, and positive actions and thoughts lead to good Karma. Karma, therefore, functions as the universal law of cause and effect that takes into account each person's actions. Like the Hindu or Buddhist concept of Karma, New Agers understand Karma as impersonal and automatic. But unlike many Hindu or Buddhist approaches that ultimately seek to minimize Karma entirely, most New Agers hope to maximize their good Karma so as to create a positive world for themselves. The more good Karma that a person obtains, the better their experience of life, and the better their experience of future lives.

Karma explains another facet of the New Age understanding of evil and suffering, namely that human beings create their own suffering in order to learn spiritual lessons. Scholars call this understanding of suffering a pedagogical explanation for evil since it looks to suffering as a form of teaching. According to this New Age approach, the world that the human mind creates forces individuals to experience events that will teach them greater spiritual truths, even if such experiences cause momentary pain. After many such experiences, individuals will obtain enough spiritual knowledge that they no longer require such lessons. Scholars note that from a psychological perspective, this approach to suffering ascribes an ultimate meaning to pain, and therefore enables New Age practitioners to understand their life experiences as meaningful. The overall New Age theory of evil and suffering therefore functions as a way of minimizing meaningless pain.

Source:
https://www.patheos.com/library/new-age/beliefs/suffering-and-the-problem-of-evil

---

Paganism

Paganism is an umbrella term and there are dozens of different traditions and earth-based faiths that fall under the umbrella title of "Paganism." The term Pagan was originally used to describe people who lived in rural areas. As time progressed and Christianity spread, those same country folk were often the last holdouts clinging to their old religions. Thus, Pagan came to mean people who didn't worship the God of Abraham, the father of both Judeo-Christian and Islamist religions. Therefore, like the term Christian, which includes Lutheran or Methodist or Jehovah's Witness, the term Pagan includes Wiccan or Asatru or Dianic or Eclectic Witchcraft.

Most Pagans would regard concepts such as salvation or justification as meaningless to their spiritual path. With no transcendent deity who acts as judge and no concept of sin, then logically there is no need for salvation or atonement, as well as any need for theodicy. Since many forms of Paganism are more oriented toward the material world rather than an abstract spiritual world, such a perspective maintains that it is more important to live well in the present than to waste time worrying about what will occur in a future that cannot be controlled anyway. Incentives to live a good life do not involve pleasing a god or goddess who is exterior to one's self; rather, virtue, honor, and nobility are their own rewards and one engages in such behavior out of a sense of love and personal pride. Because of the freedom with which individuals can form their own opinions about the afterlife, some Pagans choose either to remain agnostic about questions of what happens after death, or even reject all such ideas as mere speculation.

Questions regarding the Pagan response to suffering and evil can best be understood as two separate issues, even though they are closely related. Suffering, or the experience of pain, whether physical or emotional/mental/spiritual, is an experiential reality, whereas evil is an abstract concept. Because of this distinction, many in the modern Pagan community have distinct ways of approaching the problem of suffering versus the question of evil.

Suffering is part of life. So is loss, age, sickness, and death. Simply put, suffering is part of nature. Therefore, the problem of suffering may not impact Pagans who believe in a world where there are no moral values, no ultimate good, but what of the rest of the Pagans? How might they make sense of it? One way for these Pagans to make sense of the problem of suffering is to consider that certain kinds of life require certain conditions to manifest and develop, particularly the kind of life that eventuates in beings such as ourselves. These conditions include a geology of moving continents, earthquakes, volcanoes, floods and the like.

What appear to be disasters or imperfections in the world that cause great suffering when viewed from the local perspective of time and place, may sometimes prove beneficial when viewed more globally over long periods of time. As we learn more about our world seemingly unrelated phenomena turn out to be closely linked. For example, deserts and ice age glaciers create mineral dust that apparently enriches forests and other regions thousands of miles away and for thousands of years after the creation of those nutrients. Earth's greatest forest, the Amazon rain forest, benefits disproportionately from one valley in the Sahara desert. No such Sahara desert valley, no such Amazon forest. Volcanoes create rich soils and a more varied environment within which a greater abundance of life forms can emerge and flourish. Those places which are geologically quiet for the longest times have the poorest soils. It has been a long time since Australia had serious volcanism or massive tectonic activity, and its soils are among the worlds poorest. Processes that cause life to suffer in one context may enrich life's abundance and diversity in another context. Therefore, if life is to develop richly within a physical world like our own, then it may be necessary that earthquakes and tsunamis, droughts and deluges, be present as well.

In addition there is the universality of predators and predation in general, within the long history of life's evolutionary development. And such a long evolutionary path of suffering appears to have been required for embodied life as we know it to develop. Without the suffering of predation such an evolutionary process may not have been possible. And it may be that without such suffering it might not have been possible for the kind of life to develop which can understand and appreciate life itself, and what was required for life to get where it is now, which is a great good in itself. We Humans cannot eradicate suffering any more than we can suspend gravity or stop a tsunami, and getting caught up in explanations or arguments about such suffering simply distracts us from the real issue, which is finding ways to prevent unnecessary suffering and to alleviate or mitigate it when it does occur.

Evil, which can be defined as an abstract principle that causes suffering or harm, is more problematic than suffering itself, for while suffering can easily be described, evil, as an abstract principle, cannot. Evil, therefore, is a matter of faith, and among Pagans, no articles of faith are universally held. Therefore, while some Pagans might choose to believe in the existence of principles like good and evil, others argue that such principles are useless, and could even be harmful if used to attack or malign someone unfairly as being evil, or unjustly as being good.

Many Pagans prefer terminology like positive and negative, or order and chaos as alternatives to the categories of good and evil, in that the categories of good and evil are so heavily steeped in Judeo-Christian assumptions that their usefulness is limited. Nevertheless, because of the high degree of tolerance within the Pagan community, adherents are free to form their own opinions about the existence or the problem of evil. Whether or not evil exists as an abstract principle which causes harm, and whether or not there may be one or more beings or entities that embody evil are therefore matters of personal opinion among Pagans.

Beyond the allusions of mythology and the philosophical controversies surrounding evil, the reality of suffering remains. Since these phenomena occur within the natural world, any response to them likewise must therefore be primarily natural. This is not to preclude a spiritual or abstract response to suffering; but many Pagans would regard a purely spiritual response to a natural problem as faulty or inadequate. There is no point in casting a spell over someone bleeding without first attending to their wounds. Thus, while various Pagan paths may include a variety of spells, rituals, or prayers to help alleviate or eliminate suffering, such tools would be preceded by mundane or non-spiritual responses to the problem to begin with. While many contemporary Pagans are critical of mainstream medicine and advocate a variety of alternative healing practices, most recognize that a combination of traditional and alternative healing practices may be necessary, particularly in serious or life-threatening circumstances.

How do those who reject the idea of evil explain the existence of pain and suffering? Many say that pain and suffering are simply part of nature, and that questions about why it exists are not nearly as helpful as strategies to help alleviate it when it does occur. Regardless of whether suffering is met with natural or spiritual remedies, Pagans are free to respond to suffering in any way they deem appropriate. Seen on a purely naturalistic level, pain and suffering are markers of a condition or situation that needs to change, whether the change comes about through healing or, in extreme cases, through death.

Even when a person voluntarily embraces suffering, for example, when someone sacrifices their personal time and resources to care for an elderly relative, this suffering in itself is meaningful only because it is undertaken in service of a clearly understood greater good, in this case, the good of caring for another. There is no dogma or belief that would suggest suffering is always bad or, for that matter, always noble and virtuous. Any instance of suffering must be evaluated on its own merits, whether it is a problem that must be addressed immediately, or a sacrificial act freely undertaken in honor of a greater good. Few Pagans would subscribe to a belief that suffering is inherently virtuous, but rather would view pain as a condition that, whenever possible, should be remedied.

If undeserved suffering is not a sign of imperfection in nature, or of an imminent divine being less than good, what are we to make of human misbehavior and malice? Whether at the retail level of people deliberately hurting one another in their personal relations, or at the whole sale level of human monsters, the Mao's and Stalin's and Hitler's of this world, and a host of lesser but still deadly despots and oppressors, where both our personal lives and our history as a species are filled with frequent encounters with their specific horrific acts against others and against all of humanity in general.

Christianity, as many have encountered it, has little to no light to shed on the problem of evil. Western Christians claim to have an easy answer to this issue. They call it original sin, which along with its moral incoherence solves nothing. That is, it is posited that a perfect deity made a perfect creation where two perfect people sinned and as a result billions of others are born guilty of sin and subject to pain and suffering. To this explanation some of the more sophisticated Christians say that it is self-centeredness, this refusal to be able to respond lovingly to everyone, that is our "fallenness," i.e., our self-love is our original sin. Historically the most common Pagan answer to the problem of evil is that evil is due to ignorance, ignorance deep and dark. And from a Pagan perspective, but not only a Pagan perspective, spirituality is a means to overcome such ignorance. That is, we do not berate a child for their childish ignorance, but we do expect the child to be open to learning, to mature, and to grow out of their childish ways.

This has been an attempt to show how even the most hideous acts against others, and humanity in general, can arise from a world in which there is no inherent evil, but only ignorance among well-meaning people. If this is the case, it may mean that the world is not a good place, and that we are simply trapped here by our own ignorance, which is a kind of negative Gnostic view of the world. It may also be that such a negative Gnostic view is deeply mistaken, and that the Pagan view affirming the positive goodness and sacredness of the world and our earthly life in it, is a far wiser and more productive approach to overcoming ignorance as a solution of the problem of evil.

Source:

patheos.com/library/pagan/beliefs/suffering-and-the-problem-of-evil
learnreligions.com/wicca-witchcraft-or-paganism-2562823
https://www.patheos.com/library/pagan/beliefs/afterlife-and-salvation
https://beliefnet.com/columnists/apagansblog/2011/04/a-pagan-take-on-the-problem-of-evil-and-undeserved-suffering-part-i.html
https://www.beliefnet.com/columnists/apagansblog/2011/04/the-problem-of-evil-and-undeserved-suffering-part-ii-suffering-in-the-natural-world.html
https://www.beliefnet.com/columnists/apagansblog/2011/04/evil-and-undeserved-suffering-part-iii-the-human-dimension.html

---

Scientology

Scientology, like most religions outside of the Abrahamic tradition, does not recognize a problem of evil as such, namely the problem that arises because of the need to reconcile the existence of a loving and all powerful deity with the existence of suffering and evil. According to Scientology, God can be conceived of as the first Cause from which the Universe originates but is generally seen as that Ultimate Reality that lies ahead as the individual considers the ever-encompassing eight dynamics, the last of which is Infinity. In both instances, God is seen as largely transcendent and distant from this work, and not pictured as either concerned on a day-to-day basis with the world or actively interfering in human life. Like Deists, Scientologists do not engage in prayer and devotional activity and, like other members of other esoteric groups, would tend to relate to God by trying to attune their lives with the

Divine. In either case, how one relates to the Divine is purely an individual concern.

That said, Scientologists fully recognize the existence of suffering and evil on both the individual and group level and a significant thrust of the church's life aims at the eradication of human suffering and the elimination of social evils. Scientology originated in L. Ron Hubbard's ruminations on the suffering of people he observed in places such as the Oak Knoll Naval Hospital, where he was a patient at the end of World War II. He offered his initial observations on evil in *Dianetics: The New Science of Mental Health* (1950).

Hubbard saw the mind as divided into two parts-the analytical mind and the reactive mind. The former is that mind that operates under most normal circumstances. It observes the world, thinks about what it observes, stores memories, solves problems, and reasons abstractly. However, in times of stress and trauma, the analytical mind is suppressed, and the reactive mind takes over. The reactive mind is seen as acting purely in a stimulus-response mode. It observes what is happening, records complete three-dimensional images (including feelings) of what is occurring, and stores them uncritically in the unconscious, away from easy retrieval by the analytical mind. These images (called engrams) stored by the reactive mind can be activated by present occurrences that resonate with elements of those images. When activated, the engrams can bring to the fore feelings of pain and the spectrum of negative emotions that were stored when originally recorded. Activated engrams about which the analytical mind is unaware can cause a range of symptoms and dysfunctional behavior in the individual.

Engrams are stored in the order in which they are recorded on the mind's record of images and memories that accumulate through one's life. Scientologists refer to this record as the time track and see it as containing a rather accurate record of one's present human life. The initial phase of Scientology classes and counseling (auditing) is concerned with revisiting the time track, removing the emotive content of the engrams, and erasing the effects of the reactive mind.

In completing the first phase of church life, the Scientologist arrives at the state of Clear, defined as having erased the reactive mind. A Clear is believed to no longer have a reactive mind, and once gone, that element of his or her mind will not return. This condition brings with it a variety of benefits, including the erasure of pain and negative emotions (which should have occurred gradually during the process of reaching Clear), and the basic goodness of the person comes to the fore. It is believed that while one is still engaged in the process of dealing with the reactive mind, but short of the state of Clear, it is possible for it to revive and return, but once one has attained Clear, the reactive mind is gone forever. Engrams and the reactive mind are seen as the source of human suffering, leading to aberrant and antisocial behavior. Depending upon the nature of stored engrams, the individual can be blocked in learning, diverted into crime and other negative activities such as drug abuse, develop antisocial attitudes and behavior, and suffer from a variety of stress-related illnesses. Initially, the Church of Scientology was designed to work with individual church members to deal with their pain and suffering. That activity is still the primary purpose of the church's existence. However, along the way, it was discovered that apart from the program of church classes and counseling, particular aspects of their founder's approach to individual betterment could be utilized to deal with particular problems faced by the society. The first problem to be considered was criminality and drug abuse. It was followed by considering illiteracy and the loss of a consensus about a moral code in the modern pluralistic world. Reflections on these social issues undergirded the church's founding and nurturing of its social betterment programs.

In the early 1960s, many Scientologists assumed that becoming Clear was the ultimate goal of Scientology. However, as Hubbard continued to expand his own thinking of the human situation, he envisioned the Clear as a person who had removed the encumbrances to life and was now ready to be educated as to the free Thetan she or he had become. At the same time, he began to understand some of the implications of past lives. While the basic levels of Scientology did their work in eradicating the reactive mind, becoming Clear did not eradicate all the negativities from the individual's life. Individuals bring into this life the negative accretion of many past lives.

Thus the Operating Thetan (OT) levels are designed to educate the Thetan and invite its discovery of its potentials while at the same time introducing the OT student into the nature of the aberrations carried over from past lives and provide the resources to handle them. The exact content of the OT levels is reserved for those church members enrolled in the OT levels, and they are discussed with outsiders only in the most abstract manner. However, church leaders have acknowledged that the OT Levels offer a larger understanding of human history and address the origin of those aberrations that remain after one has become Clear. This involves a significant amount of auditing and self-auditing (in which the student runs through the auditing procedures without an auditor being present). The amount of auditing varies from individual to individual.

Source:
https://www.patheos.com/library/scientology//beliefs/suffering-and-the-problem-of-evil
https://www.patheos.com/library/scientology/beliefs/suffering-and-the-problem-of-evil.aspx?p=2

Shinto

Shinto ("the way of the gods") is the indigenous faith of the Japanese people and as old as Japan itself. And Shintoism focuses on ritual practices including divination, spirit possession, and shamanic healing. Some of their practices come from Buddhism, Taoism or Confucianism, but most come from ancient local traditions. And these practices are to be carried out diligently to establish a connection between present-day Japan and its ancient past. It remains Japan's major religion alongside Buddhism.

The introduction of Buddhism in the 6th century was followed by a few initial conflicts, however, the two religions were soon able to co-exist and even complement each other. Many Buddhists view the Shinto gods as manifestations of Buddha. Shinto does not have a founder nor does it have sacred scriptures like the Sutras or the Bible. Propaganda and preaching are not common either, because Shinto is deeply rooted in the Japanese people and traditions. And unlike many religions, one does not need to publicly profess belief in Shinto to be a believer.

Shinto gods are called kami. Kami is rendered in English as spirits, essences, or gods, and refers to energy generating phenomena that inspire a sense of wonder and awe in the beholder testifying to the divinity of such phenomenon. And kami and people are not separate; they exist within the same world and share its interrelated complexity. Early anthropologists called Shinto "animistic" in which animate and inanimate things have spirits or souls that are worshipped. That view of Shinto is no longer the current view. Kami can take the form of things and concepts important to life, such as wind, rain, mountains, trees, rivers and fertility, and some say humans become kami after they die and are revered by their families as ancestral kami.

It is common for families to participate in ceremonies for children at a shrine, and a large number of wedding ceremonies are held in Shinto style. Death, however, is considered a source of impurity, and is left to Buddhism to deal with. Therefore, most funerals are held in Buddhist style and consequently, there are virtually no Shinto cemeteries. In old Japanese legends, it is often claimed that the dead go to a place called yomi, a gloomy underground realm with a river separating the living from the dead.

Shinto has no moral absolutes and assesses the good or bad of an action or thought in the context in which it occurs: circumstances, intention, purpose, time, location, are all relevant in assessing whether an action is good or bad. And because Shinto coexists with Buddhism and Confucianism and their ethical values, it's hard, and not very useful, to isolate the distinctly Shinto elements in Japanese ethics. Confucian values in particular have inspired much of the Japanese ethical code. Specifically, Shinto ethics are not based on a set of commandments or laws that tell the faithful how to behave, but on following the will of the kami. Therefore the overall aims of Shinto ethics are to promote harmony and purity in all spheres of life. Purity is not just spiritual purity but moral purity: having a pure and sincere heart. So a follower of Shinto will try to live in accordance with the way of the kami, and in such a way as to keep the relationship with the kami on a proper footing. And it's important to remember that the kami are not perfect - Shinto texts have many examples of kami making mistakes and doing the wrong thing. This clear difference with faiths whose God is perfect is probably why Shinto ethics avoids absolute moral rules.

Shinto is an optimistic faith and Shinto ethics start from the basic idea that human beings are good, and that the world is good. Evil enters the world from outside, brought by evil spirits or kami. These can affect human beings in a similar way to disease, disaster and error, and reduce their ability to resist temptation. In fact, Shinto states that humans are born pure, and sharing in the divine soul. Badness, impurity or sin are things that come later in life, and that can usually be got rid of by simple cleansing or purifying rituals.

When human beings act wrongly, they bring pollution and sin upon themselves, which obstructs the flow of life and blessing from the kami. And anything connected with death or the dead is considered particularly polluting. However, suffering is not regarded as a form of punishment for human behavior, but, rather, as a natural element of human experience. In Shinto, the ideas closest to the western notion of evil are pollution and impurity, and these are addressed through rituals of purification. Purity is at the heart of Shinto's understanding of good and evil. Impurity in Shinto refers to anything which separates us from kami, and from musubi which is the creative and harmonizing power of matchmaking, love, and marriage. The things which make us impure are tsumi, i.e., pollution or sin, and can be physical, moral or spiritual. Tsumi means much the same as the English word sin, but it differs from sin in that it includes things which are beyond the control of individual human beings and are thought of as being caused by evil spirits.

Source:
https://en.wikipedia.org/wiki/Shinto
https://www.japan-guide.com/e/e2056.html
https://www.patheos.com/library/shinto/beliefs/suffering-and-the-problem-of-evil
https://www.bbc.co.uk/religion/religions/shinto/beliefs/purity.shtml
https://www.bbc.co.uk/religion/religions/shinto/shintoethics/ethics.shtml

---

Sikhism

Sikhism is a progressive monotheistic religion and the One God is the same God for all people of all religions. It was founded over 500 years ago in the Indian subcontinent region of Punjab, present day India and Pakistan, in the 15th century by Guru Nanak (1469-1539). Sikhism broke from Hinduism due, in part, to the blind rituals of the Hindus as well as to the Sikh rejection of the Hindu caste system. According to Sikh tradition, Sikhism was established by Guru Nanak (1469–1539) and subsequently led by a succession of nine other Gurus. All 10 human Gurus were inhabited by a single eternal Guru spirit. Upon the death of the 10th guru the eternal Guru spirit transferred itself to the sacred and principal scripture of Sikhism called Guru Granth Sahib, also known as the Adi Granth, and this scripture is regarded as the living Guru. God in Sikhism is known as the one supreme reality, the one supreme being, the eternal reality, beyond space and time, without form, the creator, without fear and devoid of enmity, immortal, never incarnated, self-existent, known by grace through the true Guru.

The word Sikh in the Punjabi language means disciple, seeker, or learner. Sikhs are the disciples of God who follow the writings and teachings of the Ten Sikh Gurus. The wisdom of these teachings are practical and universal in their appeal to all mankind. "Any human being who faithfully believes in: (i) One Immortal Being, (ii) Ten Gurus, from Guru Nanak to Guru Gobind Singh, (iii) The Guru Granth Sahib, (iv) The utterances and teachings of the ten Gurus and, (v) the baptism bequeathed by the tenth Guru, and who does not owe allegiance to any other religion is a Sikh." (Rehat Maryada, Sikh Code of Conduct)

Sikhism teaches that the strong sense of self is the primary cause of evil and suffering. When the individual puts the self at the center of everything, he or she loses reality. The Sikh truth is that each person is part of a much larger whole, a Universe in which the divine Kartar is beyond gender, beyond time, and beyond simple understanding. However, Guru Angad (1504-1552) (the second Guru) taught that self-agency is also where the cure to evil and suffering lies, by directing the self toward selfless acts: The I-Me of a self is a nasty disease, but it also contains the elixir to cure the disease. By attuning the self to the divine word, the Sikh believes that he or she is ready to receive the divine grace that will inspire righteous living and lead to the path of liberation from the cycles of reincarnation and karma, and not toward a final destination of heaven or hell

Ethics, not belief, rule the Sikh agenda. Internal spiritual practice and external daily actions must go hand-in-hand, and evil is indistinct from extreme self-centeredness, and sometimes people suffer because of the self-centered actions of others. Tyranny and oppression, far removed from all notions of compassion and empathy, are the most evil acts. Sikh history is full of stories of martyrs for the faith who were steadfast in their opposition to oppression. In the face of oppression, Sikhs have a wide array of responses from which to choose. Humility in bearing suffering is one response to oppression. This entails the ability to understand and discern that some suffering is a part of the human condition, and the enactment or sanctioning of the divine will. This also means that the Sikh is powerless to surmount the oppression of others if the oppression is in accordance with the divine will.

Nevertheless, Sikhs make appeals to Kartar for the benefit of all humanity, and the final part of the Sikh daily prayer of supplication requests just that. And human beings also possess the ability to redress the wrongs of the world, and thus make the world more just and compassionate. In the long term, then, simply bearing the self-centeredness and cruelty of others is no way to live. This is especially the case when the divine will bestows the ability for creative responses to suffering. Standing up for one's rights and those of the oppressed is another choice that also corresponds with Sikh notions of honor and justice. After the martyrdom of Guru Arjan (1563-1606) at the hands of the state, and in the midst of a succession battle for the Guru's office, Sikh savant Bhai Gurdas voiced optimism for the unfolding of divine justice that encapsulates a Sikh response to those false powers that oppress others.

The soul goes through cycles of birth and death before it reaches the human form. The goal of our life is to lead an exemplary existence so that one may merge with God. And the true path to achieving salvation and merging with God does not require renunciation of the world or celibacy, but living the life of a householder, earning an honest living and avoiding worldly temptations and sins. Sikhs should remember God at all times and practice living a virtuous and truthful life while maintaining a balance between their spiritual obligations and temporal obligations. The body takes birth because of karma, but salvation is attained through grace. Sikhism condemns blind rituals such as fasting, visiting places of pilgrimage, superstitions, worship of the dead, idol worship etc.

Sikhism preaches that people of different races, religions, or sex are all equal in the eyes of God. It teaches the full equality of men and women.

Women can participate in any religious function or perform any Sikh ceremony or lead the congregation in prayer.

The fundamental beliefs of Sikhism, articulated in the sacred scripture, include faith and meditation on the name of the one creator, the divine unity and equality of all humankind, the engaging in selfless service, the striving for justice for the benefit and prosperity of all, and the honest conduct and livelihood while living a householder's life. The scripture teaches followers to transform the "Five Thieves" (lust, rage, greed, attachment, and ego), and to remember that secular life is considered to be intertwined with the spiritual life. Guru Nanak taught that living an active, creative, and practical life of truthfulness, fidelity, self-control and purity is above metaphysical truth, and that the ideal man is one who establishes union with God, knows His Will, and carries out that Will.

Māyā, defined as a temporary illusion or unreality, is one of the core deviations humans can take from the pursuit of God and salvation. Such deviations or worldly attractions give only illusory temporary satisfaction and are inevitably followed by pain and suffering. As such these can greatly distract the person from the process of devotion to God. However, Nanak emphasized that māyā as not a reference to the unreality of the world itself, but only to the unreality of its values and promises. In Sikhism, the influences of ego, anger, greed, attachment, and lust, known as the Five Thieves, are believed to be particularly distracting and hurtful. The fate of people vulnerable to the Five Thieves is separation from God, and the situation may be remedied only after intensive and relentless devotion.

Source:
https://patheos.com/library/sikhism/beliefs/suffering-and-the-problem-of-evil
https://patheos.com/library/sikhism/beliefs/suffering-and-the-problem-of-evil.aspx
https://www.sikhs.org/
https://www.sikhs.org/summary.htm
https://www.britannica.com/topic/Sikhism
https://en.wikipedia.org/wiki/Sikhism
https://www.sikhs.org/summary.htm

Sufism

The problem of evil is among the most enduring paradoxes of religious belief. Philosophers of every era have grappled with the notion of an all-powerful and all-loving God who nonetheless allows evil, loss, and suffering to afflict even his most pious devotees. Guided by the prophet Mohammed, Job's encounter with the sublime power of God, and the Sufi perspective that hope and fear comprise an irreducible duality in life, we conclude that this problem represents a gap in our ability to understand the world: it is religion, itself, which occupies this gap, providing us a proper orientation towards the existence of evil.

Sufism is a path that seeks to reunite the soul of the believer with God, to see beyond the Unrealities of the world and to perceive the Ultimate Reality that is God. Between the believer and God's face, the Universe is something that obscures the image of God, i.e., the Universe is like a hijab/veil that was put in place by the fall of Adam. The Sufi spends life seeking to remove that veil and behold God, from whom being separated is akin to being separated from a lover. Alienation from God is expressed as estrangement from one's Beloved; it is loneliness, a sickness, and a state from which the Sufi wishes to be free.

Sufism is the phenomenon of "mysticism" within Islamic belief and practice in which Muslims seek to find the truth of divine love and knowledge through direct personal experience of God. It consists of a variety of mystical paths that are designed to ascertain the nature of humanity and of God and to facilitate the experience of the presence of divine love and wisdom in the world.

Although the overwhelming majority of Sufis are adherents of Sunni Islam, there also developed certain strands of Sufi practice within Shia Islam. In a broad sense, Sufism can be described as the interiorization, and intensification of Islamic faith and practice. It now seems established that the movement grew out of early Islamic asceticism that developed as a counterweight to the increasing worldliness of the expanding Muslim community; only later were foreign elements that were compatible with mystical theology and practices adopted and made to conform to Islam.

When it comes to the problem of evil as commonly understood by Sufis, the qualities most pertinent to understanding why evil exists and how to understand it are most immediately related to God's mercy and wrath. In Sufi thought, God's mercy far exceeds His wrath, and flows in one direction, from Him to humans. Al-Ghazali (1058-1111) considered the problem of evil to be an issue that embodied but one stage on the Sufi's path. But belief in God's exceeding mercy should reassure the Sufi, according to Al-Ghazali, that all things happen by His benevolent will. It is unclear how this resolves the issue of evil in the world. God's will is ultimately bound up in what Al-Ghazali calls His "secret," which is predestination. Therefore, the problem of evil, while not easily or handily solved in the broad and diverse tradition of Sufi interpretations, is somewhat mitigated by the principle that all of earthly reality is merely dependent on God in the first place. This does not absolve people of their responsibility to obey God and refrain from committing evil themselves, a tendency that Sufis attempt to remedy by following the Sufi path to discipline themselves and train themselves to live in a manner that is pleasing to God.

Towards a Mystical Theodicy

It may also be concluded that by presenting the notion of evil and suffering as part of the human experience and a necessary component of man's spiritual journey, the Quran refrains from articulating a systematic theodicy. The notion of evil and human suffering is not portrayed in the Islamic revelation as a "problem" to be resolved but rather as part of the human experience. Therefore, since the Quran does not engage its readers in abstract ideas and theological discussions about evil, the formulation of a classical theodicy is not presented.

Most of the Quranic verses on adversity and suffering suggest that human beings, including prophets, will be tested by difficult times. The basic nature of evil is referred to as nonexistence and privation of good by Muslim philosophers, while the theologians attribute evil to man's conduct. The Muslim mystical literature as presented in the teachings of Rumi demonstrates that trials in adversities are necessary to remove man from the state of negligence in order for him to realize his divine source and to choose to set forth on a spiritual journey. In this mystic path, exercising patience, trusting God, as well as loving God, are essential in assisting man reach the state of tranquility. Along the path, man, as the fruit of the creation, will be able to actualize the potentialities of his inner nature and purify his soul to become a perfect mirror in manifesting God's names and attributes.

The Sufi Rumi and the Problem of Evil

Rumi (1207–1273), was a 13th-century Persian poet, faqih, Islamic scholar, theologian, and Sufi mystic. Rumi's influence transcends national borders and ethnic divisions: Iranians, Tajiks, Turks, Greeks, Pashtuns, other Central Asian Muslims, and the Muslims of South Asia have greatly appreciated his spiritual legacy for many centuries. Rumi belongs to the class of Islamic transcendental philosophers or theosophists that are often studied in traditional schools throughout the Muslim world. He embeds his theosophy (transcendental philosophy) like a string through the beads of his poems and stories. His main point and emphasis is the unity of being. It is undeniable that Rumi was a Muslim scholar and took Islam seriously. Nonetheless, the depth of his spiritual vision extended beyond narrow understanding sectarian concerns. To many modern Westerners, his teachings are one of the best introductions to the philosophy and practice of Sufism. Rumi's life and transformation provide true testimony and proof that people of all religions and backgrounds can live together in peace and harmony. Rumi's visions, words, and life teach us how to reach inner peace and happiness so we can finally stop the continual stream of hostility and hatred and achieve true global peace and harmony.

In Rumi's work, there is an attempt to solve the problem of evil that is present for religions with an omniscient, omnipotent, omnibenevolent God. Rumi sees this God in all that exists as signs, forms, shadows, metaphors, manifestations, apparitions, things, creatures. All activity and rest, strife and harmony, war and peace, are forms displaying the Hidden Treasure. This implies that God is the source of evil as well as good. Given the precedence of mercy over wrath, what appears to us as evil can only be serving a greater good. Evil cannot be eliminated from the created world because that would be tantamount to destroying the world.

The first relevant account Rumi gives as a solution to the problem of evil is that evil is the logical opposite of good therefore evil is a logical necessity. This means that individuals can only know good when evil is present to provide a contrast. If evil is taken to be necessary to know good, then either both good and evil exist or neither good nor evil exist. To say otherwise would then be akin to saying that one side of a coin can exist without the other side of the same coin existing as well.

The second relevant solution is that evil is only properly understood as 'evil' relative to humanity. In contrast to evil being a logical necessity, here what is thought of as bad is only seen as such through human perception of events. What humans see as undesirable events that should be stopped or avoided, other kinds of beings may see as somehow desirable. The problem here is that it is not clear how these two solutions to the problem of evil can coexist. However, to be fair, Rumi's concern in the first place, as a poet, may not have been that these two solutions were ever to be logically consistent and reconcilable.

Source:
https://en.wikipedia.org/wiki/Sufism
https://britannica.com/topic/Sufism
https://patheos.com/library/sufism/beliefs/suffering-and-the-problem-of-evil
https://www.academia.edu/7751996/Sufi_perspective_why_would_Allah_allow_the_existence_of_evil
https://en.wikipedia.org/wiki/Rumi
https://emilystraka.agnesscott.org/philosophy/rumi-and-the-problem-of-evil
http://www.iranicaonline.org/articles/rumi-philosophy
https://medium.com/@falsabeh/in-fear-and-in-hope-a-sufi-response-to-the-problem-of-evil-ff1d44f68500

Taoism

Laozi, also rendered as Lao Tzu and Lao-Tze, was an ancient Chinese philosopher and writer. He is the reputed author of the Tao Te Ching text, the founder of philosophical Taoism, and a deity in religious Taoism and traditional Chinese religions. A semi-legendary figure, Laozi was usually portrayed as a 6th-century BC contemporary of Confucius, but some modern historians consider him to have lived during the 4th century BC. In Taoism there is no omnipotent being beyond the cosmos, which created and controls the Universe in the way that the Abrahamic

(Judaism and Islamism) religions do. In Taoism the Universe springs from the Tao, and the Tao impersonally guides things on their way.

The Taoist metaphysics does not leave the solution for the problem of evil to the future or to the other world, but rather embraces it in this life. In the Taoist metaphysics, evil and good are two parts of reality, as one sees it in the Yin-Yang relation. The bipolarity of the Tao, thus, provides not only the theoretical basis but also the ethical practicality to deal with the problem of evil. Thus, Taoism is not concerned with theodicy, i.e., justifying the ways of the Tao to humanity, but is simply interested in following the Tao effortlessly wherever it leads.

The core of the basic belief and doctrine of Taoism is that "Tao" is the origin and law of all things in the Universe. Taoists believe that people can become deities and live forever through practicing simplicity and selflessness in conformity with the Tao, leading a life of non-purposive action, a life expressing the essence of spontaneity. Taoists essentially do not think that an afterlife exists the way that many other religions do. Taoists believe that we are eternal and that the afterlife is just another part of life itself. The ultimate goal of Taoism is definitely to become a god. No matter if you are human, animals, or non-life stuff. The ultimate goal of each Taoist is to practice to become a god someday; to escape the painful reincarnation, and become a god for eternity.

Evil in Taoism

Since any aspect of the world is a manifestation of the Tao, corresponding to a different participation or mixture of the Yin and Yang principles, nothing in this world can be considered to be in itself alone an essence of evil. From this perspective, evil refers to any action that is not in accordance with the Tao. Every positive factor involves its negative or opposing one. What is usually called evil is the result of a misuse of human freewill, getting out of the natural way, causing a lack of balance between the two opposing principles of Yin and Yang and corresponds to a bigger participation of the Yin principle.

Evil belongs to the nature of the world, so humans have to subscribe to the universal harmony and respect the equilibrium of the two polarities of Yin and Yang. Tao is eternal and so are the two principles Yang and Yin, so that good and evil must be eternal, as necessary elements of our world. The general pattern in Eastern religions is to consider evil as the effect of spiritual ignorance. The only possibility of escaping suffering is to know the true nature of things and so to escape from the dominion of ignorance, karma and reincarnation. In Taoism, like other dualistic religions, evil is coeternal with good. Matter and embodied existence are evil, and our ignorance keeps us from attaining perfection.

Taoist ideas about suffering and evil reflect a variety of influences, including early Chinese religious beliefs, Buddhist beliefs, and popular religion. Different sects have different beliefs, and these change over time, and individuals also have their own personal beliefs. According to the Tao Te Ching and Zhuangzi, two primary Taoist texts, nature itself is amoral; it cares nothing for individuals. The Zhuangzi text emphasizes that death is part of a natural cycle, and that illness, death, and misfortune are inevitable aspects of human life. Thus, they are not punishments for misdeeds, or manifestations of evil.

The Tao Te Ching states that nature is not sentimental and treats people like sacrifices. Individuals are best off if they accommodate themselves to nature's laws and patterns, because to go against nature will only bring difficulty and trouble. When humans deviate from the natural order, societies will develop that are harmful to many. On the other hand, when the ruler is enlightened, or advised by an enlightened sage, the people he rules will exist in harmony with one another and with nature. Another Taoist belief is that physical health is evidence of purity, and illness is believed to be caused by one's misdeeds. The cure for illness is to confess and be purged of one's sins. If the petition is accepted, then the cause of illness will be expelled, and the sufferer will be healed. In some Taoist groups, one is also held responsible for the sins of one's ancestors, up to ten generations. Thus, sickness is viewed as the result of one's own and one's ancestors' wrongdoings. Early Taoism emphasized Confucian virtues, which encouraged harmonious community living rather than salvation from sin. Later, most Taoist sects, strongly influenced by Buddhism, adopted many moral rules. The Buddhist concept of merit was also widely adopted by Taoists. Some Taoists accepted the Buddhist belief that sin would be punished after death in some form of hellish afterlife existence, and good behavior similarly rewarded in some type of paradise. Some Taoist adepts also work to accumulate merit, sometimes for their own benefit, and sometimes for the benefit of others. From the point of view of many Taoist lay people, demons, unhappy ancestors, or orphaned souls are the cause of illness and other problems in life.

There is not a solid definition of the words "good and evil" in Taoism, but there is a solid definition when you understand what you are talking about. Just like the word "Tao", it can mean different things depending on what you are talking about, and we must be very sure about what the subject in question is, in order to use the words correctly and precisely. Good is anything that helps and flows with what your Tao is doing or leading you toward. Evil is the opposite, which is anything that interferes with your flow from the Tao. Good things help you to grow and empower you. Bad things will destroy you or break you up into pieces and push you to "death" and so that you can cycle back to neutral again.

However, "evil" is not always bad, depending on the situation and how you are using "evil." When you are teaching your child you must learn how to go against the childs flow as well as how to go with it. For example, if your child is misbehaving, should you use the "good" tactic of going with the flow of their Tao, which is directing the misbehavior? Or, should you use an "evil" tactic of going against their flow to try and change their mind? Changing their mind will change their Tao, thereby changing their intentions or motivations to misbehave. In this case, evil is sometimes useful for doing good. Therefore, evil or good is not always good or bad; we must look at the whole situation to determine if it is good or bad. Just like people saying someone "killed a person," everyone will think that it's a bad thing, but what if he killed a person that is shooting people in a massacre?

Source:
https://patheos.com/library/taoism/beliefs/suffering-and-the-problem-of-evil
https://www.academia.edu/36790239/Problem_of_Evil_in_Taoism
https://www.google.com/search?q=taoism&rlz=1C1GCEA_enUS770US770&oq=taoism&aqs=chrome..69i57j0l5.7231j0j0&sourceid=chrome&ie=UTF-8
https://prezi.com/uhgchlcaagzp/taoism-and-the-problem-of-evil/
https://www.comparativereligion.com/evil.html
https://www.bbc.co.uk/religion/religions/taoism/beliefs/gods.shtml
https://en.wikipedia.org/wiki/Laozi

Zen

In many respects, Zen's response to suffering and the problem of evil is the same as that of Mahayana Buddhism in general. Zen's understanding of these issues (with elements of Huayen Buddhism as well) is best expressed in *Xinxin Ming (Hsin Hsin Ming)*, or "*On Faith in Mind*," a prose-poem that is traditionally attributed to Sengsan, the third patriarch of Zen.

Little is known of the historical figure Sengsan. However, according to legend, he approached the second patriarch of Zen, Huike, and told him that he suffered from a terrible disease (according to several texts, it was leprosy). Sengsan asked Huike to absolve him of his sin so that he could be healed. The patriarch responded, "Bring me your sin, and I will absolve you." When Sengsan replied that he could not get at his sin to bring it, Huike told him, "Then I have absolved you." This story of the first meeting of Sengsan and Huike is also a famous koan in the Zen tradition.

There are varying theories about when and by whom *Xinxin Ming* was actually written, but scholars agree that it was written several centuries after Sengsan's death. Taoist influence on the text is clear, not only because of the philosophy that is expressed but also because of the use of common Taoist—and Confucian—phrases such as wu-wei and ziran.

Xinxin Ming proposes that all suffering and unhappiness are caused by dualistic thinking. It begins, "The Great Way is not difficult for those who have no preferences." For many, having no preferences at all may seem like a most difficult attitude to attain. Nonetheless, according to the text, the moment the smallest distinction is made, "heaven and earth are set infinitely apart." This is not simply a proposal of a psychological state of mind to aim for; it is a description of the nature of reality. Like Nagarjuna, the author of this Zen text indicated that things are neither real nor not real, neither empty nor not empty. From this point of view, to see things in an either-or fashion is to be deceived by delusion.

In an analysis similar to that of the Buddha's Four Noble Truths, which indicates that suffering is caused by desire, Xinxin Ming states that the process of creating distinctions and preferences causes human suffering.

Discriminating between "coarse or fine" leads to "for or against" thinking, which leads to notions about right and wrong, which lead, in turn, to mental confusion. There is confusion because there is no agreement about what is right or what is true. These are not characteristics innate to human existence; they are illusions caused by dualistic thinking.

The solution, according to the text, is to "simply say when doubt arises, 'Not two.'" If one recognizes the oneness of all things, then one is able to be in harmony with the world of phenomena, in which there is "neither self nor other-than-self." This is what Sengsan realized when he had his first exchange with Huike. His suffering was not separate from himself, and it was not caused by a sin or an evil deed that needed to be, or could be, removed from his body by absolution.

According to the legend, Sengsan did indeed get better physically and eventually was free of his illness. This could be viewed as a natural insistence on a happy ending, or, perhaps, as a way of countering potential nihilistic interpretations of *Xinxin Ming*. To confront doubt by saying, "not two," leads to a far more sophisticated understanding than simply passively accepting one's fate in life. It leads to the realization that, on a fundamental level, all things are one.

"Do not be attached even to this One," the text says, followed by what may be its clearest statement of relevance to suffering and the problem of evil: "When the mind exists undisturbed in the Way, nothing in the world can offend, and when a thing can no longer offend, it ceases to exist in the old way."

Source:
https://www.patheos.com/library/zen/beliefs/suffering-and-the-problem-of-evil

---

Zoroastrianism

Zoroaster, also known as Zarathustra, is best estimated to have lived sometime between 1500 and 500 BC in Persia, modern day Iran, and is the founder of Zoroastrianism, which has largely been replaced by Islam. Over the centuries, Persian thought has addressed the problem of evil more thoroughly than any other religious tradition. Evil in its various manifestations was an almost constant obsession in Zoroastrianism and ancient Iranian religions in general, exercising an influence even beyond the natural boundaries of the Iranian world.

Zoroastrians believe in one God called Ahura Mazda, meaning Wise Lord, whose goal was the eradication of evil from the world and who asked for human assistance in reaching this goal. And Ahura Mazda is omniscient, compassionate, just, and is the creator of the Universe, and is the highest spirit worshipped in Zoroastrianism, the old Mede and Persian religion which spread across Asia predating Christianity. Angra Mainyu is the evil, destructive spirit in the dualistic doctrine of Zoroastrianism. To aid him in attacking the light, Angra Mainyu created a horde of demons embodying envy and similar negative and destructive qualities.

Avesta, also called Zend-avesta, is the sacred book of Zoroastrianism containing its cosmogony, law, and liturgy, the teachings of the prophet Zoroaster (Zarathushtra). The extant Avesta is all that remains of a much larger body of scripture, apparently Zoroaster's transformation of a very ancient tradition. The voluminous manuscripts of the original are said to have been destroyed when Alexander the Great conquered Persia. The present Avesta was assembled from remnants and standardized in 3rd–7th century AD.

Prior to Zoroaster, in the ancient Iranian religious world, evil was a fact, a condition of existence. And in the eminently dualistic Zoroastrian religion the need to defeat evil was emphasized. In this view the problem of evil was omnipresent, and solutions to it took as many forms as the conceptions of dualism developed throughout ancient Iranian history. The earliest conception of dualism was apparently that of Zoroaster, which served as the basis for all subsequent elaborations.

The idea of the choice between good and evil was at the heart of Zoroastrianism throughout its entire historical development. The good choose wisely, the evil do not. The failure to make good moral choices is the root of the problem of moral evil, and Zoroaster's solution to the problem of moral evil was profoundly original. While, on one hand, Zoroaster promised the owners of truth and goodness the final triumph of good over evil in an eschatological expectation consistent with a doctrine requiring rigor and commitment from the faithful. On the other hand, Zoroaster provided a logical explanation for the existence of evil, whether through the idea of choice or through the specific conception of two existences or states of being.

The ancient Persians had another insight regarding the nature of evil. i.e., evil is not creative. In other words the actions of evil are not directed, but random. This insight is particularly instructive in understanding what is known in the philosophical community as the problem of natural evil. Natural evil refers to bad things that happen that cannot be reasonably explained as a result of human misbehavior. Unlike human moral evil, natural evil acts blindly. One is in the wrong place at the wrong time and suffers unjustly.

In orthodox Zoroastrianism, the origin of evil is somewhat vague, other than the idea of two principles of equal power, good and evil, which have the same age or date of creation. They were conceived as two eternal abstract powers, both of which manifested themselves not only in mental and spiritual phenomena, but also in the material things of this world. That is, they were both present in the beginning of things, and together they brought about the world we know and live in today. Evil, like good, is a spiritual or mental power that is wicked because of the wicked choices it makes. And like good, evil manifests itself in material existence, but, whereas the good power is manifest in its very creation, the wicked power is present through foul and violent aggression toward the good power and its creation.

In spiritual existence the powers of good and evil are equal, for each is author of its own creation, but evil can only insinuate itself in material existence, contaminating and violating that which is good. Zervanism carried this one step further, seeing the existence of the world, along with good and evil, as an act of divine purgation. The Godhead becomes perfect by purging itself of evil. In doing so the Godhead temporarily loses its omnipotence but will regain it at the end of days. Unlike many other religions, in Zoroastrianism, history has a purpose, which is the elimination of evil from the world. This divine purgation is the reason for the existence of the Universe. All is not yet well, but all will be well in the fullness of time.

Good Thoughts, Good Words, and Good Deeds comprise the core maxim of the Threefold Path of Zoroastrianism, especially by modern practitioners. All physical creation was determined and ordered to run according to a master plan inherent to Ahura Mazda, and violations of the order were violations against creation, and thus violations against Ahura Mazda. However, this concept should not be confused with Western and especially Abrahamic notions of good versus evil, for although both forms of opposition express moral conflict, the Zoroastrianism concept is more systemic and less personal, representing, for instance, chaos that opposes order; or un-creation, evident as natural decay that opposes creation; or more simply the lie that opposes the truth and goodness.

Zoroaster emphasized deeds and actions within society, and accordingly extreme asceticism is frowned upon but moderate forms are allowed. Central to Zoroastrianism is the emphasis on moral choice, to choose the responsibility and duty for which one is in the mortal world, or to give up this duty and so facilitate chaos, decay, and falsehood. Similarly, predestination is rejected in Zoroastrian teaching and the absolute freewill of all conscious beings is core, with even divine beings having the ability to choose. Humans bear responsibility for all situations they are in, and in the way they act toward one another. Reward, punishment, happiness, and grief all depend on how individuals live their lives.

The Battle Between Good and Evil

Zoroastrian religion is based on the belief that the world is a battleground between good and evil forces, with far reaching consequences for humanity. Zoroastrian texts vary in their interpretations of this epic battle. According to the traditional interpretation, the good God Ahura Mazda is constantly opposed by an evil being called Angra Mainyu. Angra Mainyu, also known as Ahirman, is the architect of evil, the anti-God principle, who represents evil, untruth, arrogance and death and subjects people to torment once they come under his influence.

Ahirman is emotionally unstable, lazy, lacks confidence, cowardly and ignorant, but has a blind ambition to overpower God and infest His creation by whatever means available. He is assisted in his effort by a host of evil entities, the Daevas and the Druj whom he created. Jeh, the primeval woman is his partner, who instigates him and reminds him of his duties, whenever he is depressed or frightened by the memory of God, and goads him into action. Despite his weaknesses and evil intentions, he is somehow endowed with the power to create his own evil forces.

Though God is omnipotent, Zoroastrian texts do not give the impression that Angra Mainyu is created by God, because God being pure light and truthfulness, cannot create evil that is centered in darkness, falsehood and malice. God will only destroy him when the time comes. Until then Ahirman exists by himself, presenting a problem to the forces of light. People have to contend with evil and do all they can to maintain the sanctity and order of the world so that Ahirman remains confined to his own domain until God destroys him in a manner already planned. The battle between the God and Ahirman will continue until the end of creation when God will ultimately triumph and confine Ahirman to Hell.

Further, according to the traditional interpretation, in the beginning there was only Infinite Time. And in Infinite Time God, i.e., Ahura Mazda and Angra Mainyu were both infinite and finite. They were infinite on one side where there were no boundaries to their domains. On the other side, they were separated by a great Void. And because the Void limited their domain on one side, they were also finite. God was not only the more powerful of the two, but was also omniscient, with the knowledge of the past, present and future. Before God even met him, He was aware of Angra Mainyu, residing on the other side of the Void. He also knew about their impending battle. But Angra Mainyu was not omniscient. He was also not as brave and courageous as God. He was weak, timid, ignorant and lazy. Fear and malice were his weapons. In Infinite Time, when there was perfect balance in the Universe, Angra Mainyu, crossed the Void and saw God for the first time and attacked Him.

As projected by God, Ahirman attacked the material world when he was instigated by his female partner, Jeh. He burst through the sky. He invaded the earth. He attacked the primeval man, the primeval ox and all the elements, namely, fire, water, earth and air. He attacked the stars, the planets, the plants and the animals. And God made a covenant with him, knowing full well that the time to contain evil was yet to come.

According to the covenant, God offered a truce to Ahirman, which would last for 9000 years. And it was further agreed that God's will alone would prevail during the first three thousand years. Then the will of both would prevail during the next three thousand years, during which the material world and things would become susceptible to the forces of evil and suffer from instability, death and decay.

The final three thousand years would begin with the birth of Zoroaster, who would spread the teachings of God among humanity and make people aware of the conflict between the forces of good and evil and prepare them for the final confrontation, teaching them the right way to live and how to support the forces of good. Another prophet would be born a thousand years after Zoroaster to continue the teachings. Finally, during the last thousand of the nine thousand years a future son of Zoroaster would manifest on earth. He would be called Saoshyant, and Saoshyant would herald the Final Judgment Day, distribute the drink of immortality among people and help God and his forces destroy evil forever.

However, there is another less traditional interpretation of the battle. At the beginning of creation, God, i.e., Ahura Mazda, created the Twin spirits Spenta Mainyu and Angra Mainyu. (Some later day texts describe the opposing Twins as children of Zurvan or Time or Infinite Time, rather than Ahura Mazda.) And God gave the Twins freedom to choose between life, light and good on one hand and death, darkness and evil on the other. Spenta Mainyu chose life, truth, light, order and goodness, while Angra Mainyu chose death, darkness, chaos and evil. Therefore, Spenta Mainyu presides over the world of truth and justice, while Angra Mainyu presides over the kingdom of lies or falsehood. The material world in between these two is a playground in which the opposing forces meet and determine the fate of human beings. Angra Mainyu is presently trapped in metals and material things and will continue to trouble people until God brings him to justice on Judgment Day.

According to Zoroastrianism, the presence of evil in the material plane makes our world unstable and ever changing. Evil renders the things in our world susceptible to decay, death and disintegration. Mountains were formed when evil pierced through the otherwise plain earth and caused earthquakes deep inside. Evil is also responsible for droughts, deserts and the stench that sometimes comes from the earth. Smoke and black soot is formed when evil overtakes the fire. It makes air noxious with stinking smells, water susceptible to pollution and impurities, plants and animals susceptible to fever and sickness, and the sun and the moon to eclipses.

Human beings are also susceptible to the invasion of evil forces. Especially, their minds and bodies can succumb to the influence of evil. Their minds and bodies can fall prey to evil thoughts and evil temptations. They can intentionally or unintentionally come into contact with evil things such as dead or putrid matter or contaminated water, air or earth. The Zoroastrians scriptures therefore urge people to be very careful in their day to day lives, living very responsibly, religiously and ethically, remembering God all the time and practicing righteousness by observing the three commandments taught by Zoroaster, namely: Good Thoughts, Good Words, and Good Deeds. And people are advised to protect themselves by chanting the sacred mantras and abide by the instructions given in the scriptures to keep their minds, bodies and environment as pure and clean as possible.

The concept of duality, or the battle between good and evil forces, is found in all religions. Rejection of evil and adoration of the divine for one's own good is the common theme that runs through all religious scriptures. However Zoroastrianism presents it in a rather dramatic way, not as something that has been happening only in some higher worlds between beings of light and darkness, but as something that has been happening right here, right now, in oneself and in every aspect of the material creation, in everything that one can see, touch, smell and feel. It presents this duality of good and evil as a problem inherent in our existence, from which escape is possible, by a conscious and ethical choice, by practicing righteousness and emulating all the qualities represented by God.

Source:

https://en.wikipedia.org/wiki/Zoroastrianism

https://www.britannica.com/topic/Avesta-Zoroastrian-scripture

https://iranicaonline.org/articles/evilhttp://zoroastrian.org.uk/vohum an/Article/Zarathushtrian%20Theodicy.htm

https://hinduwebsite.com/zoroastrianism/ahirman.asp

Part VII

Addenda

Addendum 1

Suffering In Life
By Jordan Peterson

Above all, he [Jordan Peterson] alerted his students to topics rarely discussed in university. Such as the simple fact that all the ancients knew, from Buddha to the evangelical authors, what every slightly worn-out adult knows, that life is suffering. If you are suffering, or someone close to you is, that's sad. But alas, it's not particularly unusual.

We don't only suffer because "politicians are dimwitted" or "the system is corrupt." Or because you and I, like almost everyone else, can *legitimately* describe ourselves, in some way, as a victim of something or someone.

It is because we are born human that we are guaranteed a good dose of suffering. And chances are, if you or someone you love is not suffering now, they will be within five years unless you are freakishly lucky.

Rearing kids is hard, and work is hard, aging, sickness, and death are hard. And Jordan emphasized that doing all that totally on your own without the benefit of a loving relationship, or wisdom or the psychological insights of the greatest psychologists only makes it harder.

He wasn't scaring the students. They found this frank talk reassuring, because, in the depths of their psyches, most of them knew what he said was true, even if there was never a forum to discuss it.

That is, they may never have discussed it before because the adults in their lives had become so naively overprotective that they deluded themselves into thinking that not talking about suffering would in some way magically protect their children from it.

Source:
12 Rules for Life by Jordan B. Peterson pgs xvi-xvii

Addendum 2

A Brief History of Theodicy

A Brief History of
The Problem of Evil &
The Problem from Evil*
In Western Culture

The origin 'of' evil (what is the cause of evil) and the consequences resulting 'from' evil (pain, suffering, hardship) can be thought of as two separate problems. What is written here often conflates these two problems. When the phrase 'problem of evil' is used, it may be understood to include the 'problem from evil.'

The problem of evil is undoubtedly the greatest obstacle to belief in God — both for the Christian and the non-Christian.
(William Lane Craig)

The sheer crushing weight of the pains suffered by women, children, and men, and also by the lower animals, including that inflicted by human greed, cruelty, and malevolence, undoubtedly constitutes the biggest obstacle that there is to belief in an all-powerful and loving Creator.
(John Harwood Hick)

Karl Rahner calls the problem of evil "one of the most fundamental questions of human existence . . . which is universal, universally oppressive, and touches our existence at its very roots."

Alvin Plantinga catalogs the constellation of questions that comprise the problem of evil: "Why does God permit evil, or why does he permit so much of it, or why does he permit those horrifying varieties of it?"

"Why does God permit evil?" is known as the "logical problem of evil."

"Why does he permit so much of it?" is known as the "evidential problem of evil."
"Why does he permit those horrifying varieties of it?" is known as the "existential problem of evil."

Such questions call into question the very existence of a 'good' God.

Also, if a good God exists, what possible morally sufficient reason could there be for such a God to allow the amounts and kinds of pain, suffering, and hardship that also exist?

The attempt to answer these two questions in a positive way is called a 'theodicy,' which means to 'justify' or 'vindicate God.'

Regarding what is written here, the existence of a 'good' God is a given.

Further, it is given that the 'good' God who does exist is the Omni-Perfect God of the Bible.

That leaves the question of the morally sufficient reason the Omni-Perfect God of the Bible has for allowing evil to exist in the world He created and declared to be 'very good.' (Gen 1:31)

The term theodicy was coined in 1710 by the German philosopher Gottfried Leibniz in a work entitled "Essay of Theodicy About the Benevolence of God, the Freewill of Man and the Origin of Evil."

However, before Leibniz, Epicurus, the Greek philosopher who lived from 341-270 BC, is often cited as one of the earliest expositors of the question, 'Whence Cometh Evil?'

Is God willing to prevent evil but not able?   Then He is not omnipotent.
Is He able, but not willing?   Then He is not omnibenevolent.
Is He both able and willing?   Then, 'Whence Cometh Evil?'
Is He neither able nor willing?   Then why call Him God?

A theodicy should attempt to meet the following three sets of criteria.

I. From Website: "Problem of Evil Defined." Theodicy: An Overview, www3.dbu.edu/mitchell/documents/TheodicyOverview_009.pdf

a) It should leave one with one's sense of reality intact; i.e., it tells the truth about reality.
b) It should leave one empowered within the intellectual-moral system in which one lives; i.e., it should not deny God's basic power or goodness.
c) It should be as intellectually coherent as possible; i.e., it is an answer which is both coherent and life-satisfying.

II. These are five criteria for a sound Christian theodicy.
From Book: *Pathways in Theodicy* (2015) pp. 65-66

a) Fidelity: Does it utilize the sources of theology, especially scripture and tradition?
b) Coherence. Does it make sense logically? Is it internally consistent?
c) Relevance. Does it speak to contemporary experiences of evil?
d) Creativity. Does it creatively engage the problem of evil?
e) Humility: Does it recognize and respect the limits of theodicy?

These five criteria are not equally weighted. Nevertheless, the first and second criteria are primary, while the latter three are secondary, which does not diminish their value; it simply subordinates them to the definitive criteria of fidelity and coherence. All five will factor into our analysis of the viability of theodicial models and trends.

III. A theodicy should attempt to answer two questions:

a) What is the greater good that comes from God permitting evil?
b) Could this greater good have been achieved some other way?

Undoubtedly, the problem of human pain, suffering, and hardship has been a chief concern for human beings from the beginning. The question of how to avoid and alleviate pain, suffering, and hardship arising from both disobedient choices (moral evil) and natural disasters (natural evil) has always been at the center of human thought and life.

From Book: *The Problem of Evil by Peterson* (2017) p.1

The Old Testament book of Job is considered by many to be the oldest book in the Bible. Fittingly it is a dramatic treatment of the issue of God and suffering. One insight that emerges in the book is that human life and God are too complex for simplistic formulas and that good people can indeed suffer. This insight is linked to the higher insight that a relationship with God is to be valued above all, regardless of one's circumstances.

A poem by Voltaire was inspired by the Lisbon earthquake of 1755, one of the great natural disasters in human history. The quake killed sixty thousand people in Lisbon alone. When the quake occurred on November 1, All Saints' Day, much of the population was attending church services, and thousands were killed or injured as churches collapsed. This event was a turning point in intellectual history because rationalist religious systems supporting unqualified optimism were seen by many in a different light.

In Fyodor Dostoyevsky's final novel "The Brothers Karamazov," the fictional character Ivan Karamazov, a university professor, denies that there is any rationally or morally acceptable reason for God to allow the suffering of innocent children. His brother Alyosha, a novice clergy, reluctantly agrees that he would not, if he were God, consent to the suffering of a single child, even if that one child's suffering was necessary to the higher harmony of all things. However, Dostoyevsky does not stop there but also states that the love Christ showed to all people and for all people, which is Alyosha's final stance in the novel, is the only good, and in the face of evil, the beauty that will save the world.

These writings are a sample of the poignant treatments of evil outside technical philosophy and theology, where a vivid sense of the reality and perplexity of evil is expressed in emotionally gripping terms.

Theodicy from a Christian Perspective

Numerous Christian theodicies have been proposed during the two millennia of the Christian era.

John Hick (1922–2012) was a British philosopher of religion and perhaps the most influential philosopher of religion and theodicy of the twentieth century. His framework-setting, discussion-shifting book, *Evil and the God of Love* (1966), details his theodicy, which revolutionized discourse on the problem of evil.

In it, he describes two basic types of theodicy. One type is the more standard theodicy of Augustine (354-430 AD), and the other is the older, less well-known theodicy of Irenaeus (130-202 AD).

Hick labeled Augustinian type theodicies 'soul-deciding' theodicies and Irenaean type theodicies 'soul-making' theodicies.

Full Disclosure: Later in life Hick became known for his advocacy of religious pluralism, which is radically different from the traditional Christian teachings he held when he was younger.

Augustinian Theodicy (Soul-Deciding Theodicy)

In Part From Website:
www.tutor2u.net/religious-studies/blog/the-problem-of-evil

Based on the narratives of Genesis 1-3, Augustine's theodicy argues that God created the world and it was perfect, without the existence of evil or suffering. Genesis 1:31: "God saw all that he had made and saw that it was very good".

Augustine defined evil as the privation of goodness, just as blindness is a privation of sight. Since evil is not an entity in itself, just like blindness is not an entity in itself, God could not have created it.

The existence of evil originates from freewill, possessed by angels and humans, who turned their back on God and settled for a lesser form of goodness thus creating a privation of goodness, which the narrative of 'the fall' in Genesis 3 tries to explain. As a result, the state of perfection was ruined by disobedience to God, i.e., sin.

Augustine reasoned that all humans are "seminally present in the loins of Adam" and are therefore deserving of the punishment for Adam & Eve's Original Sin.

God has the right not to intervene and put a stop to evil and suffering since he is a God of justice and all are deserving of punishment. However, it is by his grace and infinite love that we are able to accept his offer of salvation and eternal life in heaven. Augustine posited the idea of an interim place where the souls of the faithful departed will be purged of their sin prior to Heaven; i.e., Purgatory.

However, Augustine believed in the existence of a physical Hell for any who did not accept God's offer of salvation in this life. Therefore, Augustine proposes a rather pessimistic view of humanity since many will not accept this offer.

Moral evil and suffering derive from human freewill disobedience and is ordained by God as punishment for disobedience.

Natural evil occurred because of the loss of order in nature, defined by Augustine as the 'penal consequences of disobedience.'

Criticisms

One of the principal critics of the Augustinian Theodicy is Friedrich Schleiermacher. He argued that it was a logical contradiction to claim that a perfectly created world went wrong. This implies that evil created itself ex nihilo, out of nothing, which is a logical contradiction. Either the world was not perfect to start with, or God made it go wrong – if this is the case, it is God and not humans who are to blame, and the existence of evil and punishment of humans is not justified.

If the world was perfect and there was no knowledge of good and evil, how could Adam and Eve have the freedom to disobey God if goodness and evil were as yet unknown? The disobedience of Adam and Eve and the angels implies that there already was knowledge of good and evil. Augustine's interpretation of the tree of knowledge therefore is questionable.

Augustine's view is also inconsistent with the theory of evolution, which asserts that the universe began in chaos and is continually developing, not diminishing over time. And the evolution of life from chaos to order is due to the great amount of energy emanating from the sun to the earth, and therefore the 2nd Law of Thermodynamics is not violated.

Augustine's view that every human in seminally present in the loins Adam is biologically inaccurate and the question can be raised; is God really justified in allowing punishment of one human being for the sin of another human being?

Irenaean Theodicy (Soul-Making Theodicy)

The Irenaean soul-making theodicy (Irenaeus 130-202 AD) asserts that even though God ordained evil and the consequent pain, suffering, and hardship, He did so for a good reason, which is to prod humans to moral maturity. Therefore, a world that contains moral and natural evil is the best of all possible worlds.

In this best of all possible worlds, God takes humans created in the image of God with freewill and uses pain, suffering, and hardship to teach them obedience, thereby maturing them into a likeness of God.

God created Adam & Eve in the Garden of Eden as young children in the image of God, and they were perfect in every way, just as young children are perfect. Even though they were perfect, they were not fully developed. They still needed to grow and mature into an adult likeness of God. And this maturation process requires the person's freewill cooperation and agreement with God.

Throughout this life and lives to come, all people will eventually freely cooperate with God, mature into a likeness of God and live forever in the New Jerusalem.

Therefore, this is an optimistic view of humanity in that there is no Hell, and all will be saved. And once evil and its consequences have served their disciplinary purpose of prodding humans to maturity of obedience, God will remove evil from existence.

Irenaeus used the Biblical example of Jonah as someone whose suffering and eventual obedience brought about a greater good. Hick labeled this type of theodicy 'Irenaean' in honor of Irenaeus being the 'father' of its main ideas. And the Irenaean theodicy is considered the first of the greater-good, optimistic, soul-making theodicies.

Moral evil is ordained by God and derives from human freewill and the necessary and inevitable disobedience that arises from having it.

Natural evil is also ordained by God and has the divine purpose of developing human qualities such as compassion through the soul-making process.

Hicks Reformation of The Irenaean Theodicy

John Hick highlighted the importance of God allowing humans to develop themselves. He reasoned that if God made us perfect, we would have the goodness of robots, which would love God automatically without any further deliberation. God wants humans to love and therefore gives them freewill genuinely.

Further, Irenaeus argued that for humans to have freewill, God must be at an 'intellectual distance' from humans, far enough away that belief in God remains a free choice. If humans were too close to God intellectually, they would have no real choice except to believe in Him, and if too far away, humans would never be able to believe in Him.

Criticisms

a) The idea that everyone goes to heaven is not justice, and it is inconsistent with Orthodox Christianity and 'The Fall' of Genesis 3. It also demotes Jesus' role from 'savior' to 'moral role model.'

b) Is the magnitude of suffering that humans experience and witness necessary for soul-making, e.g., the Holocaust?

c) D.Z. Phillips in *The Concept of Prayer* (2015) argued that the continuation of evil and suffering is not a demonstration of love from an Omni-benevolent God.

Counter Arguments

a) If life suddenly ceased to exist, God would not have achieved his purpose in that He desires all to be saved.

b) The supreme life in Heaven is required to justify the amplitude of suffering and evil on earth.

c) Some 'evil people' cannot be held responsible for their evil actions; for example, developmentally disabled people.

Differences Between Augustinian and Irenaean Theodicies
By John Hick – *Evil and the God of Love* (1966)

1. The primary motivating interest of the Augustinian tradition is to relieve the Creator of responsibility for the existence of evil by placing that responsibility upon dependent beings who have freely and willfully misused their God-given freedom.

In contrast, the Irenaean type of theodicy in its developed form, as we find it in Schleiermacher and later thinkers, accepts God's ultimate responsibility for evil. And it seeks to show for what good, justifying, and satisfying reason God has created a universe in which evil was inevitable.

2. The Augustinian tradition embodies the philosophy of evil as non-being, with its Neo-Platonic accompaniments of the principle of plenitude, the conception of the great chain of being, and the aesthetic vision of the perfection of the universe as a complex harmony.

In contrast, the Irenaean type of theodicy is more purely theological in character and is not committed to the Platonic or to any other philosophical framework.

3. The Augustinian theodicy, especially in the thinking of Thomas Aquinas and the Protestantism of the eighteenth-century 'optimists,' sees God's relation to God's creation in predominantly non-personal terms. That is, people are only a part, albeit the most important part, of God's creation.

The eighteenth century was the golden age of theodicies, when the problem of evil was often at the center of discussion and when comprehensive solutions to it were confidently offered.

In that century of the Enlightenment the conception of evil as serving a larger good — a conception derived, as we have seen, from Plotinus and Christianized by Augustine — was developed to the ultimate conclusion that despite all that is bad within it our universe is nevertheless the very best that is possible.

Then, according to the Augustinian type theodicy, God's goodness is His overflowing plenitude of being bestowing existence upon a dependent realm where man has accordingly been created as part of a hierarchy of forms of existence which would be incomplete without him.

Evil is traceable to the necessary finitude and contingency of a dependent world, which exhibits an aesthetic perfection when seen from the divine standpoint, and the existence of moral evil is harmonized within this perfect whole by the balancing effect of just punishment. These are all ideas that relegate the 'person' to the periphery.

However, on the other hand, according to the Irenaean type of theodicy, the 'person' is central to God's creation, having been created for fellowship with his Maker and is valued by the personal God of love as an end in itself. The world exists to be an environment for a person's life, and the world's imperfections are integral to its fitness as a place for the making and perfecting of the person's soul.

4. For the explanation of the existence of evil in God's universe, the Augustinian type of theodicy looks to the past, to a primal catastrophe in the Fall of angels and/or men.

In contrast, to explain evil, the Irenaean type of theodicy looks to the future where God is bringing an infinite good for all people out of the temporal process, employing both moral and natural evil.

5. Accordingly, in the Augustinian tradition, the doctrine of the Fall plays a central role.

However, in the Irenaean type of theodicy, while the doctrine of the Fall is not necessarily denied, it becomes much less important. The notions accompanying the Fall of an original but lost righteousness of man and the lost perfection of his world, and of inherited Original Sin as a universal consequence of the Fall, which jointly render that event so catastrophic and therefore so crucial for the Augustinian theodicy, are rejected in the Irenaean type of theodicy.

6. The Augustinian tradition points to a final division of humanity into the saved and the damned. In contrast, Irenaean thinkers (at any rate since Schleiermacher) have been inclined to see the doctrine of eternal Hell, with its implicates of permanently un-expiated sin and unending suffering, as rendering a Christian theodicy impossible.

Points of Hidden Agreement
Between Augustinian and Irenaean Theodicies
By John Hick – *Evil and the God of Love* (1966)

Despite these considerable differences, there are also points of agreement between the two types of theodicy. These are not obvious at first but are perhaps for that all the more significant an unintended witnesses to certain basic necessities of Christian thought concerning the problem of evil.

1. The aesthetic conception of the perfection of the universe in the Augustinian tradition has its equivalent in the Irenaean type of theodicy in the thought of the eschatological perfection of the creation.

This is the belief that the Kingdom of God, as the end and completion of the temporal process, will be a good so great as to justify all that has occurred on the way to it, so that we may affirm the unqualified goodness of the totality which consists of history and its end; i.e., the end justifies the means.

Augustine's 'To thee, there is no such thing as evil' is matched by Mother Julian's eschatological 'But all shall be well, and all shall be well, and all manner of thing shall be well.' Thus, despite the significant difference that the Augustinian tradition attributes to the world the goodness of a balanced harmony of values in space and time, while the Irenaean type of theodicy sees it as a process leading to an infinitely good end, each proclaims the unqualified and unlimited goodness of God's creation as a whole.

2. Both alternatives acknowledge explicitly or implicitly God's ultimate responsibility for the existence of evil. Theodicies of the Irenaean type, from Schleiermacher onwards, do this explicitly. They hold that God did not make the world as a paradise for perfect beings but rather as a sphere in which persons made in the 'image' of God may be brought through their own free responses towards the finite 'likeness' of God. From this point of view, both moral and natural evil are inevitable aspects of the creative process.

The Augustinian tradition, on the other hand, implicitly teaches an ultimate divine responsibility for the existence of evil by bringing the free and culpable rebellion of men (and angels) within the scope of divine predestination. Augustine and Calvin both see the Fall as part of the eternal plan which God has ordained in His sovereign freedom.

The real issue between the two theodicies at this point is not so much the fact of the ultimate divine responsibility for evil, so much as the proper attitude of a theologian to that fact.

The Augustinian thinks it is impious to state explicitly what his doctrine covertly implies; the Irenaean, in a more rationalist vein, is willing to follow the argument to its conclusion.

3. The 'O Felix culpa' (O fortunate fault) theme is common to both types of theodicy. The profound paradox expressed in the famous words (of unknown authorship) of the ancient Easter liturgy --- '0 fortunate crime, which merited such and so great a redeemer' --- is quoted with approval by theologians in both traditions. See: Alvin Plantinga

In agreement with this paradox Augustine explicitly affirms that 'God judged it better to bring good out of evil than not to permit any evil to exist,' and Aquinas that 'God allows evils to happen in order to bring a greater good therefrom;' though neither of them permits this insight to affect his theodicy as a whole, as it does those of the Irenaean type.

Nevertheless, the recognition in both kinds of theodicy that the final end-product of the human story will justify the evil within that story points to an eschatological understanding of the divine purpose, which gives meaning to human life.

4. Both types of theodicy acknowledge logical limitations upon divine omnipotence, though neither regards these as constituting a real restriction upon God's power; for the principle of the inability to do the self-contradictory does not reflect impotence in the agent but a logical incoherence in the task proposed.

This principle was misused, i.e., over-extended by Leibniz, who regarded all empirical relationships as logical and accordingly saw the characters of all possible worlds as determined by logical necessity rather than by the divine will.

The principle is invoked more modestly by the developed Irenaean type of theodicy when it claims that there is a logical impossibility in the idea of a free person being 'ready-made' in the state of having learned and grown spiritually through conflict, suffering, and redemption.

5. The Augustinian tradition affirms while theodicies of the Irenaean type need not deny the reality of a personal devil and a community of evil demonic powers.

The traditional notion of Satan as the prince of darkness can have permanent value for Irenaean thought, at least as a vivid symbol of 'the demonic' in the sense of evil solely for the sake of evil, as we meet it in utterly gratuitous cruelty.

On the other hand, for the Irenaean, the notion of Satan is misused if it is used to provide a solution to the problem of evil. A permissible doctrine of Satan must be logically peripheral to Christian theodicy in both its Augustinian and Irenaean forms.

6. The Augustinian tradition affirms a positive divine valuation of the world independently of its fitness as an environment for human life.

The Irenaean way of thinking is not concerned to deny this, although it is inclined to stress that we can know God's purposes and evaluations only in so far as He has revealed them to us in their relation to humankind.

Again, neither type of theodicy has any interest in denying the possibility, or indeed the probability, that there are divine purposes at work within the created universe other than and in addition to that of providing a sphere for man's existence.

This thought has, however, been more cherished in Augustinian and Catholic than in Irenaean and Protestant thought, and probably represents a point at which the latter should be willing to learn from the former.

Heavily influenced by Augustine, the great Christian philosopher, and theologian Thomas Aquinas (1275-1274 AD) argues that a supremely good God created all things good and cannot create evil. He noted that, although goodness makes evil possible, it does not necessitate evil. He attested that God being all good, must have a morally sufficient reason for allowing evil to exist. He believed that evil is acceptable because of the good that comes from it, and that evil can only be justified when it is required for something good to occur.

Attempting to relieve God of responsibility for the occurrence of evil, Aquinas insisted that God merely permits evil to happen rather than willing it. Evil in the creaturely world, then, is a defect in or corruption of what is originally good, and like Augustine, evil is the privation or absence of good.

Augustine's works also influenced John Calvin (1509-1564) and the Reformers. Modern Reformers accept that God has ordained evil and that all evil glorifies God. But, unlike Augustine, Calvin was willing to accept that God is responsible for evil and suffering; however, he maintained that God could not be indicted for it. Calvin continued the Augustinian approach that sin is the result of the fall of man and argued that the human mind, will, and affections are corrupted by sin. He proposed that humanity is predestined, divided into the elect and the reprobate: the elect are those who God has chosen to save and are the only ones who will be saved.

Luis Molina (Augustinian type theodicy)

Gottfried Leibniz (1646-1716 AD) maintains that an absolutely perfect being must create the best of all possible worlds. So, evil in the world must be part of its being the best possible world among alternative worlds that God could have chosen to instantiate. This idea of a perfect being follows from Anselm (1033-1109 AD) where, in his Proslogium Ch II, he stated, "And indeed, we believe that thou art a being than which nothing greater can be conceived."

David Hume claims that it is not possible to infer the existence of a good God from the facts of evil but that the simultaneous presence of good also blocks an inference to a completely malicious being. Since the world contains a perplexing mix of good and evil, the most reasonable inference is to a creator who is indifferent to his sentient creatures.

In that climate of opinion, in 1955, J. L. Mackie published his argument that was designed to expose a logical contradiction between the existence of God and the existence of evil. In its simplest form, following Epicurus, the logical problem of evil is this: God is omnipotent; God is wholly good; and yet evil exists; therefore God does not exist. An argument that, if valid, is a direct disproof of theism.

During the renewal of the philosophy of religion that began in the late 1970s, theistic responses to the problem of evil proliferated.

In 1974, 1977 Alvin Plantinga's response to the logical problem of evil, known as the freewill defense, became classic. Plantinga points out that Mackie's definitions—particularly of omnipotence—need not be accepted by theists. If God grants a kind of freewill to creatures that is incompatible with any form of determinism, Plantinga argues, then it is not within God's power to control the outcome of their choices, thus allowing the possibility for evil.

Note that the point of Plantinga's defense is not to argue for the truth or plausibility of a good God but to show that the coexistence of a good God with evil is not a logical contradiction, as Mackie proposed.

Many theists and non-theists came to agree that the freewill defense of Plantinga shows that the logical argument against theism, as exemplified in Mackie, fails. Consequently, many nontheistic professional philosophers developed a different type of argument to show why evil is still a problem for theism.

What became known as the evidential argument claims that some facts about evil count against the credibility or probability of theistic belief.

This argument assumes that God would prevent or eliminate any evil, i.e., gratuitous evil, which does not lead to a greater good. Therefore, a greater good for every evil or type of evil must be specified for a theodicy to be adequate.

One critical issue in the ongoing discussion concerns the concept of gratuitous evil. A gratuitous evil is an evil that is not necessary to achieve some greater good or prevent another evil equally bad or worse.

The controversy pertains to two key questions: whether it is rational to believe that gratuitous evils exist and whether standard theism requires God to prevent them.

William L. Rowe articulated his rendition of the evidential argument in 1979. Rowe claims that it is reasonable to think that at least some of the intense suffering in our world could have been prevented without losing a greater good or allowing an equally bad or worse evil in its place.

Since Rowe assumes that theism entails that God is justified in permitting evils only if they are necessary to a greater good, he believes he has a good argument for atheism.

For Rowe and others who advance the evidential argument from evil, God reveals to human beings neither the specific reasons nor the fact that he even has reasons for permitting gratuitous evil.

On the good-parent analogy, it is reasonable to think that the goods for the sake of which a loving, self-revealing God would allow such evils would not be totally beyond our ken.

The version of the evidential argument from evil offered by Paul Draper frames the matter in the following way. He states that although theism may provide an explanation of evil that has some degree of plausibility on its own, there may be a competing hypothesis that explains evil better by comparison.

Paul Draper argues that atheism explains the actual pattern of pain and pleasure in the world better than theism does. The focus here is not on our inability to see a justifying reason but on our supposed ability to see that an atheistic explanation is superior to a theistic one.

Willam Rowe's evidential argument gains traction by claiming that it is likely that there are evils that are not necessary for obtaining any greater goods. For example, Bambi dying in a forest fire. Following Augustine, that the creature is unable to perceive all aspects of the divine plan, skeptical theism is now a well-known line of response to the evidential argument from evil.

Skeptical theists argue that God perceives and pursues goods beyond our comprehension for all we know.

Skeptical theists Daniel Howard-Snyder and Michael Bergmann are prominent representatives of this response known as the skeptical theist defense. The essential point is that the human inability to discern God's reasons for some evils does not constitute evidence that there are no such reasons.

Their argument for this point is that we have no reason to think that our finite minds are able to grasp either all of the connections between goods and evils or all of the goods that there are to which evils may be connected. Yet such connections may well be known by infinite divine wisdom.

In addition to philosophical work on the logical and evidential versions of the problem of evil, some work has also been done on what has been called the existential version. This label calls attention to the "real-life" dimension of the problem and the more abstract and general lines of reasoning that are typically pursued.

Marilyn Adams explores the redemptive or salvific nature of human suffering, providing what we might consider being a forthrightly spiritual solution to the existential problem of evil. Adams advocates 'the logic of compensation' for the victims of evil, a postmortem healing of divine intimacy with God. This goes so deep, she believes, that eventually, victims will see the horrors they suffered as points of contact with the incarnate, suffering God and cease wishing they had never suffered them.

———————

John Hick published Evil and the God of Love in 1966, in which he developed a soul-making theodicy based on the work of Irenaeus. Hick supported the Irenaean view that the world is ideally suited for the moral development of humans and that this justifies the existence of evil.

The Irenaean theodicy does not attempt to protect God from being responsible for evil as the Augustinian theodicy does. Rather, it argues that God is responsible but justified for it because of its benefits for human development. Therefore, bringing such good out of evil is preferable to the evil not occurring in the first place.

Hick framed his theodicy as an attempt to respond to the problem of evil in light of scientific development, such as Darwin's theory of evolution, and as an alternative to the traditionally accepted Augustinian theodicy.

Rejecting the idea that humans were created perfectly and then fell away from perfection, Hick instead argued that humans are still in the process of creation. He interpreted the fall of man, described in the book of Genesis, as a mythological description of the current state of humans.

According to Hick, God's soul-making process is not completed in temporal existence but continues into the afterlife. And Hick rejected Augustine's belief in the existence of Hell.

———————

Second-century philosopher and theologian Irenaeus (130-202), after whom the theodicy is named, proposed a two-stage creation process in which humans require freewill and the experience of evil to develop.

Another early Christian theologian, Origen (184–253), presented a response to the problem of evil which cast the world as a schoolroom or hospital for the soul; theologian Mark Scott has argued that Origen, rather than Irenaeus, ought to be considered the father of this kind of theodicy.

One of the principal critics of the Augustinian Theodicy is Friedrich Schleiermacher (1768-1834). He argued that it was a logical contradiction to claim that a perfectly created world went wrong, since this implies that evil created itself ex nihilo, which is a logical contradiction.

Schleiermacher argued in the nineteenth century that God must necessarily create flawlessly but not perfectly, so this world must be the best possible world because it allows God's purposes to be fulfilled naturally.

In 1966, philosopher John Hick (1922-2012) discussed the similarities of the preceding theodicies, calling them all "Irenaean." He supported the view that creation is incomplete and argued that the world is best placed for the moral development of humans, as it presents real moral choices. And he supported the view that everyone will eventually be saved.

French theologian Henri Blocher (1937) criticized Hick's universalism, arguing that such a view negates the freewill choice of rejecting God.

British philosopher Richard Swinburne (1934) proposed that, to make a free moral choice, humans must have experience of the consequences of their actions and that natural evil must exist to provide such choices.

The development of process theology has challenged the Irenaean tradition by teaching that God's power is limited and that he cannot be responsible for evil.

D. Z. Phillips (1934-2006) and Fyodor Dostoyevsky (1821-1881) challenged the instrumental or practical use of suffering, suggesting that love cannot be expressed through suffering. However, Dostoyevsky also states that the beauty of love is evident, in that love can continue to grow, withstand and overcome even the most evil acts.

Michael Tooley (1941) argued that the magnitude of much suffering is excessive and that, in some cases, cannot lead to moral development.

In *God, Power, and Evil: A Process Theodicy*, published in 1976, David Ray Griffin criticized Augustine's reliance on freewill and argued that it is incompatible with divine omniscience and omnipotence as presented by Augustine.

Griffin argued in later works that humans cannot have freewill if God is omniscient. He contended that if God is truly omniscient, he will know infallibly what people will do, meaning that they cannot be free. He proposed that original sin, as Augustine conceived it, must itself be caused by God, rendering any punishment he wills unjust.

He also criticized the Irenaean soul-making theodicy, which supposes that God inflicts pain for His own ends, which Griffin regarded as immoral.

The process doctrine proposes that God is benevolent and feels the world's pain (both physically and emotionally) but suggests that his power is restricted to persuasion rather than coercion and cannot prevent certain evil events from occurring.

God is not omnipotent and does not limit Himself in some way for the sake of His creation, but that His power is limited in a metaphysical sense. God has all the power it is possible for Him to have.

In his introduction to process theology, C. Robert Melse argued that, although suffering does sometimes bring about good, not all suffering is valuable, and that most suffering does more harm than good.

Process theology also teaches that God created the world out of pre-existent chaos rather than creating the world ex nihilo (as Augustine proposed).

Against David Ray Griffin, Bruce Reichenbach defends a more nuanced theistic view of God's power. In the end, says Reichenbach, the process deity is not even a personal being and therefore does not resemble the God of the Bible as understood by the community of faith.

In *God, Freedom, and Evil* (1974 & 1977), Alvin Plantinga presented a version of the freewill defense as an alternative response to the problem of evil. He demonstrated that the existence of an omnipotent, benevolent God and the existence of evil are not logically inconsistent.

Plantinga supported this argument by claiming that there are some things that an omnipotent God could not do yet remain omnipotent – for example, if an omnipotent God has necessary existence, he could not create a world in which he does not exist. For this reason, Plantinga argued that an omnipotent God could not create any universe that he chooses, as Leibniz had proposed.

Plantinga's version of the defense embraces Augustine's view of freewill but not his natural theology. Rather than attempt to show the existence of God as likely in the face of evil as a theodicy does, Plantinga's freewill defense attempts to show that belief in God is still logically possible, despite the existence of evil.

Theologian Alister McGrath has noted that because Plantinga only argued that the coexistence of God and evil are logically possible, he did not present a theodicy but a defense.

That is, Plantinga did not attempt to demonstrate that his proposition is true or plausible, just that it is logically possible that God might have a morally sufficient reason for allowing evil, without specifying what that reason is.

Contrary to Calvinism and Reformed Theology, there is an argument for a view of divine providence that is general and not meticulous such that the world contains genuine contingencies, including contingencies of evil free choice, and contingencies in the way natural order intersects human interests.

A position called open theism is one such argument. Open Theism follows from and extends Arminianism. Open Theism has attracted a great deal of interest since it arose in the early 1990s.

Its explanation of evil draws heavily from two of its most basic themes: that God limits his own power by creating personal beings with genuine freedom, and that God's knowledge is contingent upon creaturely choices rather than being timeless and fixed.

In brief, the openness vision is that God and his creation are profoundly relational. God's overarching goal is for personal beings to freely seek a personal relationship with God and their fellow personal beings.

Genuine human-divine relationship, according to openness thinkers, requires both that God is open to creaturely choices that he does not meticulously control and that the human future is open as persons interact with God's overtures toward them. So, this kind of genuinely relational universe involves the real possibility of evils that serve no greater good.

From Calvinism and the Reformed tradition, Paul Helm argues, on the contrary, that God takes no risks in creating and guiding the universe. Elaborating on what he considers a biblical view, Helm takes the position that divine providence as it applies to personal evil is indeed "meticulous."

Attaching extreme views of power and knowledge to God, Helm argues that God always chooses to prohibit or allow evil, thus guaranteeing that his creation is free from the risk of an action being chosen or an event occurring outside of his control.

Alvin Plantinga, departing from his usual defensive stance that the logical problem of evil argument against theism fails, articulates a "felix culpa" or "fortunate fault" theodicy similar to Augustine. Based on this ancient theme, the human fall into sin is an exceedingly fortunate event because, in addressing sin, God enacts a plan of redemption that involves the incomparable good of the Incarnation and Atonement.

So, suppose God intended to create a highly valuable world that includes the good of God's existence and the good of the Incarnation and Atonement. In that case, logically, God must will that the world contains sin, suffering, and evil.

Kevin Diller responds by questioning Plantinga's strategy of interpreting evil as a means to God's far greater ends. Diller argues that this makes evil a functional good, somehow rational and fitting in God's economy, thus distorting its true theological significance as needless and harmful, but permitted, rebellion and damage.

British philosopher Richard Swinburne proposed a version of the Irenaean theodicy based on his libertarian view of freewill, a view that one's free actions are not caused by any outside agent.

It is a great good that humans have a libertarian moral freewill, able to make free and responsible moral choices. This is a version of the "greater good morally freewill" theodicy.

It is not logically possible that God could give humans such freewill and yet ensure that they always use it correctly. However, if humans do have such a morally freewill, there will necessarily be the possibility of moral evil. And having such a freewill is worth the cost of the evil consequences that may result from humans having it.

He also argued that, for people to make free moral decisions, they must be aware of the consequences of such decisions. Knowledge of these consequences must be based on experience—Swinburne rejected the idea that God could implant such knowledge, arguing that humans would question its reliability.

Swinburne argued that humans must have firsthand experience of natural evil to understand the consequences of moral evil. For God to give humans moral freewill, he must also allow humans to suffer from natural evil.

Swinburne conceived Hell as a separation from God, rejecting the notion of eternal physical punishment, and argued that people who had chosen to reject God throughout their lives would continue to do so after death.

James F. Sennett, regarding the greater good morally freewill theodicy, argues that if there is freedom in heaven, then it seems that there is the possibility of evil in heaven, which violates standard intuitions.

That is, there is a dilemma in heaven. If there is no evil in heaven, then heaven lacks a great good which in this world is worth the presence of great evil. So then, how can God be justified in omitting such a great good from heaven?

Catholicism indirectly addresses this problem by postulating an afterlife, i.e., Purgatory, where those entering atone for their sins, making them eligible for Heaven, even while retaining their free will.

A number of Protestant theodicists, such as Greg Boyd, Kevin Tiempe, and others, address the Heaven dilemma directly by following Irenaeus' "soul-making" theodicy where the human soul is perfected before Heaven. During this life and an afterlife, the person's character is perfected to the point where committing a sin is no longer an option, even though they retain their libertarian freewill.

Another controversy in the overall discussion of evil considers the role of natural evil. The familiar line of argument is that a world run by natural laws is necessary for a stable environment for the conduct of our lives. However, the regular operation of natural laws also creates pain, suffering, disaster, and other evils.

According to Swinburne, natural evils are necessary to humans having meaningful freedom to commit morally good or evil actions. Natural processes alone give humans knowledge of the effects of their actions without inhibiting their freedom, and if evil is to be a real possibility for them, they must know how to allow it to occur.

Eleonore Stump rejects Swinburne's argument that natural evils are necessary for the knowledge that is connected to moral freedom because the relevant knowledge of how to bring about moral evil is available by other avenues (such as divine revelation or scientific study) rather than by induction from actual natural evils.

Others declare that certain kinds of good and meaningful acts of heroism and sacrifice would be absent without such natural evils.

The theodicies mentioned in this brief history of the problem of evil in Christian literature cover a wide range of Christian theodicies. That is, other theodicies emphasize certain aspects of those mentioned, but they do not differ in a significant way.

For example, Thomas Jay Oord, has presented a theodicy that says God does not have the power to control humans. That is, the God of infinite love not only does not have the power to control humans now, but that God never had that power.

Oord defines this as "essential kenosis." This would seem similar to David Ray Griffin's view that a limitation of God's power is not divine self-limitation but a metaphysical feature of God's being.

The problem of evil arguably commands more attention than any other issue in the philosophy of religion, and will very likely continue to do so, not only because of its intellectual complexity but also because of its grounding and importance in real life.

Addendum 3

The Family of God

God is a Trinity of Persons, each Omni-Perfect, i.e., omnipotent, omniscient, omnibenevolent, and so forth., co-equal and fully divine.

However, there are not three Gods, but One True God in Three God Persons, suggesting that the Trinity of God is the Family of God.

It is suggested that there is the Person of the Father, the Person of the Holy Spirit, which could be understood to be the Person of the Mother, and the Person of the Son.

The Person of the Son has a divine nature, the Son of God, and a human nature, the Son of Man. And it is the human nature of Jesus the Son of Man that is resident in both female and male members of the human family.

And members of the human family can freely choose to become a part of the bride of Christ. And the bride of Christ is joined together with the Divine Family of God, through Jesus the Son of Man, as Human Children of God.

"He came to His own, and those who were His own did not receive Him. But as many as received Him, to them He gave the right to become children of God, even to those who believe in His name, who were born [again], *not of blood nor of the will of the flesh nor of the will of man, but of God. (John 1:11-13* NASB)

Addendum 4

The Genders of God

"God created man in His own image, in the image of God He created him; male and female He created them." (Genesis 1:27 NASB)

From this verse in Genesis, it would seem that God created male and female humans in the Image of God, and therefore God could be said to be both male and female.

"The earliest Christians – all of whom were Jews – spoke of the Holy Spirit as a feminine figure. The present article [See source above] discusses the main proof texts, ranging from the 'Gospel according to the Hebrews' to a number of testimonies from the second century."

"The ancient tradition was, in particular, kept alive in East and West Syria, up to and including the fourth century Makarios and/or Symeon, who even influenced 'modern' Protestants such as John Wesley and the Moravian leader Count von Zinzendorf."

"This does not mean that in this way God has been 'defined;' it just means that in the Image of God the Holy Spirit as Mother, one may attain a greater appreciation of the fullness of the Divine Nature as both Female and Male."

From this perspective, Gen 1:27 might be paraphrased: 'Mother & Father God created men and women in Their Image, in the Image of Themselves They created them; male and female They created them.'

Source:
https://en.wikipedia.org/wiki/Gender_of_the_Holy_Spirit
https://hts.org.za/index.php/hts/article/view/3225/7763

Addendum 5

Jesus The Son of Man

Jesus used the expression 'Son of Man' almost fifty times in the Gospels. However, even after two millenniums of debate, there does not seem to be a consensus among theologians on how to interpret this expression.

According to Delbert Burkett, in his book *The Son of Man Debate* (2007), subtitled 'A History and Evaluation,' currently, there are three popular interpretations of the 'Son of Man,' among other less popular ones.

1) "Son of Man," an expression of Jesus' humanity
2) "Son of Man," a messianic title derived from Daniel 7:13
3) "son of man," an idiom by which a man could refer to himself

It would seem that one or the other of these interpretations may best explain what Jesus is saying in each of the occurrences where He used this expression, but that no one of them seems satisfactory in all occurrences.

However, we know that God is the Father of Jesus (Matthew 1:18). In this way, Jesus is the Son of God, and therefore He is in every respect divine.

"For this reason therefore the Jews were seeking all the more to kill Him, because He not only was breaking the Sabbath, but also was calling God His own Father, making Himself equal with God." (John 5:18 NASB*)*

And we know that Mary is the mother of Jesus. So, in this way, Jesus is in every respect a human being. Therefore as a human being, He could go to the Cross as a representative of all of humanity. As it says,

"And He Himself is the propitiation for our sins; and not for ours only, but also for those the whole world." (1 John 2:2 NASB*)*

Since it may be understood that the name of a person in the Bible symbolizes the nature of that person, then the nature associated with the 'Son of Man' is considered here to be 'humanity.'

It is understood then that Jesus is both the Divine Son of God and the Human Son of Man. He is one person with two natures, and these two natures represent Jesus' divinity and His humanity.

It is also understood here that Jesus acted primarily as the Son of Man during His Incarnation. That He emptied Himself of His divine attributes so that He could identify Himself with every other person and that all other persons could identify themselves with Him.

"Have this attitude in yourselves which was also in Christ Jesus, who, although He existed in the form of God, did not regard equality with God a thing to be grasped, but emptied Himself, taking the form of a bond-servant, and being made in the likeness of men." (Philippians 2:5-7 NASB*)*

Addendum 6

The Personhood of God

"Thus the LORD used to speak to Moses face to face, just as a man speaks to his friend. (Exodus 33:11 NASB)

The Bible speaks of God as the living Personal God where the Personhood of the One True God is a rational being, conscious of Their own existence. And as the living Personal God, God possesses all the attributes of what we know and consider, at the very least, to be a person.

As Persons, among other things, God can speak, love, express anger, and show mercy. The Bible also says that God has a will and an intellect. All of these characteristics are consistent with personhood.

Furthermore, the Bible contrasts the Personal living God with impersonal idols that are dead things. Indeed, the idea that we are created as persons in the image of God suggests that God is a person.

One of the defining characteristics of a person is the ability to engage in relationships and express love, i.e., the love of another person. In every way that human people exist and love, God exists and loves as a Person.

https://www.thebrooknetwork.org/2012/02/07/the-personhood-of-god/
https://carm.org/is-god-a-person
https://www.blueletterbible.org/faq/don_stewart/don_stewart_1277.cfm

---

https://www.thebrooknetwork.org/2012/02/07/the-personhood-of-god

The Personhood of God

What is a person? You are a person; a stone isn't. You have self-awareness; a tree doesn't. You can be moral; electricity is amoral. You are alive; a corpse is not. "Person" usually refers to a living human being, although from a Christian point of view "person" also refers to God, and we assume that we are persons with personalities because it was a personal God who created us.

Some do acknowledge that God is absolute, mighty, and rational, but more a supernatural force than a divine person. But the God of the Bible is a person. He is intelligent, creative, and moral. He speaks of himself as "I."

Indeed, the idea that God speaks at all assumes that he is a personal being. God plans; God acts; God intends. He has will and wisdom. He has many names. He wants us to know him. If God were not personal, we could not pray, and we would not worship. If God were merely a force, we would have no guidance, no comfort, no discipline.

One of the defining characteristics of a person is the ability to engage in relationships. Rocks don't have relationships. Persons talk to each other, they seek to understand each other, they make choices that shape their relationships with each other. Persons (from *persona*, "mask") have faces, or public presentations of themselves.

Unlike stars, water, or trees, there is a dynamic interaction between persons. Persons know other persons—not just know about or store information on, but comprehend, care for, and commit to.

I have to admit that when our children were born, I probably didn't really see them as persons. They appeared to be little creatures whom we served by putting food in one end and getting by-products out the other.

My wife, of course, saw this as a wonderful relationship, but I was really waiting for the first ball game or the first swim in the lake. But it didn't take that long. All it took for me was the day the first responsive smile spread across that small face—eyes wide open, a gutteral "g-aaaaa," which meant something-or-other.

See a smile, and the first thing you think is, there's a person in there! And I want to know what's behind the smile.

———————————

https://blueletterbible.org/faq/don_stewart/don_stewart_1277.cfm

Is God a Personal God?

While most of the religions of the world believe that God is an impersonal being, the God who is revealed in the Bible is a personal God. This means that He has the characteristics of a person. A person can be defined as someone who is rational, conscious of his own being. This is how the Bible portrays God. He is a person, not an impersonal force.

He Is The Living God

The Bible speaks of Him as the living God.

Joshua said, "By this you shall know that among you is the living God who without fail will drive out from before you the Canaanites, Hittites, Hivites, Perizzites, Girgashites, Amorites, and Jebusites" (Joshua 3:10).

As a youth, David realized that the giant Goliath was defying "the living God" (1 Samuel 17:26).

David later wrote in the Psalms.

For with you is the fountain of life; in your light we see light (Psalms 36:9).

The prophet Jeremiah proclaimed.

But the Lord is the true God; He is the living God and the everlasting King (Jeremiah 10:10).

God Has The Characteristics Of A Person

The Scriptures attribute characteristics to the living God that can only be those of a person.

1.   He Has Personal Names

We find in Scripture personal names used in reference to God.

But God said to Moses, "I AM WHO I AM." And he said, "Thus you shall say to the children of Israel, "I AM has sent me to you' " (Exodus 3:14).

Jesus referred to God as His "Father."

At that time Jesus answered and said, "I thank you Father, Lord of heaven and earth, because you have hidden these things from the wise and prudent and have revealed them to babes" (Matthew 11:25).

2.   He Is A God Of Love

The Bible speaks of God having the capacity to love.

The Lord has appeared of old to me, saying: 'Yes I have loved you with an everlasting love' (Jeremiah 31:3).

Paul wrote.

But God demonstrates his own love toward us, in that while we were still sinners, Christ died for us (Romans 5:8).

3.   He Is A God Who Has Feelings

Scripture attributes feelings, or emotion to God. He can show love.

He loves righteousness and justice; the earth is full of the lovingkindness of the Lord (Psalm 33:5).

The Lord can be grieved.

And the LORD was sorry that he had made humankind on the earth, and it grieved him to his heart. (Genesis 6:6).

He can feel sorrow.

Jesus wept (John 11:35).

God is compassionate.

We count those blessed who endured. You have heard of the endurance of Job and have seen the outcome of the Lord's dealings, that the Lord is full of compassion and is merciful (James 5:11).

4.   God Can Show Anger

At times, we find that God can show His anger.

And the Lord said to Moses . . . 'Now therefore, let me alone, that my wrath may burn hot against them and I may consume them' (Exodus 32:10,11).

5.   He Has A Will To Choose

The Bible says that God has a will or self-determination. He is free to do whatever He chooses. The psalmist wrote.

But our God is in the heavens; he does whatever he pleases (Psalm 115:3).

Isaiah testified the following abilities of God.

Declaring the end from the beginning, and from ancient times things which have not been done, saying, 'My purpose will be established, and I will accomplish all my good pleasure.   Truly I have spoken; truly I will bring it to pass. I have planned it, surely I will do it (Isaiah 46:10,11).

Although God has the ability to make choices, they are not responsive to outside stimulus as is often the case with human beings. God makes choices based on His own determination.

6.   He Is A God Of Mercy

The Scriptures teach that God has the ability to show mercy.

Then God saw their works, that they turned from their evil way; and God relented from the disaster that He had said He would bring upon them, and He did not do it (Jonah 3:10).

The Bible speaks of God as wanting or desiring things.

The Lord is not slack concerning his promise, as some count slackness, but is longsuffering toward us, not willing that any should perish but that all should come to repentance (2 Peter 3:9).

7.   God Has An Intellect

The Bible says that God has an intellect. He has a mind that thinks. God uses His mind to instruct His people concerning what they should do.

Thus says the Lord, your Redeemer, the Holy One of Israel: 'I am the Lord your God who teaches you to profit, who leads you by the way you should go' (Isaiah 48:17).

In Proverbs it says.

The eyes of the LORD are in every place, keeping watch on the evil and the good. (Proverbs 15:3).

Jeremiah wrote.

For surely I know the plans I have for you, says the LORD, plans for your welfare and not for harm, to give you a future with hope (Jeremiah 29:11).

In the Book of Acts we read.

Says the Lord, who makes these things known from long ago (Acts 15:18).

The writer to the Hebrews stated.

And there is no creature hidden from his sight, but all things are open and laid bare to the eyes of him with whom we have to do (Hebrews 4:13).

These are some of the attributes that the Bible says God possesses. They are all consistent with personhood. By demonstrating these in His character God has shown that He is a personal God.

8.   He Is Contrasted With Idols

The Bible also contrasts the personal living God to idols, which neither hear nor speak. The Apostle Paul told a crowd at Lystra:

Men, why are you doing these things? We also are men with the same nature as you, and preach to you that you should turn from these vain things to the living God, who made the heaven, the earth, the sea, and all things in them (Acts 14:15).

There Is A Distinction Between The Living And Non-Living

When he wrote to the church at Thessalonica Paul again brought out the distinction between the living God and non-living idols.

For they themselves declare concerning us what manner of entry we had to you, and how you turned to God from idols to serve the living and true God (1 Thessalonians 1:9).

Hence the Bible contrasts the living God who hears, sees, thinks, feels, and acts like a person with idols which are things, not persons.

Summary

The Bible designates God as the living God. He is a rational being, conscious of His existence. As the living God He possesses the attributes of a person. For, among other things, He can love, express anger, and show mercy. The Bible also says that God has a will and an intellect. All of these characteristics are consistent with personhood. Furthermore, the Bible contrasts the personal living God with impersonal idols that are mere things. We conclude the Bible clearly teaches that God is personal.

Addendum 7

How Do You See and Love God?
God's Self-Portrait, Part 1
By Greg Boyd

https://www.reknew.org/2021/12/how-do-you-see-god-gods-self-portrait-part-1

December 16, 2021

When ReKnew first launched a year and a half ago, I planned on initially using the blog primarily to flesh out the theology and significance of the ReKnew Manifesto.

As happens all-too-frequently in my ADHD world, that project got sidelined primary because of my obsession with finishing The Crucifixion of the Warrior God. Well, the book is almost finished, so I feel its time to return to our original plan.

We'll continue to post other Kingdom related blogs, and I'll continue to use the blog to address questions sent into us and other topics from time to time, but—God willing (James 4:13-5)—the focus of three or more blogs a week will be on the Manifesto.

And since I believe the single most important aspect of our theology concerns our mental picture of God, that is the topic I'd like to start with. For some these initial reflections on God may be radically new, while for long-time followers of ReKnew some of this will be review— but it's material that I don't believe we can be reminded of too often.

Only a relatively small percentage of people on the planet flat out refuse to believe in some sort of God, and for good reason. Not only do most have a deep intuitive sense of a transcendent power, but there are a multitude of compelling arguments pointing to God's existence.

For example, it's very hard to explain how a completely irrational universe could evolve rational beings like humans by sheer time and chance. It's even harder to explain how it is that our reason succeeds in making sense of reality (as in science).

So too, its extremely difficult to explain how the universe could evolve beings like humans who long for ultimate meaning unless there is in fact an ultimate purpose to our existence. And it's close to impossible to account for how an amoral universe could produce beings that are convinced that good and evil exist and that good should overcome evil. (Even those who claim moral convictions are nothing more than culturally conditioned preferences act like they're not when you cut them off in traffic!).

It's not surprising, then, that most people believe in some kind of "god".

While there's widespread consensus regarding God's existence, there's very little agreement on what God is like. Many imagine God to be an angry and austere judge who punishes people by sending things like diseases and catastrophes upon them. Some go so far as to hold that God is a cosmic tyrant who orchestrates every single thing that happens and even predestines people to go to heaven or hell. Others picture God as being too preoccupied running the universe to be interested in the details of their lives or as being a quaint old grandpa in the sky who just wants his grandkids to have fun. (See America's Four Gods, a book by Baylor sociologists who report their research on the various ways that people see God).

Most classical theologians in church history have conceived of God as "too exalted" to be genuinely affected by us little humans. They claim that God never experiences change (he's "immutable"), for he exists in a timeless present moment. So too, they claim God never experiences passions and never suffers (he's "impassible"), for he is "above" allowing anything outside of himself to affect him or disturb his perfect bliss.

And there are an increasing number of people in our post-modern world who simply conclude that God is too mysterious to know, let alone have a relationship with, while many others today imagine him as an impersonal mystical force or metaphysical principle.

As I said at the start, the way you envision God in your mind is the single most important fact in your life, for it completely determines the quality of your relationship with God. In fact, all of our emotions are associated with the images we entertain in our minds. So how you imagine God determines how you feel and relate to God.

If you imagine God as an angry judge or controlling tyrant, you will not only live in fear of him, but you'll find it impossible to passionately love him. If you think that God is uninterested in your life, you aren't likely to be genuinely interested in him. If you conceive of God as an old grandpa, you might occasionally be grateful towards him, but you won't be passionate about being disciplined to conform your life to his holy will.

If you imagine God as one who is above being affected by you and above change or emotion, you'll find it extremely difficult to develop a deeply personal relationship with him. And if you conceive of God as too mysterious to know or as an impersonal force or metaphysical principle, you may be curious about God now and then, but you aren't likely to make loving him the central point of your life.

We have to always remember that the quality of our love for God can never outrun the beauty of the God we mentally envision. Loving God isn't something we can just will ourselves to do. You can hear a thousand sermons about how you ought to love God and even about how you're going to hell if you don't love God, but while these sorts of sermons may succeed in motivating you to say you love God and even to crank out apparently loving behaviors, they can't succeed in helping you actually love God. Quite the opposite: in making you fear God, these messages ensure that you can't love God, for as John says,

There is no fear in love. But perfect love drives out fear, because fear has to do with punishment. The one who fears is not made perfect in love (1 John 4:19).

The only way we can genuinely love God is by being convinced that "he first loved us" (1 John 4:20). And since all of our affections are associated with the mental images in our minds, the only way for this love to affect us is to imagine it, as vividly as possible. If we regularly envision God loving us, it invariably evokes in us a love for God.

If you understand that we are called to love God with all our mind, heart, body and soul, as Jesus taught us, then the all important first step in moving in this direction is to pay attention to the mental pictures of God you entertain in your mind and to spend time asking God to help you develop and nurture the true one, letting God pour his passionate love on you.

Greg

P.S. If you want to go deeper on the importance of our mental pictures of God and on how to use your imagination in prayer in ways that are transforming, you might want to check out my book, Seeing Is Believing (Baker, 2004).

Addendum 8

How Does God See and Love You?

First and foremost, it is given that God knows and loves every person. The more we see ourselves as being different from the Person of Jesus, Son of Man, the more difficult it is for us to understand and believe just how and how much Mother & Father God loves each of us.

Mother & Father God love each of us in the same way and to the same degree that They love Jesus, Son of Man.

Further, nothing anyone could ever think, say, or do could change what Jesus the Son of Man accomplished in His incarnation and death on The Cross.

Therefore, there is nothing that can change the love Mother & Father God have for Jesus Son of Man or change the love Mother & Father God have so Graciously offered to humanity based on the finished work of Jesus Christ.

To some extent, each of us can understand how much Mother & Father God must love Jesus, Son of Man, and what Mother & Father God must think and feel about Him, and that is exactly how They think and feel, see and love every one of us.

Imagine just how much Mother & Father God love Jesus the Perfect Son of Man, and then put yourself in place of Jesus; He put Himself in our place on The Cross so that we can put ourselves in His place in the heart of Mother & Father God.

Mother God's love and support for Jesus, Son of Man, was always unconditional. Several verses in the Bible mention God's unconditional love for humanity regarding a mother's love for her child.

God asks rhetorically in, *"Can a woman forget her nursing child and have no compassion on the son of her womb? Even these may forget, but I will not forget you."* *(Isiah 49:15* NASB*)*

273

Even if it were possible for a human mother to forget her child, Mother God would not forget us. And, it may be that women can better understand this kind of unconditional love for their children than men.

Unlike Mother God, Father God's love and support for Jesus Son of Man was conditional during the period of His incarnation.

And that was because the human nature of the Son of Man had to be tested and proven worthy of continuing to receive the Father's love and support by willingly obeying the Father in every way, including the Son of Man's obedience to death on a cross.

As the Son of Man continued to obey the Mosaic Law and obey the Father during His Incarnation, then the Father continued to love and support the Son of Man without reservation.

However, if Jesus Son of Man had failed during this period, he and all humanity would have been cut off from the Father's support, and not even the love of Mother God could have saved Him, and all humanity would have perished. However, Jesus, Son of God, as a member of the Trinity, would not have been lost.

Thankfully, as we know, Jesus was successful in completing the work the Father had given Him to accomplish in this world. Jesus Son of Man met all the Father's conditions for His continued love and support.

Therefore, the Father's conditional support for Jesus Son of Man was cemented at the cross and was no longer in jeopardy of being withdrawn. It may be that men can better understand this kind of conditional performance-based love and support for their children than women.

Therefore, all the blessings and promises of God that result from obedience to God were granted by Grace to humanity because of the finished work of Jesus Son of Man culminating on the Cross.

That is, in addition to Mother God's unconditional love and support for the Son of Man, the Father's conditional love was also extended to all humanity.

Through no merit of its own, humanity was awarded the same love, approval, and acceptance that Mother & Father God have for the Son of Man.

It is this combined love and support of Mother & Father God that humanity can receive and experience as a free gift for what Jesus, Son of Man, accomplished in His incarnation.

Addendum 9

Heaven Before the Angelic Rebellion
And Paradise Before the Fall of Adam & Eve

This is a highly speculative account of what conceivably could have taken place in Heaven before the Angelic Rebellion and before the Fall of Adam & Eve in the Garden of Eden, i.e., Paradise.

God created Angels with libertarian freewill, which is the freewill power to either obey or disobey God, i.e., the power to either love or not love God.

And God explained that since They did not know if they would obey or disobey in the future, they were created open to temptation to determine their willingness to obey and their willingness not to disobey Them.

Then, God told the angels that:

"… God is faithful, who will not allow you to be tempted beyond what you are able, but with the temptation will provide the way of escape also, so that you will be able to endure it" (1 Corinthians 10:13 NASB)

Then God explained that they could escape the suffering of temptation by asking to have their power to disobey removed. And once that was done, they would no longer suffer from temptation since they could no longer give in to it. Then temptation would have served its purpose in their life and would cease to exist for them.

God also explained to the angels that if they ever disobeyed God, they would be expelled from Heaven, with no possibility of returning.

However, Lucifer, wanting to be like God and not wanting to serve Jesus and His bride in Paradise, refused God's way of escaping temptation and knowingly and willfully disobeyed God by leading other angels in a rebellion against God and were expelled from Heaven forever.

Of course, God knew there was always this possibility. However, giving in to temptation and disobeying God was avoidable, in that God had provided a way of escape.

Other angels, witnessing this rebellion and fearing they too might fall into temptation, took the way of escape and asked God to remove their power to disobey. And, of course, God honored their request, and they remained in Heaven.

In the end, about two-thirds of the angels remained in Heaven with their power to obey intact. In this way, the good angels showed their love for God by laying down their life for Him by voluntarily sacrificing their power to disobey.

After the Angelic Rebellion, Adam & Eve, like the angels before them, were created with the power of freewill. And like the angels before them, it was not inevitable they would exercise their power to disobey God.

It is conceivable that Adam & Eve knew of the Angelic Rebellion, the actions of the good and bad angels, and the consequences following each group. And when tempted to disobey God, they could have followed the example of the good angels and showed their love for God by laying down their life for Him by asking Him to remove their power to disobey.

Then Adam & Eve would have remained in the Garden Paradise uncorrupted, and God's best of all worlds creation project would have gone forth. If Adam & Eve had denied themselves in this way, then their progeny, generation after generation, would have faced the same decision regarding giving up their power to disobey.

However, as we know, Adam & Eve chose not to deny themselves but to disobey God. And this evil act not only caused them to be expelled from the Garden, but it also caused them to be changed entirely by becoming thoroughly corrupt in spirit, mind, body, and soul.

Further, it opened the door for Satan (Lucifer renamed) to rule over the First Earth and for him and his cohorts to influence humankind to bring forth human misery, death, and destruction.

Importantly, however, God only allowed these fallen angels to bring this forth by indirect means. They were allowed to influence human beings but not allowed to take control of a person's freewill power.

Then the LORD said to Satan, *"Behold, all that he has is in your power, only do not put forth your hand on him."* (Job 1:12 NASB)

And Jesus said, *"I do not ask You to take them out of the world, but to keep them from the evil one."* (John 17:15 NASB)

Then God said, *"Let Us make man in Our image, according to Our likeness; and let them rule over the fish of the sea and over the birds of the sky and over the cattle and over all the earth, and over every creeping thing that creeps on the earth."* (Gen 1:26 NASB)

The 'rule' over creation that God had given to Adam & Eve was now given by Adam & Eve to Satan through obedience to Satan. And Satan and his cohorts used it to instill fear in all living creatures and wreak havoc and destruction over the earth through their influence on Adam & Eve.

Upon becoming aware of their fallen, corrupted state in the First Earth, Adam & Eve may have implored God to forgive them, remove their power to disobey, and return them to their original uncorrupted glorious state in the Garden.

However, it was too late. First, they would have to wait until they died physically to the First Earth and for their souls to go to Hades. Then, in Hades, they would await the Atonement of their sin to be made by Jesus the Son of Man.

Once Atonement had been made, they could ask God to remove their power to disobey and usher them to the New Earth, Paradise, where they would receive their new body and renewed soul. Alternatively, they could use their power to disobey to request Annihilation.

Why does a person have to wait until Hades to have their power to disobey removed? Why can a person's power to disobey not be removed in the First Earth, thereby eliminating them as a source of evil?

It may be that to remove a person's power to disobey in this world, however much they may desire, would leave the world untenably asymmetric, with one group of people able to disobey God and another group unable to do so.

However, God did not leave humankind alone and helpless in their fallen, corrupt state. God will send the Helper, the Holy Spirit, to come alongside that person and ease their burden when anyone asks.

That is, the Helper encourages and strengthens people in their struggle to resist temptation, and in that way, God helps lessen the amount of evil, hardship, pain, and suffering in the First Earth. And because God is yoked to them, when people fall into temptation, God is there to help them.

"And we know that God causes all things to work together for good to those who love God, to those who are called according to His purpose." (Romans 8:28 NASB*)*

However, even though God can bring something good out of evil, it is not to be understood that the reason for the evil events in the first place was so He can demonstrate mercy toward them.

These mercies express God's love and concern for His creatures and creation but only provide temporary relief in this life. The full expression of God's love and mercy toward a person awaits the removal of their power to disobey, followed by their acquiring a new human nature of spirit, mind, body, and soul, available in the New Earth. Only in the New Earth can an uncorrupted creature without the power to disobey dwell in perfect peace.

It may be that when people first arrive on the New Earth, they will undergo a period of healing.

"Then he showed me a river of the water of life, clear as crystal, coming from the throne of God and of the Lamb, in the middle of its street. On either side of the river was the tree of life, bearing twelve kinds of fruit, yielding its fruit every month; and the leaves of the tree were for the healing of the nations." (Rev 22:1,2 NASB*)*

After this period of healing, the New Person in the New Earth will be able to enjoy the fullness of living and working for all eternity in peace and harmony in the community of saints under the rule of, and in the presence of Jesus, Son of God and Son of Man, in the midst of the Beatific Vision of God in the New Heaven.

————————————

Addendum 10

Freewill Theism

https://www.en.wikipedia.org/wiki/Open_theism

Open theism, also known as openness theology and freewill theism, is a theological movement that has developed within Christianity as a rejection of the synthesis of Greek philosophy and Christian theology.

Open theism arises out of the freewill theistic tradition of the church, which goes back to the early church fathers.

Open theism is typically advanced as a biblically motivated and logically consistent theology of human and divine freedom (in the libertarian sense), emphasizing what this means for the content of God's foreknowledge and exercise of God's power.

While several versions of traditional theism picture God's knowledge of the future as a singular, fixed trajectory, open theism sees it as a plurality of branching possibilities. Some possibilities become settled as time moves forward. In short, open theism says that since God and humans are free, God's knowledge is dynamic and God's providence flexible.

Thus, the future and God's knowledge of it are open, hence the term 'open theism.'

Other versions of classical theism hold that God fully determines the future, entailing that there is no free choice (the future is closed). [Calvinism]

Yet other versions of classical theism hold that even though there is freedom of choice, God's omniscience necessitates God foreknowing what free choices are made (God's foreknowledge is closed). [Molinism]

Open Theists emphasize that God's most fundamental character trait is love and that this trait is unchangeable. They also (in contrast to traditional theism) tend to hold that the biblical portrait is of a God deeply moved by creation, experiencing a variety of feelings in response to it.

---

5 Ways the Bible Supports Open Theism
By Greg Boyd

https://reknew.org/2019/07/5-ways-the-bible-supports-open-theism/

July 9, 2019

Open Theism refers to the belief that God created a world in which possibilities are real. It contrasts with Classical Theism which holds that all the facts of world history are eternally settled, either by God willing them so (as in Calvinism) or simply in God's knowledge (as in Arminianism).

Open Theists believe God created humans and angels with free will and that these agents are empowered to have "say so" in what comes to pass. In Open Theism, therefore, what people decide to do genuinely affects God and affects what comes to pass. In particular, by God's own sovereign design, things really hang on whether or not God's people pray.

The primary reason Open Theists believe what they do is because they find that Scripture presents the future as partly open. While there are certainly passages that depict God predetermining and foreknowing some aspects of the future, there are at least as many passages depicting God as facing a future partly comprised of possibilities. A small sampling of these sorts of passages are the following:

1. The Lord frequently changes his mind in the light of changing circumstances, or as a result of prayer (Exod. 32:14; Num. 14:12–20; Deut. 9:13–14, 18–20, 25; 1 Sam. 2:27– 36; 2 Kings 20:1–7; 1 Chron. 21:15; Jer. 26:19; Ezek. 20:5–22; Amos 7:1–6; Jonah 1:2; 3:2, 4–10). At other times he explicitly states that he will change his mind if circumstances change (Jer. 18:7–11; 26:2–3; Ezek. 33:13–15). This willingness to change is portrayed as one of God's attributes of greatness (Joel 2:13–14; Jonah 4:2). If the future were exhaustively and eternally

settled, as classical theism teaches, it would be impossible for God to genuinely change his mind about matters.

2. God sometimes expresses regret and disappointment over how things turned out—even occasionally over things that resulted from his own will. (Gen. 6:5–6; 1 Sam. 15:10, 35; Ezek. 22:29–31). If the future was exhaustively and eternally settled, it would be impossible for God to genuinely regret how some of his own decisions turned out.

3. At other times God tells us that he is surprised at how things turned out because he expected a different outcome (Isa. 5:3–7; Jer. 3:6-7; 19–20). If the future were eternally and exhaustively settled, everything would come to pass exactly as God eternally knew or determined it to be.

4. The Lord frequently tests his people to find out whether they'll remain faithful to him (Gen. 22:12; Exod. 16:4; Deut. 8:2; 13:1–3; Judges 2:20–3:5; 2 Chron. 32:31). If the future were eternally and exhaustively settled, God could not genuinely say he tests people "to know" whether they'll be faithful or not.

5. The Lord sometimes asks non-rhetorical questions about the future (Num. 14:11; Hos. 8:5) and speaks to people in terms of what may or may not happen (Exod. 3:18–4:9; 13:17; Jer. 38:17–18, 20–21, 23; Ezek. 12:1–3). If the future were exhaustively and eternally settled, God could never genuinely speak about the future in terms of what "may" or "may not" happen.

So the Bible presents God as interacting with a world that is moving into a partly open future. This doesn't mean that God could ever be caught off guard or that his overall purposes for the world are ever threatened. Because they believe God is infinitely intelligent, Open Theists affirm that God anticipates each and every possibility from the foundation of the world, as though it were a certainty.

Whatever comes to pass, God has a plan in place to respond to it, bringing good out of evil when this is necessary. But, unlike Classical Theists, Open Theists are confident that God is so smart, he can sovereignly rule the world effectively without needing to have everything pre-settled in his will or mind ahead of time.

A Very Brief History of Open Theism
By Greg Boyd

https://reknew.org/2019/10/a-very-brief-history-of-open-theism/

October 29, 2019

While the open view of the future has always been a very minor perspective, it has had its defenders throughout Church history and it has never been called "heresy" (until in mid 1990s when some started using this label).

According to some African American church leaders, it has been the predominant view in the African American Christian tradition (e.g., in The Color of God: The Concept of God in Afro- American Thought [Mercer Press, 1987]. Major Jones argues that the African Christian experience of oppression has enabled them to seize a dimension of the biblical portrait of God which the classical western tradition missed because of its overemphasis on control and its indebtedness to platonic philosophy).

More research needs to be done on the history of the open view, but my own research thus far has found advocates as far back as the fourth century (e.g., Calcidius). What's most interesting about Calcidius is that his view is espoused in his Commentary on Plato's Timaeus, which was used extensively throughout the middle ages. Yet, so far as I've been able to discern, no middle scholar thought his view was heretical enough to comment on.

In the early eighteenth century, a man named Samuel Fancourt published an essay entitled Concerning Liberty Grace and Prescience which led to a good deal of discussion about the topic in England. His arguments largely parallel those used by Openness advocates today. Also, it appears that Andrew Ramsay, a contemporary of John Wesley, espoused the teaching that God doesn't know the future strictly as a domain of settled facts.

The topic was much discussed in the nineteenth century, being advocated by the renowned Bible commentator Adam Clarke, the popular Methodist circuit preacher Billy Hubbard, and some within the Stone-Campbell Restoration movement such T.W. Brents, whose 1874 book The Gospel Plan of Salvation puts the Open View of the future on center stage. This book was widely used as a theology textbook in the Stone-Campbell movement. On top of this, the Methodist professor and chancellor of Ohio Wesleyan University, L. D. McCabe, wrote several books espousing Open Theism on biblical as well as philosophical grounds.

At the turn of the century, the view was espoused by Finnis Dennings Dake, author of the famous and influential Dakes Annotated Bible. The view had occasional defenders throughout the twentieth century and became a standard teaching among the early founders of Youth With a Mission.

This is brief (very brief) history only hits the highlights. But it demonstrates that the open view of the future has been a part of historic orthodoxy. The modern expression, propelled in an accessible form through the publication of The Openness of God by Clark Pinnock and others, falls in line with Protestant thought of theological reform. The entire Protestant movement has been rooted in the conviction that the church always needs more reforming, and whether particular theological claims contribute to this on-going reformation or not needs to be tested against Scripture.

Unfulfilled Prophecies and the Open Future
By Greg Boyd

https://www.reknew.org/2008/12/unfulfilled-prophecies-and-the-open-future

December 2, 2008

I've been reading Volume II of John Goldingay's excellent two volume work, Old Testament Theology, 2 Vols (IVP, 2006). Among other things, Goldingay highlights an important, but almost universally overlooked, aspect of Old Testament prophecy.

In sharp contrast to the standard ancient Greek view of prophecy, inspired prophecies in the Old Testament (and, I would add, at least one in the New Testament, see Ac 21:10-11, cf. 26-33) are not always fulfilled, at least not in the exact way they were originally prophesied.

For example, Jeremiah prophesied that Jehoiakim would die a dishonorable death. It is said that no one would mourn for him and that his corpse would be dragged around and thrown outside the gates of Jerusalem, left unburied to decompose in the sun (Jere. 22:18-19, cf. 36:30).

Not only this, but it was prophesied that no descendent of his would sit on the throne (Jere. 36:30-31). As it turned out, however, Jehoiakim received a proper burial and his son succeeded him as king (2 Kg. 24:6). What are we to make of this?

Something similar is true of Jeremiah's prophecy to Zedekiah. Jeremiah declares to Zedekiah that the Lord says "You will not die by the sword" but will rather "die peacefully." The Lord adds that people will mourn his death (Jere. 34:4-5). As it turned out, however, Zedekiah was captured by the Babylonians, had his eyes plucked out and died in prison (Jere. 52:8-11).

What's most interesting is that both the prophecy and the record of events revealing that it wasn't fulfilled are included in the same book, demonstrating that Jeremiah and/or the compilers of this work weren't at all bothered by the fact that the prophecy didn't come to pass.

Perhaps most impressively, in Ezekiel 26-28 we find a lengthy prophecy against the city of Tyre. It is said that Nebuchadnezzar, King of Babylon, would utterly defeat Tyre, killing its inhabitants, plundering all its wealth and leveling all its walls so that it ends up being flat as a rock.

Indeed, it is prophesied that it would virtually vanish from the earth and never be found again. Well, it didn't quite happen that way, as Goldingay notes.

Nebuchadnezzar did lay siege to Tyre, but, while he did gain some control of the city, it was "nowhere near as decisive as Ezekiel had implied" (Old Testament Theology, Vol. II, 83). The city wasn't completely conquered and laid flat until Alexander did this several hundred years later.

Because his campaign failed, Nebuchadnezzar failed to get much of Tyre's wealth. So, says Goldingay, Yahweh made " a new decision." He decided to turn Egypt over to him in order to repay him for his expenses in his "vain effort" to take Tyre (Ezek. 29:17-20; Goldingay, ibid.,84).

The amazing thing is that this campaign also seems to have failed! Nebuchadnezzar invaded Egypt, but "the achievement did not amount to conquest" (op.cit.).

As with Jeremiah, Goldingay is impressed with the fact that Ezekiel and/or the compilers of this work seem totally untroubled by these"unfulfilled" prophecies. He surmises that this is due to the fact that, despite Ezekiel's strong emphasis on divine sovereignty, he accepts that "human beings exercise real freedom in the world and do not have to cooperate with God's will."

The prophecies announce God's plan, but as Goldingay repeatedly emphasizes, a plan is not an unalterable script. When humans resist his will, Yahweh "reworks the plan" rather than coercively bulldoze over them (op. cit.)

When the Old Testament speaks of a divine plan therefore, "this is not a design for the detail of history…but an intention for the present context."

So, Goldingay concludes, "The assumption that everything that happens in the world emerges from God's plan stands in contrast with the more concrete way in which the Scriptures speak of God's plan. God's plan refers to the way God works out specific details of an overall vision as decades unfold, in interaction with human actions." (ibid., 85).

The phenomenon of unfulfilled prophecy tells us a lot about how different ancient Hebrews viewed prophecy from the way ancient Greeks viewed it and the way most today view it. It also reveals how flexible the sovereign Lord is in his dealings with humans as free agents (on this, see also Jere. 18:1-10).

Though Goldingay doesn't draw this conclusion, I would suggest that the phenomenon of unfulfilled prophecies implies that the future is somewhat open and that the omniscient God knows it as such.

At the very least, it seems to me the Open View of the future can accommodate unfulfilled prophecies much easier than the classical view in which all facts about the future are eternally settled and known by God as such.

Think about it.

The Open View of Messianic Prophesies
By Greg Boyd

https://reknew.org/2015/02/the-open-view-of-messianic-prophesies/

February 16, 2015

A number of passages speak of particular events being foreknown by God, even events resulting from individuals' freewill. For example, dozens of prophesies in the OT accurately predict details about the coming Messiah (e.g., he would be born in Bethlehem; arise out of the lineage of Abraham; be executed with criminals; have his side pierced; be buried with the rich; atone for the sins of many). Most of these predictions seem to involve future free decisions of individuals.

How are the messianic prophesies possible unless God possesses exhaustive definite foreknowledge?

In point of fact, however, these passages present no difficulty for the view of the future which is partly open. While the open view holds that humans must be free to the extent that they are capable of love, this freedom obviously has limits. Indeed, the concept of freedom is only meaningful against a backdrop of limited determinism.

Our freedom is conditioned (but not extinguished) by our genes, our environment, our previous choices and acquired character, and most certainly God's will. The open view of the future thus affirms that many aspects of the future are determined either by God or by inevitable consequences of present causes.

It is therefore compatible with the biblical portrait of God as the sovereign Lord of history who knows all settled aspects of the future ahead of time, and who is able to determine whatever he wants to ahead of time to accomplish his objectives. There is therefore no logical problem in reconciling the biblical truth that the Lord predestined and foreknew various details about the Messiah.

However, in Acts 2:23 and 4:28, God seems to predestine a wicked deed (crucifying Jesus) while at the same time holding the perpetrators responsible for it. Does this undermine the claim that morally responsible free acts cannot be part of the future that is settled? Two points.

First, neither of these passages suggest that the individuals who crucified Jesus were predestined and foreknown. These verses only affirm that it was preordained and foreknown that the Messiah would be crucified. That Jesus would be killed was predetermined. Who would do it was not. As long as God knew that in certain circumstances there would be a certain percentage of people who would act as the wicked people spoken of in these passages acted, he could predestine and thus foreknow that the Messiah would be crucified without undermining the freedom of any individuals.

Second, the open view affirms that God at times predestines certain acts of wicked individuals, while denying that this predestining occurred before these individuals had freely resolved their own character. God would be morally culpable if he predestined people to carry out wicked acts prior to their birth. But he is not morally culpable if he chooses to direct the path of people who have already made themselves wicked.

Moral responsibility applies to the acquired character of self-determining agents even more fundamentally than it applies to the particular decisions agents make which reflect and reinforce their character. There is no contradiction in the claim that a person is morally responsible for an act even though they could not have done otherwise, so long as the character that now rendered their action certain flowed from a character they themselves acquired. It was not "infused" into them by God.

Hence, a person who has solidified his character as a greedy person by making multitudes of free decisions is morally culpable not only for all the further greedy acts he performs but also and even more fundamentally for being the kind of person he has freely become.

Moral culpability is not just about people acting certain ways when they could have and should have acted differently. It's more about people becoming certain kinds of people when they could have and should have become different kinds of people. If God decides that it fits his providential plan to use a person whose choices have solidified his character as wicked, God is not responsible for this person's wickedness.

One final illustration: Scripture suggests that the Messiah's betrayal was predestined and Jesus foreknew that Judas would betray him (John 6:64, 70-71, 13:18-19). This doesn't contradict the view that morally responsible, self-determining actions cannot be predestined or foreknown as long as Judas was not in particular chosen to carry out this deed before Judas had made himself into the kind of person who would carry out this deed.

After Judas unfortunately hardened himself into this kind of person, God wove his character into a providential plan. Jesus could then foreknow that Judas would be the one to betray him. But nothing suggests that it was God's plan from eternity that Judas would play this role.

—Adapted from *Satan and the Problem of Evil* (2001), pgs 119-123

What Unfulfilled Prophesies Say About the Open View
By Greg Boyd

http://www.reknew.org/2015/02/what-unfulfilled-prophesies-say-about-the-open-view

Yesterday, we posted about how Messianic prophesies are understood in the open view of the future. Today, this post will look at prophesies that are not fulfilled in the way predicted and what that can tell us about the open view of the future.

In John Goldingay's excellent multi-volume work, Old Testament Theology, he highlights an important, but almost universally overlooked, aspect of Old Testament prophecy.

In sharp contrast to the standard ancient Greek view of prophecy, inspired prophecies in the Old Testament (and, I would add, at least one in the New Testament, see Ac 21:10-11, cf. 26-33) are not always fulfilled, at least not in the exact way they were originally prophesied.

For example, Jeremiah prophesied that Jehoiakim would die a dishonorable death. It is said that no one would mourn for him and that his corpse would be dragged around and thrown outside the gates of Jerusalem, left unburied to decompose in the sun (Jer 22:18-19, cf.36:30).

Not only this, but it was prophesied that no descendent of his would sit on the throne (Jer. 36:30-31). As it turned out, however, Jehoiakim received a proper burial and his son succeeded him as king (2 Kg. 24:6). What are we to make of this?

Something similar is true of Jeremiah's prophecy to Zedekiah. Jeremiah declares to Zedekiah that the Lord says "You will not die by the sword" but will rather "die peacefully." The Lord adds that people will mourn his death (Jer. 34:4-5). As it turned out, however, Zedekiah was captured by the Babylonians, had his eyes plucked out and died in prison (Jer. 52:8-11).

What's most interesting is that both the prophecy and the record of events revealing that it wasn't fulfilled are included in the same book, demonstrating that Jeremiah and/or the compilers of this work weren't at all bothered by the fact that the prophecy didn't come to pass.

Perhaps most impressively, in Ezekiel 26-28 we find a lengthy prophecy against the city of Tyre. It is said that Nebuchadnezzar, King of Babylon, would utterly defeat Tyre, killing its inhabitants, plundering all its wealth and leveling all its walls so that it ends up being flat as a rock. Indeed, it is prophesied that it would virtually vanish from the earth and never be found again. Well, it didn't quite happen that way, as Goldingay notes.

Nebuchadnezzar did lay siege to Tyre, but, while he did gain some control of the city, it was "nowhere near as decisive as Ezekiel had implied" (Old Testament Theology, Vol. II, 83). The city wasn't completely conquered and laid flat until Alexander did this several hundred years later.

Because his campaign failed, Nebuchadnezzar failed to get much of Tyre's wealth. So, says Goldingay, Yahweh made " a new decision." He decided to turn Egypt over to him in order to repay him for his expenses in his "vain effort" to take Tyre (Ezek. 29:17-20; Goldingay, ibid., 84). The amazing thing is that this campaign also seems to have failed! Nebuchadnezzar invaded Egypt, but "the achievement did not amount to conquest" (op.cit.),

As with Jeremiah, Goldingay is impressed with the fact that Ezekiel and/or the compilers of this work seem totally untroubled by these "unfulfilled" prophecies. He surmises that this is due to the fact that, despite Ezekiel's strong emphasis on divine sovereignty, he accepts that "human beings exercise real freedom in the world and do not have to cooperate with God's will." The prophecies announce God's plan, but as Goldingay repeatedly emphasizes, a plan is not an unalterable script.

When humans resist his will, Yahweh "reworks the plan" rather than coercively bulldoze over them (op. cit.) When the Old Testament speaks of a divine plan therefore, "this is not a design for the detail of history…but an intention for the present context."

So, Goldingay concludes, "The assumption that everything that happens in the world emerges from God's plan stands in contrast with the more concrete way in which the Scriptures speak of God's plan. God's plan refers to the way God works out specific details of an overall vision as decades unfold, in interaction with human actions." (ibid., 85).

The phenomenon of unfulfilled prophecy tells us a lot about how different ancient Hebrews viewed prophecy from the way ancient Greeks viewed it and the way most today view it. It also reveals how flexible the sovereign Lord is in his dealings with humans as free agents (on this, see also Jere. 18:1-10).

Though Goldingay doesn't draw this conclusion, I would suggest that the phenomenon of unfulfilled prophecies implies that the future is somewhat open and that the omniscient God knows it as such.

At the very least, it seems to me the Open View of the future can accommodate unfulfilled prophecies much easier than the classical view in which all facts about the future are eternally settled and known by God as such.

Addendum 11

The Future Has Not Been Decided

What is the difference between classical Newtonian physics and modern Quantum physics?

Classical physics is generally regarded as deterministic or causal. Complete knowledge of the past and present allows for complete and comprehensive knowledge of the future.

Quantum physics introduced genuine uncertainty into physics, uncertain knowledge of the future. Given complete knowledge of the past, only probabilistic predictions of the future can be made.

Experiment after experiment has shown that Nature works according to the rules of Quantum physics.

Addendum 12

God in Heaven Before the Rebellion
A Highly Speculative Account

Before the beginning, there was God the Father, God the Holy Spirit, and God the Son in Heaven. And it is understood here that God the Holy Spirit is God the Mother. See: Addenda 4 The Genders of God

Together, Mother, Father, and Jesus the Son of God are the "uncaused cause" of all things that exist, and They began the chain of existence ex nihilo.

"For by Him all things were created, both in the heavens and on earth, visible and invisible, whether thrones or dominions or rulers or authorities -all things have been created through Him and for Him. He is before all things, and in Him all things hold together." (Colossians 1:16,17 NASB)

Then, God Begat Jesus the Son of Man into existence, as it was in God's heart and mind to provide a Home and a bride for Jesus.

The Home is Paradise, beginning with the First Heaven and First Earth, the Garden of Eden, and ending with the New Heaven and New Earth.

And the bride is all of Humanity created in the image of God, male and female they were made, starting with Adam & Eve.

Also, the Angels were created in Heaven to serve God, and to love, obey, and serve Jesus and His bride in Paradise.

Addendum 13

Angels in Heaven Before the Rebellion
A Highly Speculative Account

God created the angels in Heaven to serve God and serve Jesus the Son of Man and His bride in their work to subdue and rule in Paradise.

"God blessed them; and God said to them, "Be fruitful and multiply, and fill the earth, and subdue it; and rule over the fish of the sea and over the birds of the sky and over every living thing that moves on the earth." (Genesis 1:28 NASB*)*

And God explained to the angels that for them to be truly free to serve and obey Jesus they were created with the power to disobey. For obedience to be real, there has to be the possibility of disobedience.

And God also explained that for them to be truly free to obey or disobey, He had to relinquish His power to know beforehand what they would choose to do. He could know everything they were doing or had done, but not what they would do so that their choice would be valid.

To test their willingness to obey Jesus, God would tell them what they should do, and to test their willingness to disobey Jesus, God would tell them what they should not do.

To this end, they were created to think and feel what it would be like to obey or disobey Jesus.

And God explained further that these thoughts and feelings to disobey were a kind of suffering, a warning of danger ahead. But that this suffering was nothing compared to the suffering they would experience if they disobeyed.

God also explained that He would never tempt them to disobey. He only ever wanted them to obey Jesus and His bride in their lives and work in Paradise.

God then told the angels that they could escape this suffering of temptation by asking God to remove their power to disobey.

"God is faithful, who will not allow you to be tempted beyond what you are able, but with the temptation will provide the way of escape also, so that you will be able to endure it" (1 Corinthians 10:13 NASB*)*

(Although this Scripture was given later to people, it is conceivable that God would have instructed the angels in Heaven in the same way.)

And once God had removed their power to disobey, they would no longer suffer from temptation. Since they could no longer give in to it, temptation would have served its purpose and ceased to exist for all practical matters.

God also explained that if they ever disobeyed God, they would be expelled from Heaven, with no possibility of returning.

And God explained that even though they would never again be able to disobey, they would still be able to obey in the many ways provided. They would not be like robots, only able to obey when and as directed.

However, the Arch Angel Lucifer considered himself superior to Jesus and more worthy than Jesus to rule and reign in Paradise.

He rebelled at the thought of leading the angels in the building of Paradise for Jesus; he wanted it for himself. He wanted to be the god of Paradise.

Therefore, he refused to have his power to disobey removed and willfully led angels in a rebellion against God, and they were expelled from Heaven.

However, many more angels, witnessing this rebellion and not wanting to be expelled, but wanting to escape the suffering of temptation, demonstrated their love for God by asking that their power to disobey be removed, and God granted their request.

Also, a few angels requested annihilation. God granted them their request after doing everything possible to persuade them to change their minds, but without going so far as to overrule their power to disobey.

By the end of the rebellion, about two-thirds of the angels remained in Heaven. In this way, these good angels showed their love for God by laying down their lives for God by freely asking God to remove their power to disobey, thereby escaping any further suffering of temptation.

———————————————

Addendum 14

The ReKnew Manifesto
By Greg Boyd

https://www.reknew.org/2012/07/a-reknew-manifesto

July 18, 2012

As our curious name indicates, ReKnew exists to encourage believers and skeptics alike to re-think things they thought they already knew.

We want to promote a beautiful, Jesus-looking vision of God and his kingdom. We want to promote a host of related theological convictions that we believe were compromised or lost in traditional Christianity— especially since the 5th century when the Church first acquired political power and became the religion of "Christendom."

And we want to be a catalytic resource for the new tribe of Jesus-followers who are rising up and re-thinking their faith now that Christendom—which has been dying for over a century—is gasping its last breaths.

This does not mean we aren't deeply appreciative for the multitude of true and beautiful aspects of the Church throughout history. To the contrary, we believe that all theological reflection should be humbly carried out in a respectful dialogue with the Church tradition.

Yet the focus of ReKnew is to challenge those aspects of the tradition we don't believe are consistent with the movement Jesus birthed, and with the teachings of the New Testament.

What follows is an overview of these core convictions stated in their simplest form. You might think of this as the first draft of a "ReKnew Manifesto."

1. ReThink the Source of Life

Because traditional Christianity has often held that people get right with God by believing the right things, many Christians tend to get their "life" (their core sense of identity, worth, significance and being loved) from the rightness of their beliefs (as discussed here).

Our conviction is that followers of Jesus should get all of their "life" from the love that God has shown them on Calvary. Every other source of "life"—including the rightness of our beliefs—is an idol.

2. ReThink the Nature of Faith

Many Christians throughout history (and still today) have assumed that a person's faith is only as strong as the degree to which they feel certainty and free from doubt.

Likewise, many have assumed faith is opposed to reason, antithetical to historical-critical approaches to Scripture, and at odds with much of the scientific enterprise—especially evolutionary theory.

Our conviction is that faith is not the absence of doubt, but the willingness to commit to a course of action even though one is not certain. However, that is not to say faith is irrational. While faith always goes beyond reason, we don't believe it should ever go against it.

We thus believe Jesus-followers should never be afraid of wrestling with biblical criticism, evolutionary theory, or any other field of rational inquiry.

Along the same lines, we do not believe the goal of faith is to arrive at a point at which we convince ourselves we possess all the right beliefs, and therefore close off further inquiry.

Rather, when we get all our "life" from Christ (and not from the rightness of our beliefs), and when we understand that faith is not the absence of doubt, we are free to view faith instead as a process of honest, open-ended inquiry.

It's our conviction that the fearful, dogmatic rigidity that characterizes so much of contemporary Evangelicalism reflects an idolatrous relationship with beliefs, which in turn causes many to become hostile and unloving when debating doctrinal issues.

We are convinced God is more concerned with the love with which we debate than the content of what we debate.

3. ReThink Our Picture of God

The dominant image of God espoused in the religion of Christendom has been a composite picture in which the revelation of God in Christ has been fused with violent images derived from the Old Testament, as well as other philosophical sources.

Our conviction is that Jesus is the one and only perfect revelation of God's true nature (Hebrews 1:3). Jesus doesn't merely reveal part of what God is like. Rather, the fullness of God is in Christ, and revealed through Christ (Colossians 1:19; 2:9). As Jesus himself tells us, when we see him, we see the very character of the Father (John 14:7-9).

Moreover, it's our conviction that Jesus' self-sacrificial death on the cross expresses the theme that weaves everything Jesus was about together. From his incarnation, to his ministry, to his ascension, Jesus reveals the truth that God's nature is other-oriented, self- sacrificial love.

We thus believe that all of our thinking about God, as well as all of our reading of Scripture, must be done through the lens of the cross and with this cruciform understanding of God's love.

4. ReThink the Kingdom of God

Once the Church was given political power in the 4th and 5th century, it has more often than not looked like a "Christianized" version of the kingdoms of the world, often relying on political and military power to advance its own self-interest.

As the one sinless person in history, we believe Jesus is the one and only perfect reflection of what it looks like for God to fully reign over a person's life. Jesus is thus the perfect embodiment of "the kingdom of God" (the "dome" over which God reigns).

We at ReKnew therefore believe Jesus-followers are individually and corporately called and empowered by the Spirit to look like Jesus and reflect God's humble, self- sacrificial love toward all people. To the extent that an individual or group doesn't look like Jesus, the kingdom of God is not present—regardless of what the individual or group professes to believe.

Given the massive harm that has been done throughout Church history when the Church has become too closely aligned with versions of the kingdom of the world, and given that the Church continues to be co-opted by political regimes (especially in America), we believe it's vital that Jesus-followers today strive to keep the kingdom "holy"—which means separate and distinct from the kingdoms of the world.

Of course we are called to assume responsibility for poverty, side with the oppressed, and fight injustice as well as all other social ills. But the way followers of Jesus are to do this is not by telling governments what they should do. We are to do it the way Jesus did it—by sacrificing our time, energy, and resources on behalf of others.

5. ReThink Providence

The dominant image of God within Christendom after Augustine (5th century) has been that of an all-controlling deity. The Church has therefore tended to espouse a "blueprint worldview" in which it has assumed every event that comes to pass conforms to a meticulous "blueprint" God had before the creation of the world.

In this view, God wills (or at least allows) every particular event for a specific good reason—including each and every evil.

Our conviction is that the cross reveals the kind of power on which God relies: not power over others, but power under others. It is the power of self-sacrificial love— which is the greatest power there is, for it alone is able to transform hearts.

Along with every church father before Augustine, therefore, our conviction is that "God is a God of persuasion, not coercion"—as Irenaeus (2nd century) put it.

While God remains in control of the big picture, we believe God has given humans and angels freewill, which means we have a degree of "say-so" over what comes to pass. We can either use that "say-so" to further God's purposes, or to resist them.

As such, we believe all evil is the result of the misuse of created freewills, whether human or angelic.

In place of the "blueprint worldview," therefore, we advocate a "warfare worldview" in which the creation is viewed as a battlefield between God and Satan, along with all created human and angelic agents who align themselves with one or the other.

Moreover, since creation includes free agents who have the power to resolve possible courses of actions into actual events, we believe the future is partly comprised of possibilities and that the all-knowing God therefore knows them as such. Yet, because God is infinitely intelligent and can anticipate future possibilities as effectively as certainties, we don't believe God loses any providential advantage.

Whatever comes to pass, God had been preparing a plan, from all eternity, on how he would bring good out of it in case it came to pass. So while we don't believe everything happens for a good purpose, we believe everything happens with a good purpose—namely, the eternally prepared good purpose God had in place in case any given event came to pass.

6. ReThink the Atonement

The majority of Evangelicals today believe that the main significance of what Christ has done on the cross (the atonement) is that he satisfied the Father's wrath against sin by being punished in our place, thereby allowing the Father to accept us despite our sin.

While the Church has always understood that Jesus died in our place, as our substitute, the depiction of the Father venting his wrath on Jesus instead of on us — the "penal substitution" view of the atonement — originated with Calvin and Luther.

The Church has always embraced a variety of atonement theories, but it's worth noting that the "Christus Victor" view of the atonement was the dominant view for the first 1000 years of Church history. This view holds that "[t]he reason the Son of God appeared was to destroy the works of the devil" (1 John3:8; Heb.2:14), which in turn liberated humanity and all creation from his oppression and reconciled everything to God.

With the historic-orthodox Church, we affirm that Jesus died as our substitute and experienced the death-consequences of sin in our place. But we do not believe this means the Father needed to "satisfy" his own wrath by violently pouring it out on his Son in order to forgive us and reconcile us to himself.

And while we affirm that Christ accomplished a variety of things by his life and death and resurrection, we believe that Christ's victory over Satan and the powers of darkness lies at the base of them all.

We thus consider the "Christus Victor" view of the atonement to be the foundation to all other views.

7. ReThink Salvation

With the rise of the penal substitution view of the atonement, the western church began to think of salvation increasingly in legal categories. God has thus come to be viewed as the judge, humans as the guilty defendants, and Jesus as our defense attorney who allows us to be acquitted by suffering our sentence in our place.

As a result, salvation has come to be thought of primarily as an acquittal (escaping hell) that people receive when they simply believe that Jesus did this for us.

Among the many unfortunate consequences of this view is the fact that Christianity has become much more focused on how we benefit from what God has done for us in the afterlife than it is focused on the beautiful things God wants to do in our present life—the relationship God wants with us, the character that God wants to cultivate in us, and the things God wants to accomplish through us now.

304

While legal metaphors are sometimes used to express salvation in the New Testament, the dominant way of expressing it is as a covenant—like marriage. Salvation, in our view, is not primarily about being acquitted by God, or about the afterlife.

Rather, salvation is about becoming part of "the bride of Christ" and participating in—and being transformed by—the fullness of God's life that he opens up for us in the present. For this reason, salvation is not merely about believing in Jesus; it's even more profoundly about being empowered to follow Jesus' example.

Salvation thus cannot be divorced from the call to follow Jesus' example of loving enemies and refraining from violence; of caring for the poor, the oppressed, and the marginalized. It's about manifesting God's fullness of life by cultivating a counter-cultural lifestyle that revolts against every aspect of society that is inconsistent with the character of God and his will for the world.

It's about living and praying in a way that actualizes the fullness of the Lord's prayer that the Father's will would be done "on earth as it is in heaven" (Matthew 6:10).

9.   ReThink Hell

The earliest Christians understood "hell" in several different ways. Some viewed it as annihilation, others as eternal conscious suffering, and others redemptive process that will result in everyone being saved ("universalism"). After Augustine however, the view of hell as eternal conscious suffering became dominant. Annihilationism quickly became a marginal view and universalism was eventually officially condemned.

In light of the love that God has revealed for all humans in Christ, we are convinced that if there is any way that God could save all, he most certainly would save all.

Moreover, we don't see how anyone who genuinely loves all people—as Christ commands and empowers us to do—could fail to hope that God's love will eventually rescue and transform everyone. At the same time, our belief in freewill rules out the Universalist's belief that there will come a time when everyone must be saved. Moreover, we don't see in Scripture sufficient warrant for being confident that all will be saved.

What is more certain to us is that the fire of God's love will salvage and purify everything in a person that is consistent with God's loving character and will burn up (metaphorically speaking) everything that is not.

If it unfortunately turns out that people can sink to the point where there is nothing salvageable, it's our conviction God will justly, yet mercifully, withdraw his sustaining hand, allowing them to return to nothingness – "as though they had never been" (Obadiah 16).

When Scripture speaks of hell as "eternal," we believe this most likely refers to the effect of this punishment, not the duration of anyone's experience of it.

However, we are convinced that what is more important than the particular views we hold is the manner in which we hold them.

Since the biblical material on this topic is ambiguous, and since the witness of the early church is not uniform on this matter, we encourage Jesus- followers today to not christen their own view as the orthodox view, but rather to allow all views to be entertained and lovingly debated.

10. ReThink Humanity

Against the long-standing patriarchal mindset of the Church tradition, ReKnew is passionate about encouraging husbands and wives to assume an egalitarian mindset in their marriages, and passionate about urging local Church communities to empower women to serve in any leadership capacity for which they are gifted and called to serve.

So too, against the ethnocentrism of the western Church tradition, we believe Jesus died to create "one new humanity" (Ephesians 2:15) that has done away with the separating walls erected from the curse of Babel.

Racial reconciliation is thus not something a church can choose to engage in or not. We believe it is one of the reasons for which Jesus died and that it must therefore be proclaimed and practiced by all followers of Jesus.

Conclusion

This is, in a nutshell, what ReKnew stands for. There are a host of other beliefs and practices ReKnew hopes to challenge people to reconsider that need not necessarily be elaborated in this "manifesto."

We of course don't expect all who get onboard with ReKnew to agree with each and every particular thing we espouse.

But if you're one of those who believe it's time to thoroughly re-think the Christian faith—especially our picture of God and our understanding of his kingdom—we are here to help you do that and to help build a network of like-minded, open-minded, passionate disciples.

———————————

Addendum 15

Another Argument Against Molinism

Luis de Molina was a 16th-century Spanish Jesuit theologian and philosopher who lived about thirty years after John Calvin, and he took exception to Calvin's teaching on divine sovereignty and human libertarian freedom.

Calvin believed that God's omniscience included perfect knowledge of all events past, present, and future. God, from His perspective, sees the past, present, and future of the world as altogether one thing, an eternal now. Rational thinking would lead people to reject a good and just God who predestines and foreknows every event and yet condemns people to Hell.

Calvin's response was his willingness to accept that God is responsible for the entry of evil into the world. However, he maintained that God could not be blamed for it since He uses evil to bring about a great good that He could not achieve were it not for the evil.

Consequently, Molina proposes to go further than Calvin and attempts to remove from God all responsibility for evil since to think otherwise would detract from God's glory.

Molinists argue that God sovereignly and perfectly accomplishes His will in the lives of genuinely free individuals through the use of His omniscience. To be clear, Molina means specifically that God's detailed and absolute knowledge of the future applies to the future choices of individuals who have libertarian freedom. Molinism is an attempt to hold fast the attribute of God's meticulous foreknowledge regarding all future human choices while at the same time maintaining libertarian freedom for those same humans.

In support of his thesis, Molina advanced the following three texts: 1 Samuel 23:8-14, Proverbs 4:11, and Matthew 11:23.

Prominent Molinist William Lane Craig calls Molinism one of the most fruitful theological ideas ever conceived, because it serves to explain not only God's meticulous foreknowledge of the future, but divine

308

providence and predestination as well. Craig cites the following passages: Matthew 17:27, John 21:6, John 15:22-24, John 18:36, Luke 4:24-44 and Matthew 26:24.

Suppose these texts better apply to groups of individuals rather than to individuals within the group. And suppose that predicting the behavior of a group is different from predicting the behavior of individuals within the group. If these Scriptures better apply to groups of individuals, rather than individuals within the group, then his attempt to remove from God all responsibility for evil would seem to fail.

The question is, do the following supporting Scriptures refer to:
a) Individuals within a group or a group of individuals.
b) Miracles having nothing to do with libertarian freedom of individuals.
c) Nothing having to do with human libertarian freedom.
d) General principals aside from human libertarian freedom.

Of all these supporting Scriptures, it would seem that only 1 Sam 23:11 refers to knowing what a specific individual, Saul, would have done in a future situation. However, anyone who knew Saul at that time could probably guess that he would go against David. The remainder of these Scriptures seems to refer to groups of individuals.

Biblical Texts Supporting Molinism

1 Samuel 23:8-14
11 "Will the men of Keilah surrender me into his hand? Will Saul come down just as Your servant has heard? O LORD God of Israel, I pray, tell Your servant." And the LORD said, "He will come down."
12 Then David said, "Will the men of Keilah surrender me and my men into the hand of Saul?" And the LORD said, "They will surrender you."

Proverbs 4:11
11 I have directed you in the way of wisdom; I have led you in upright paths.

Matthew 11:23
23 "And you, Capernaum, will not be exalted to heaven, will you? You will descend to Hades; for if the miracles had occurred in Sodom which occurred in you, it would have remained to this day.

Matthew 17:27
27 "However, so that we do not offend them, go to the sea and throw in a hook, and take the first fish that comes up; and when you open its mouth, you will find a shekel. Take that and give it to them for you and Me."

John 21:6
6 And He said to them, "Cast the net on the right-hand side of the boat and you will find a catch." So they cast, and then they were not able to haul it in because of the great number of fish.

John 15:22-24
22 "If I had not come and spoken to them, they would not have sin, but now they have no excuse for their sin.
23 "He who hates Me hates My Father also.
24 "If I had not done among them the works which no one else did, they would not have sin; but now they have both seen and hated Me and My Father as well.

John 18:36
36 Jesus answered, "My kingdom is not of this world. If My kingdom were of this world, then My servants would be fighting so that I would not be handed over to the Jews; but as it is, My kingdom is not of this realm."

Luke 4:24-44
24 And He said, "Truly I say to you, no prophet is welcome in his hometown.

Matthew 26:24
24 "The Son of Man is to go, just as it is written of Him; but woe to that man by whom the Son of Man is betrayed! It would have been good for that man if he had not been born."

Can an analogy from the physical world be used to support the proposition that describing the behavior of a group of individuals is different from describing the behavior of individuals within the group?

Classical Physics applies to macroscopic particles like a coin or a chair. In contrast, Quantum Physics applies to microscopic particles, such as the atoms which make up a coin or a chair.

Quantum Physics states that if one knows a microscopic particle's precise momentum, it is impossible to know its precise position, and vice versa. Therefore, all of the properties of a microscopic system cannot be known simultaneously. In contrast, all of the properties of a macroscopic system, say a coin, can be known quite well at the same time.

Properties of a macroscopic system can be considered something like the average of the microscopic systems' properties. When there are many microscopic particles, predictions of the properties of the macroscopic system become significant; the greater the number of microscopic particles, the more significant the prediction.

Suppose the properties of a macroscopic physical system can be thought analogous to the behavior of a group of individuals, and the properties of a microscopic physical system analogous to the behavior of individuals who make up that group.

From this analogy, the behavior of a group of individuals is not necessarily a good indicator of how individuals within that group would behave. The actions of a group can be predicted quite well, especially by God, whereas individuals within the group can have true libertarian freedom.

Addendum 16

Process Theology

In recent times, Process Theology and its associated Theodicy have gained support among Christian theologians, philosophers, and Christian scientists. It is a derivative of Irenaeanism in that it espouses a gradual development of human beings toward a perfection of the human character and Christlikeness.

One reason it has gained this support is its effort to reconcile the science of Darwin's theory of evolution, with the Biblical account of the origin and development of life on earth.

BioLogos, founded by Francis Collins, is currently one of those organizations at or near the front of this reconciliation effort. BioLogos explores God's Word and God's World to inspire authentic faith for today.

What is BioLogos?
https://biologos.org/common-questions/what-is-evolutionary-creation

Evolutionary Creation (EC) as taken from the BioLogos website.

EC is a Christian position on origins. It takes the Bible seriously as the inspired and authoritative word of God, and it takes science seriously as a way of understanding the world God has made. EC includes two basic ideas. First, that God created all things, including human beings in his own image. Second, that evolution is the best scientific explanation we currently have for the diversity and similarities of all life on Earth.

God Is the Creator – Evolution Is Compelling Science

So what are the central ideas that define EC? ECs believe that God created and sustains all things. We believe that God acts purposefully in creation, just as he does in our lives, and that he continues to actively uphold and sustain creation. We believe in the Trinity, the full divinity and full humanity of Jesus Christ, and the bodily resurrection of Jesus Christ from the dead. We believe that all humans are made in the image of God and all humans have a sinful nature. We believe in salvation by grace through faith in Christ alone.

ECs accept evolution as the best scientific explanation we have for how life on Earth has changed over time. In biology, evolution refers to "descent with modification," which includes the idea that all species are descended from a common ancestor over many generations. We therefore accept the scientific evidence that all life on Earth is related, including humans, which does not negate the image of God in us.

EC is neither science nor theology, but an explanatory system that seeks to incorporate the best scholarship from each. It also includes some ideas about how theology and science relate to one another. For how EC compares to other views on origins, see How is BioLogos different from Evolutionism, Intelligent Design, and Creationism?

Evolutionary Creation Is Distinct From Theistic Evolution

The term "Evolutionary Creation" was probably first used in the early 1990s. Theistic Evolution (TE) is an older and more widely used term than EC, and many people use both terms interchangeably. However, we at BioLogos prefer EC over TE for at least three reasons.

First, we prefer EC because we are, essentially, creationists. We are not mere theists. We believe that God, by the authority of the Father, through the Son, in the power of the Holy Spirit created all things. Our beliefs about God and creation come first. "Evolutionary" is simply an adjective that describes creation and marks our acceptance of evolutionary science as the best scientific explanation we have for the diversity and similarity of life.

Second, we do not talk about "theistic chemistry" or "theistic physics." Neither should we speak about "theistic evolution." We do not propose a special Christian version of scientific facts. Science provides powerful tools for investigating God's creation. When we look at the insights science provides through the eyes of faith, we get an even fuller picture of reality. As Johannes Kepler wrote long ago, science, by discovering a deeper understanding of the world, is like thinking God's thoughts after him.

Third, many people have historically accused TEs of being deists. TE has at times been associated with the idea that God created the world and all the natural laws, but is no longer actively governing or involved in the cosmos.

This is very different from how most ECs understand God's involvement. In the BioLogos community we affirm the biblical miracles (most centrally the Resurrection), believe God answers prayer, and recognize that God works providentially through natural processes to accomplish his purposes. Natural processes and supernatural miracles both result in God's handiwork.

It is worth noting that BioLogos Founder Dr. Francis Collins coined the term BioLogos as an alternative to TE. The name comes from the Greek words bios (meaning "life") and logos (meaning "word" a reference to how John 1:1 describes the Son of God). As he wrote in his 2006 book *The Language of God*, "'BioLogos' expresses the belief that God is the source of all life and that life expresses the will of God" (p. 203). BioLogos didn't stick as the name of the view, but it fits well as the name of our organization.

ECs Have Diverse Views on Many Biblical and Scientific Questions

In any community, not everyone believes exactly the same things. Some beliefs are primary and help to define the group. Others are secondary and open to debate. The EC community here at BioLogos is no exception.

The BioLogos Statement of Beliefs includes beliefs affirmed by all staff and Board members, and convictions shared by most in our community. However, on many topics a range of views exists within our community. On those topics we do not champion one particular view.

For example, everyone at BioLogos believes all humans are made in the image of God, but there are different ideas about what exactly this means. For some, the image of God refers to our cognitive capacities, while others emphasize our unique spiritual capacity to enter into a relationship with God. Still others view the image of God as being God's chosen representatives to the rest of creation.

Or consider Adam and Eve. ECs generally agree that people were made by God and that humans are biologically related to other creatures, but they differ on how best to interpret the early chapters of Genesis. Some ECs believe Adam and Eve were a historical couple. Others see the story as a symbolic retelling of Israel's story, or as a symbolic story about humanity as a whole. Many interpretations have been put forward and this remains an exciting area of scholarship.

Finally, all ECs believe the Bible is God's inspired and authoritative word. But like the broader church, we disagree about how certain passages should be interpreted, and we disagree about whether biblical "inerrancy" is a helpful term.

On the science side, all ECs accept that common ancestry is true, but they might disagree about which biological mechanisms drive evolutionary change over time.

Regarding the origin of first life, some ECs envision a supernatural miracle, while others see a variety of natural explanations, each under the providential guidance of God.

Commitments of the BioLogos EC Community

The groundswell of interest and support for EC over the past decade has coalesced into a thriving community at BioLogos. Communities are defined not just by ideas, but by values and commitments. In addition to our commitment to the historic Christian faith and EC, at BioLogos we are committed to truth-seeking. Truth-seeking requires community, exploration, and discussion. Questions, and even doubts, are welcome here, as we seek to understand both the Bible and the natural world.

We value the expertise of scientists, biblical scholars, theologians, and philosophers. We value the sensitivity and spiritual understanding of pastors and leaders in the Christian community. We value the experiences and gifts of many, many lay people who love God and science. We value those who are simply exploring the claims of Christianity. Many people distrust organized religion or have been hurt by Christians, and we welcome them to look for healing here.

Another commitment for us at BioLogos is humility and gracious dialogue. Of course we don't get it right every time, but we strive to love those who think differently than we do. This doesn't mean watering down our message, but it does mean engaging in principled civility. We recognize that all people are loved by God and should be treated with respect.

Finally, we aim for excellence in all areas. This includes recognizing that science is both powerful and limited. Science has vast explanatory value when it comes to describing natural history and natural phenomena. Yet, it isn't the right tool to answer some of the really big questions, like why there is something rather than nothing, and whether there is a creator God who loves us.

We don't aim to create an alternate Christian version of scientific facts. Instead, we aim to trust scientific consensus where it exists, since it is based on evidence, testing, and peer-review, and allow for a range of views where it doesn't. And we aim to hold our scientific understanding with open palms in case new discoveries overturn consensus.

In our approach to the Bible, excellence means reading with sound principles of interpretation in mind. We seek to understand the purpose of a given passage and what it meant to the original audience, even if that understanding doesn't answer our own modern questions.

We don't expect the Bible to reveal scientific facts that the original authors wouldn't have understood. We don't try to explain away the Bible's evidence that people in biblical times had pre-scientific ideas and concepts. We prayerfully seek guidance from the Holy Spirit as we learn from teachers and scholars whose work can deepen our understanding of God's word.

All of this means we can reject the fear, cynicism, and suspicion that can sometimes cause people to disengage from either science or faith. We have freedom to approach both science and the Bible with a sense of wonder, confidence, and joy.

How Is Evolutionary Creation Different From Evolutionism, Intelligent Design, and Creationism?

biologos.org/common-questions/how-is-biologos-different-from-evolutionism-intelligent-design-and-creationism

At BioLogos, we present the Evolutionary Creation (EC) viewpoint on origins. Like all Christians, we fully affirm that God is the creator of all life, including human beings in his image. We fully affirm that the Bible is the inspired and authoritative word of God. We also accept the science of evolution as the best description for how God brought about the diversity of life on earth. But while we accept the scientific evidence for evolution, BioLogos emphatically rejects Evolutionism, the atheistic worldview that so often accompanies the acceptance of biological evolution in public discussion.

Evolutionism is a kind of scientism, which holds that all of reality can in principle be explained by science. In contrast, BioLogos believes that science is limited to explaining the natural world, and that supernatural events like miracles are part of reality too.

According to Young Earth Creationism (YEC), a faithful reading of Scripture commits Christians to accepting that the earth is young, between 6,000 and 10,000 years old. YEC claims that Scripture is not compatible with the idea that humans share common ancestry with other life forms on earth, and most YEC proponents feel that evolution is a direct threat to Christianity.

According to Old Earth Creation (OEC), the scientific evidence for the great age of the earth (4.6 billion years) and universe (13.7 billion years) is strong. This view typically maintains that the days of creation in Genesis 1 each refer to long periods of time. OEC does not accept the common ancestry of all life forms, often opting instead for a theory of progressive creation in which God miraculously created new species at key moments in the history of life.

We at BioLogos maintain that the scientific evidence from many branches of modern science would make little sense apart from common ancestry and evolution. We also believe that the cultural and theological contexts in which Scripture was written are key for determining the best interpretation of the creation accounts.

In contrast to EC, YEC, and OEC, Intelligent Design (ID) does not explicitly align itself with Christianity. It claims that the existence of an intelligent cause of the universe and of the development of life is a testable scientific hypothesis. ID arguments often point to parts of scientific theories where there is no consensus and claim that the best solution is to appeal to the direct action of an intelligent designer.

At BioLogos, we believe that our intelligent God designed the universe, but we do not see scientific or biblical reasons to give up on pursuing natural explanations for how God governs natural phenomena. We believe that scientific explanations complement a robust theological understanding of God's role as designer, creator, and sustainer of the universe.

While Christians differ on their views of the age of the earth and evolution, we all agree on the essentials of the faith: that all people have sinned and that salvation comes only through the death and resurrection of Jesus Christ. We agree that the God of our salvation is the same God we see in the wonders of his creation. Whether we ponder the intricacy of DNA, the beauty of a dolphin, or the vastness of the Milky Way, we can lift our hearts together in praise to the divine Artist who made it all.

————————————

Addendum 17

Theodicy in Process Theology

biologos.org/series/divine-action-a-biologos-conversation/articles/divine-action-theodicy-and-the-holy-spirit

The plausibility of the approach I am proposing to the problem of divine action in a scientifically understood world can be appreciated only given a certain set of presuppositions.

Presuppositions About God's Action

First, I assume a revised faith-seeking-understanding posture that is derived from a more or less orthodox notion of Christian faith. I understand this to be fallibilistic and constantly responding to various criteria. Among these I count continuity with scriptural and theological traditions, correlation with the ongoing advance of human knowledge in its various domains, and capacity to bring about the greater good as agreed upon by the world religions.

I embrace a Pentecostal Christian form of life, although I am always exploring its coherence with the broader Christian tradition, testing its adequacy with respect to progress in human inquiry, and examining its ability to engage apologetically and constructively with other world and life views for the common good.

Second, and more specific to the theology and science interface, I presume as a (Pentecostal) Christian that God works through the creation, and its natural laws or creatures and agents. I do not believe, however, that it is possible from a scientific perspective to know when God works interventionistically or specially. There are both positive and negative aspects of this premise.

Positively, according to my reading of the creation narrative in the book of Genesis, the evolutionary history of the cosmos unfolds pneumatologically, or "ruahologically." That is to say, the ruah elohim (the wind of God) hovered across and over the primordial waters (Gen. 1:2), and creation developed from there. Hence there is nothing purely "natural" (in the reductive and Enlightenment sense of that term) in the evolutionary processes of the world. There is also nothing "supernatural" to divine action since no divine work occurs apart from the creational dynamics, and since creation's unfolding can be understood to proceed only via divine activity. So I believe we ought to jettison the natural-supernatural binary as too heavily saddled with Enlightenment baggage.

Negatively, however, I also posit that the most we can say about how God acts comes from what we can empirically detect about the ways in which creation's processes work, which is precisely the domain of science.

Science and Theodicy

From a scientific perspective, of course, the concerns of theodicy, the justification of an omnipotent and omnibenevolent God in the face of evil, do not arise, and that for at least two interrelated reasons.

First, scientific inquiry is primarily an activity focused on increasing our understanding of how the world works. Second, questions about nature's processes concern matters of cosmic causality more than they do ethical morality.

Within this framework, that and how earthquakes happen can be explained geologically and illuminated from a variety of perspectives provided by the natural sciences. But the claim that earthquakes are evil is not something that science is designed to define. Further, even if science can play a role in clarifying why people suffer, for instance, genetics can elucidate chromosomal aberrations that result in severe or profound disabilities and their attendant painful effects and tragic impacts on human life, science does not presume, one way or another, that God is related to such experiences. So even if the various natural and human sciences help us to understand better from whence and how suffering emerges in the human condition, they do not respond directly to theodic questions and concerns.

Models of Theodicy

Various theodicies have been proposed historically, each with strengths but none with definitive resolutions. I cannot give an exhaustive discussion of the approaches to theodicy in the Christian tradition, but will briefly note here three types of theodicies representative of, in my view, the dominant models, the monotheistic, the cosmic, and the crucicentric.

First is what might be called the divine sovereignty response that insists suffering is allowed by the one creator God for various soul-making or otherwise inscrutable reasons. In the end (eschatologically) God will make right the perceived wrongs and vindicate these divine decisions. Some believers find comfort in the idea that human knowledge is limited and divine omnipotence will justify history finally. Others feel that God's goodness seems unreliable in the face of what seems to be gratuitous evil, and so it is difficult to trust that monotheism will make things right for distressed souls in the end.

Second is a kind of cosmic dualism in which God is the most powerful but perhaps not all-powerful being who works variously against the recalcitrant forces of the world. These are usually understood either to have always existed in some way alongside God or as emergent from the freedom given to angelic or other non-human creatures that have rebelled against God, to bring about life, goodness, and beauty.

This view in effect locates evil in the world that is either perennially distinct or has fallen away from God (thus preserving divine transcendence and goodness). It does not, however, assuage the worry that such evil will also persist everlastingly into the future, as there is no apparent means of guaranteeing divine victory once-and-for-all over such cosmic obstinacy.

Last but not least is a theodic rejoinder that is distinctively Christian in focusing on the central symbol of the cross of Christ as revealing not where evil and sorrow come from, but that God does not stand aloof from human hurt and actually enters deeply into such, even to the point of death. Advocates emphasize how such a reply invites pastoral presence with and praxis in support of the afflicted, but others are unsatisfied that this rejoinder adequately addresses the origins of evil or that the idea of divine solidarity with human sufferers sufficiently undergirds optimism for ultimate triumph over pain and tragedy.

I am not naïve to think that my pentecostal-pneumatological-and eschatological theology will prove thoroughly adequate where these others have valiantly strived. Yet perhaps when situated as a complementary proposal, what I am suggesting buttresses the weakest links of the other chains toward a more robustly trinitarian theological construct.

If the theodicy question is fundamentally theological, then my pentecostal and pneumatological notion is necessary in order to fill out the trinitarian potential inherent within but underdeveloped by the incarnational and crucicentric model. So without taking away anything from the important truth that God enters into the human condition in Jesus Christ and experiences fully its suffering and pain on the cross, the pentecostal outpouring of the Spirit on all flesh additionally proclaims that the creator of the world seeks to redeem the broken cosmos by coming upon and even inhabiting from within the hearts, bodies, and lives of all human sufferers. Hence crucicentric embrace of the generality of human flesh in the carnal being of Jesus is followed by pentecostal infusion into the particular carnal bodies of human beings by the Spirit of Jesus.

Such a trinitarian theodicy foregrounds the work of both the Son and the Spirit in the eschatological redemption of God. If the theodic models proposed above each relies on some kind of eschatological resolution to the problem of evil, the outpouring of the Spirit on all flesh in the last days (Acts 2:17) not only indicates how God is present amidst human misery but also accentuates how the Spirit empowers human participation in the mission of the triune deity to redeem such an aggrieved world and enables witness to the good news of the now-but-not-yet reign of God amidst the evil and calamity of the present age. In other words, such a pneumatological and eschatological view invites human creatures to be open to being conduits of charismatic signs and wondrous manifestations that extend hope in the current era of agony and torment, and provide glimpses of the full redemption to come.

Coming back full circle, such a pentecostal and pneumatological theodicy asks how followers of Jesus Christ can make full use of the various realms of human knowledge, the broad scope of the natural and human sciences included, in order to bring comfort and healing to a stricken world.

If the reign of God is already here in some sense through Christ and the Spirit (Luke 17:21), then those filled with the Spirit of Christ are co-laborers with the triune God in embodying and announcing the good news of salvation, perhaps not innoculation from anguish and travail but certainly in and through them.

To the degree that science unveils the causes of suffering and to the degree that scientific interventions and technologies can alleviate such in the present time, to these same degrees those committed to the mission of the triune God can embrace, urge on, underwrite, and support scientific inquiry for redemptive purposes, all as part of the Spirit's empowering witness in this pentecostal dispensation.

If this theodic vision, like the others, does not account for the ultimate genesis of evil, its trinitarian purview provides vigorous theological support for the eschatological hope that the divine will and goodness eventually prevail, even as the presence and activity of the Spirit of Pentecost instigates and arouses human inquiry, scientific and otherwise, and action toward such redemptive ends.

———————————

How Could God Create Through Evolution? A Look at Theodicy
biologos.org/articles/how-could-god-create-through-evolution-a-look-at-theodicy

Introduction

"How could a good God create through a process that involves so much pain and death?" For many people, accepting evolution is less a scientific question than a theological one. After all, seeing evolution as God's method of creation requires affirming that death, pain, and natural disasters are part of God's creative toolbox instead of a result of the Fall.

In this three-part blog series, I will first look at how theologians and scientists have seen the world in contrary ways, and then reflect theologically on how a world created through evolutionary means can be good.

First, let's see how theologians have thought about our world. Theologians, academic and popular, contemporary and ancient, have almost universally affirmed the connection between sin and physical death. Drawing from passages such as Genesis 3 and Romans 5 & 8, they have argued that death came through sin. In regard to the natural world, this means invoking a Cosmic Fall scenario in which not only human death came through the Fall, but earthquakes, tornadoes, pain, predation, and disease as well.

Consider this quotation from John Calvin: "For it appears that all the evils of the present life, which experience proves to be innumerable, have proceeded from the same fountain. The inclemency of the air, frost, thunders, unseasonable rains, drought, hail, and whatever is disorderly in the world, are the fruits of sin. Nor is there any other primary cause of diseases." Pretty clear, right? God did not want these "evils" to be part of the world, and the only reason they exist is because of human sin.

What's more, theologians see the redemption by Christ on the cross as the denunciation of these natural evils. For example, T. F. Torrance writes "The Cross of Christ tells us unmistakably that all physical evil, not only pain, suffering, disease, corruption, death, and of course cruelty and venom in animals as well as human behaviour, but also 'natural' calamities, devastations and monstrosities are an outrage against the love of God and a contradiction of good order in his creation."

Scientists, on the other hand, have looked at these same natural phenomena, and have come to the conclusion that realities like pain, earthquakes, and death are in fact necessary to good and flourishing lives. How do they do this? Let's look at two examples: earthquakes and pain.

When discussing plate tectonics, the media tends to focus on the negative effects of our planet's mobile plates. We hear about volcanic activity that shuts down European flight zones, tsunamis that devastate whole populations, and of course earthquakes, which have caused major devastations and cost many people their lives in Haiti, China, and Chile. How can earthquakes be good? What else does the plate cycle do?

First, plate tectonics, through the rotation of the mantle below, contributes to the magnetic field which surrounds our planet, keeping the atmosphere in and warding off deadly cosmic rays from the sun, which would destroy life if they reached the planet. Second, plate tectonic movement involves the solid plates being forced down into the liquid mantle and melting in some places, while in other places the plates separate and allow hot magma to rise and solidify. This recycling uses up heat produced by the interior radiation of the earth. This process is so effective that it uses up almost 90% of the heat produced by the Earth. In comparison, on Venus, the lack of plate tectonics means that the same heat produced by the core does not get recycled, and the pressure and heat build up so high that the distinction between mantle and crust gets lost, the whole planet goes molten. The rest of the time, surface temperatures average around 500 degrees Celsius. There are many other advantages to plate tectonics, including stabilizing atmospheric carbon dioxide, maintaining temperatures for liquid surface water, renewing nutrients in the soil, and keeping a distinction between ocean and continent.

Life, and certainly human life in this world, simply does not have a chance without plate tectonics. I do not want to understate the great human and animal cost associated with earthquakes, volcanoes, and tsunamis, but without plate tectonics, there would be no life at all. I would affirm that this world's plate tectonics are part of God's very good creation.

What about pain? If any of us were given the choice to live without pain, most of us would say an enthusiastic "yes please!" Until, that is, we saw what a life without pain really looks like. In our mind's eye we would imagine striding untouched though hardship and peril, like a real-life Superman, able to conquer all the aches and pains that keep us from reaching our full potential. In reality, a painless life is a horror show. In reality, painlessness looks like leprosy.

Leprosy, also known as Hansen's Disease, is a bacterial infection that invades the body's pain nerves and ultimately destroys them, leaving the person with an inability to feel pain. That is, in fact, almost all that leprosy does. The subsequent damage that we associate with leprosy, fingers falling off, open wounds, and missing limbs, does not actually come from the bacteria themselves, but from the resulting painlessness. Patients burn themselves and do not pull back; they walk on broken limbs and do not notice.

In the book *The Gift of Pain*, Paul Brand describes how in one African clinic, rats were coming in the night and feeding on patients fingers, and because they felt no pain, they slept on. Pain is a good thing, our ever-present protector, developed through an evolutionary process to help us live good lives. Now, this is not to say that pain never goes wild. It does, and with realities like chronic pain or torture, pain can become an enemy. But that does not undermine the fact that our ability to feel pain is a great gift; it just means that sometimes that gift becomes twisted in its expression. The solution is not to wish for a world with no pain, but for a world where pain is appropriately experienced.

Now let me insert one caveat here: in no way do I want to say that just because pain is "natural" that we have no responsibility to help relieve it. That is not what I am arguing. I would say that pain serves important purposes, which are needed for a good life. At the same time, we should look to the example of Jesus, who walked into pain-filled situations and brought healing, regardless of the cause of the suffering. It is our recognition of suffering in the other and our responsibility of stewardship to one another that must motivate our medical ethics.

There is a lot more that we could talk about here. We could speak of predation, which encourages biodiversity and drives evolutionary innovation. We could explore how physical death is a good and necessary part of a world that has limited resources, keeping organisms from becoming cancerous (cancer cells never die on their own and are thus "immortal"). These are important, but they roughly follow the same type of argumentation as above.

Why Didn't God Create Heaven in the First Place?

We looked at how our very good evolutionary world necessarily includes unpleasant realities like earthquakes and pain. Now we are going to look at why God might have created a world through evolutionary processes. What is the advantage of a world where pain and death are necessities? What is gained by an evolutionary process that would not be present in an unchanging, static, 'perfect' world? Why did God not simply create heaven in the first place? These are questions of huge theological significance and are not going to be satisfactorily answered here. I do, however, hope to offer some starting points for discussion.

I began to look at these questions by researching Irenaeus's theology of creation. Irenaeus of Lyons was a second-century Church Father, and one of the Church's greatest theologians. One of the most intriguing parts about his theology is that he understood the creation as being made in immaturity.

Most of us imagine the world of Genesis 1-2, or the original creation, as a perfect world, where everything is already completed, and where Adam and Eve were meant to live out their lives in a perfect existence. Apart from multiplying and filling the earth, there is not a lot of room for growth, either physically or spiritually, for humans or for creation because everything has already "arrived."

In a radical re-imagining of this story, Irenaeus pictures Adam and Eve in the garden as children not perfect, but on a journey toward maturity and perfection. This is because perfection is not something you can give to an infant; it must be grown into. Irenaeus argues, "For as it certainly is in the power of a mother to give strong food to her infant, [but she does not do so], as the child is not yet able to receive more substantial nourishment; so also it was possible for God Himself to have made man perfect from the first, but man could not receive this [perfection] being as yet an infant."

So, God does not force something on to humanity that it is not ready for. Perfection was not something that could be implanted; it had to be journeyed toward. And so Irenaeus gives us our first value of an evolving world: room for the growth and development of humans.

Now, let's extend this argument to the wider cosmos. Just as humanity is not created in static perfection, the world around is not fully completed either. Colin Gunton, reflecting on Irenaeus, writes, "Creation is a project... It has somewhere to go." There is value in saying that creation has the freedom to grow, that it is an ongoing project. A world with freedom must have choice, and this is present in a world with a long evolutionary history.

The cosmos, like humanity, is created very good, but it is not created in its final state. This giving of freedom (and perhaps even limited autonomy) to the creation is, I would argue, more consistent with the nature of divine love than a creation where everything is determined.

God gives true freedom to humanity, leading to moral choice, and true freedom to creation, leading to evolutionary development. This is God's act of love, and this is why God did not just make heaven in the first place. Freedom and growth are valuable, and God delights in them.

A third value given through evolution is the ability to move toward a goal. And that begs the question: "Where is evolution going?" I would argue that evolution was moving toward developing a community of beings which carries God's image and amongst which God would be made incarnate. The Incarnation was not a contingency plan brought in when humanity sinned, but rather was one of the original purposes of creation. This concept is one of the great contributions of Irenaeus, creation was always headed for the Incarnation!

Also, this creation was always part of the journey toward new life. God's promise of a new creation is not a contingency plan either! The new (or, rather, renewed) creation, as described at the end of Revelation, was always part of the plan. I don't think that any theodicy can say "this world is good" without also pointing forward to the time when there will be no pain, no death, and no tears, under some new and unimaginable reconstruction of the universe.

Keep in mind that we do tend to imagine the new future as static in some ways. Many of the values that are achieved here (such as having children or freedom of moral choice) are not imagined to exist there in the same way. In no way does saying "this is a good world" undermine the Christian hope in the world to come.

Actually, recognition that this life was always meant to be renewed can help our Christian walk. The spiritual growth coming from this world is seen most easily, perhaps, with the example of death.

In the present world, physical death is the most poignant reminder of our mortality. While we grasp at immortality through various means, we find it is always beyond our reach. The suffocating horror and fear that accompanies many of our encounters with death reminds us finally that we are not God. Yet it is in those moments of deepest agony that our need for the hope of resurrection is the strongest.

What Do We Do With Death?

328

In light of the new creation, death is a transition from this life to the new life. It is a leap of faith that God always intended, and one which God himself did not avoid. In the lives of saints and martyrs, we see a taste of what physical death was intended to be (I am speaking here of physical death without sin; our present experience of death is horridly marred by sin and the reality of spiritual death). We see how many of the martyrs approached death with peace, acceptance, and even joy, to lay down their lives and be called into the presence of God. I believe that this was the original intention of death. Death was to be a transition, a final giving up of oneself into the enfolding arms of God. Our bodies go to decompose and support new life, while our trust is placed in the promise of the resurrected life.

I want to be careful here. This does not mean that we should not grieve death. Even Jesus, when he was at the tomb of Lazarus, wept openly, even though he knew that he was about to raise Lazarus from the dead. There can be a strange disconnect, where if we Christians say something is good or natural, we sometimes feel we should then be able to avoid a real emotional response to the situation, or that faith means not being broken by certain situations. This is not what I am advocating.

Encountering death should make us weep, because the loss we experience is real. Christian hope makes us more human, not less, we should feel more deeply, not less. But we should also feel differently. We grieve, knowing that there is hope and life and renewal ahead. We know that physical death does not have the last word, because of the life, death and resurrection of Jesus. We hear Paul's triumphal cry "Where, O death is your victory? Where, O death is your sting?...The sting of death is sin, and the power of sin is the law. But thanks be to God! He gives us the victory through our Lord Jesus Christ." Our path is not to avoid pain and death, but to walk through them, following our Lord and Savior in life, in death, and in resurrection life.

Doesn't Paul Say That Death Came Through the Fall?

I have been trying to show that the world we inhabit is in fact a very good world. It is marred by human sin, but the operations of the natural world express the values of freedom and growth, just as God intended them. We have come to what is likely to be my most contentious section.

How do we deal with the biblical language about death? We started with quotations from John Calvin and T. F. Torrance in which they asserted that the unpleasant realities of this world (predation, natural disasters, and so on) were not part of God's original creation but were the results of human sin. This theology is usually taken from the curse language of Genesis, and Paul's explanation of death in Romans 5, 8, and 1 Corinthians 15.

There are, however, several more things going on here than meets the eye. The two major issues that need to be dealt with are the varying biblical perspectives on death and the influence of cultural accommodation in the text.

Starting with the first of these, we must acknowledge that the Bible treats the issue of death in several different ways, and that it recognizes several different types of death. First we must draw a distinction between physical death and spiritual death. This is particularly evident in Paul's writing to the Romans. In Chapter 7, speaking of the effects of sin, Paul writes, "For sin, seizing the opportunity afforded by the commandment, deceived me, and through the commandment put me to death" (Romans 7:11). Now obviously, a man put to death physically could not have later written those words! An even more telling passage is 1 Corinthians 15:31 where the apostle writes, "I die every day, I mean that, brothers."

It is interesting to note that in both places where Paul explicitly states that death came through Adam, he speaks of his own death as a past reality. This is not conclusive of Paul's use of the word "death" but it is suggestive that we should be careful of assuming a simple one-level meaning. Certainly we see other places where Paul is clearly indicating physical death, such as 1 Corinthians 15:35-42, as he speaks of the physical resurrection of the body after (what is clearly) physical death.

This leaves us with the question: Which kind of death is Paul referring to when he states that death came through Adam? Unfortunately, this is not always clear. In Romans 5, Paul seems to be speaking of spiritual death, as he speaks of effects of death in contrast to eternal life and later (in v.18) uses "condemnation" as a substitute for death. However, considering Paul's reliance on Genesis 3 where the curse language clearly indicates physical death through the phrase "dust you are and to dust

330

you will return" (Genesis 3:19) it is likely better to adopt what Douglas Moo calls a "physico-spiritual" death which keeps both the physical and spiritual aspects in mind. These two are closely entwined in Paul's mind, and the enmeshing of the two will become important later. The same multi-layered concept of death is true of 1 Corinthians 15:20-22, where Paul speaks of death and then future physical resurrection.

How does this view of death interact with modern science? It is clear that death was present in the world long before human sin, indeed, death has been present as long as life. It is also clear that death is necessary in order to renew resources and allow for evolutionary development. Paul, however, would not have known this. He would not have recognized the importance of death in ecosystems, nor would he have understood the horror of the limited types of "immortality" that we see in the natural world, such as cancer. Paul was an ancient thinker. Just as Pete Enns wrote about Paul's views on Adam not necessarily determining our scientific and historical understanding, I would propose that Paul's views on death need not keep us from accepting the insights of modern science.

This is where the issues of biblical interpretation get interesting. Most of us take for granted that if we read the Bible, we need someone who can translate from the original languages of Greek, Hebrew, and Aramaic before we have a hope of understanding what is being said. What is less acknowledged is that worldviews and cultural assumptions must also be translated. Ancient perspectives, whether in science or history, must be moved into forms that make sense to a contemporary audience and to the questions a modern mind is asking.

Remember I said earlier that Paul entwines together spiritual and physical death? Both in the ancient world are seen as evil, as opposed to the will of God and against the flourishing of His creatures. Part of translating Paul into our culture means distinguishing between these two types of death, and acknowledging the necessity of physical death, while maintaining the sin-death connection in relation to spiritual death. Death did come through sin, but spiritual death, not physical death.

This in no way undermines Paul's main argument in Romans. Paul is explaining our need for Christ to redeem us from our sin, and our need for life that swallows up death. This remains true in two ways. First,

Christ redeems us from our spiritual death, from the separation from God which sin instills. Second, Christ assures us of the future life of physical resurrection. While Christ deals with our sin problem completely, believers still die. If sin were the cause of physical death, we would expect Christians to live forever. But this is not the case. Our hope, as it ever was, lies in the resurrection, which is a direct consequence of Jesus' work. Physical death will one day be defeated, but this comes from walking through the valley of the shadow of death, not around it. Where Paul attributes a conditional immortality to the figure of Adam, and sees eternal life as a past historical reality, we must instead root the cessation of death in the eschatological future.

While this brief treatment is in no way complete, I hope it will open up discussion and allow for new ways of seeing the truth, goodness, and beauty in the creation we inhabit.

About the Author
Bethany Sollereder
Dr. Bethany Sollereder is a research coordinator at the University of Oxford. She specialises in theology concerning evolution and the problem of suffering. Bethany received her PhD in theology from the University of Exeter and an MCS in interdisciplinary studies from Regent College, Vancouver. When not reading theology books, Bethany enjoys hiking the English countryside, horseback riding, and reading Victorian literature.

Addendum 18

When Did Sin Begin in Process Theology

Process theology attempts to reconcile faith in science with faith in the Bible. In particular, it attempts to reconcile the science of evolution with the Biblical account in Genesis of when life began and when did sin first occur.

Typically, Darwinian evolutionists do not claim to understand how life first originated. They only espouse that all life today has evolved from a single life form, a single common ancestor.

Loren Haarsma, a scientist, has written the book, *When Did Sin Begin* (2021), and was interviewed by Jim Stump of BioLogos. The interview covers in depth Haarsma's four approaches to the origin of sin and the fall, from a wide range of possibilities, and the pros and cons of each.

Haarsma takes the position that, "When you look at the wide range of possibilities, you realize, yeah, the data of science and the data of theology and church tradition actually allows for quite a wide range of possible scenarios, which I would say are still compatible with everything we know about what science is telling us and still compatible with the core doctrine of original sin."

Four Approaches to Original Sin

There are a range of ways that people have thought about original sin, Adam and Eve, and the spread of sin throughout the world. Scientific knowledge, including the science of human evolution, has contributed to that conversation but science has not identified a definitive position.

Loren Haarsma lays out four different approaches in his book, *When Did Sin Begin?* (2021) and talks with us in the episode about the approaches, as well as the benefits and theological challenges of each approach.

Haarsma: I've read many books by theologians that I've found and by scientists who have been very helpful to me where they say, here's my understanding of human evolution and the science. Here's how I think we put our theology with it. Here's how I think sin entered the story. And they've offered a lot of different ideas. In most of the books, the authors sort of say why they think their particular favorite scenario works best. But when you look at the wide range of possibilities, you realize, yeah, the data of science and the data of theology and church tradition actually allows for quite a wide range of possible scenarios, which I would say are still compatible with everything we know about what science is telling us and still compatible with the core doctrine of original sin.

My name is Loren Haarsma. I'm an Associate Professor of physics at Calvin University. And I've also spent a lot of time thinking, reading and writing about science and theology topics.

Stump: Welcome to Language of God. I'm Jim Stump.

At BioLogos we think that faith and science can go hand in hand, that you can find harmony between science and theology. That doesn't mean, however, that science and theology will always give you one easy answer for every question that might arise. One place where that becomes especially evident is when trying to work out the details of the doctrine of original sin. Science, and especially the science of human origins and human evolution, has contributed to a conversation about sin and Adam and Eve, but there remains a wide range of possibilities that are still compatible with the Christian faith.

Loren Haarsma is a physicist by training but he has been thinking, reading and writing about these theological issues for many decades and his most recent book, *When Did Sin Begin*, lays out several scenarios for answering that question, considering the pros and cons of each, without landing on any one 'correct' position. I think it's fun to talk through these with Loren.

Full disclosure: Loren Haarsma is married to my boss, the president of BioLogos. But I can confirm that she had nothing to do with selecting the guest for this episode and had no input on the contents thereof! Disclaimer aside, let's get to the conversation.

Interview Part one

Stump: Well, Loren Haarsma, welcome to the podcast, we're glad to have you here.

Haarsma: Thank you very much. I'm very happy to be here.

Jim: You have a new book out recently called *When Did Sin Begin.* There's nothing too unusual about us talking to someone with a book like that, but the path by which you yourself came to write such a book is a little unusual. And there are at least two surprising turns in this that I'd like you to talk about. The first is a kid growing up in rural Iowa ends up getting a PhD in physics from Harvard. How did that come about?

Haarsma: Well, I always loved science. I remember as a kid getting books on astronomy as a high school student going into the public library and finding popular level books on particle physics. And I always liked math puzzles. I was encouraged to study science by my parents, by my school, by my church. So I went off to Calvin College as an undergraduate to study physics and I found many more people like me, Christians who saw science, in general, and physics, in particular, as their calling.

Jim: Give us just a little overview of the kind of physics that you have specialized in and continue to work on today.

Haarsma: For my graduate work, I focused on particles, antimatter particles, trapping them, studying them. But then I made a shift into biophysics, studying the electrical activity of molecules called ion channels, which allow electrical information to flow into and out of cells and between cells.

Jim: So this brings me to the second surprising turn to your story, which is that a professor with a PhD in physics from Harvard and studies things like ion channels, ends up writing a book called *When Did Sin Begin?* Walk us through a little bit of that part of the story, if you would, as well.

Haarsma: I grew up going to church and hearing wonderful Calvinist sermons twice each Sunday, and I loved learning systematic theology, even as a kid. I was encouraged also to put them together, I remember, pastors and teachers talking about how we can believe that God feeds the birds of the air and also we can study that scientifically, that God governs the motion of the planets, but we can also learn about gravity.

So when I was at college, I learned that when it came to the age of the Earth and interpretations of Genesis, there were multiple different interpretations within the church. I didn't pay a great deal of attention then. But when I went off to graduate school, I really began to pay attention to the talks on cosmology and geology and to some extent on evolutionary biology. I saw there was really wonderful, cool science going on. I wasn't too worried about what that meant for God being in charge of everything, because I'd been taught all along that we can have scientific explanations and still see God in charge. But I did need to think a little bit about how to interpret Genesis. So I started reading more theology at that point, of Old Testament scholars who helped me understand interpretations of Genesis. What they said made sense to me, that we could have an evolutionary understanding of creation and still see Scripture as inspired by God and teaching us important things about God's relationship to the world and our relationship to God.

Jim: Why this question in particular then, original sin and the fall, or where does this come into your saying that's what I really want to focus in on, trying to understand better?

Haarsma: Yes. So I remembered all those theology lessons growing up and I knew about the doctrine of original sin. I knew if there was one particular topic in all of the science and faith areas having to do with origins where there might be a conflict between the theology I learned and the science I was learning, it would be in human origins, human evolution, and the doctrine of original sin. I just felt called, I think, by God to study that area to read whatever books I could find back in the 1990s. Then in the decades that followed, read as many books as I can and try to work through the implications.

Jim: Well, very interesting. We will talk very specifically about your book and some of the proposals that you have there in just a second. I'm curious, before we get to that, though, to do a little more what we, in philosophy at least, call the methodology of this. I think, we have here with you, in your work, the very embodiment of the two books metaphor that's so often referred to in science and religion work. We have the book of God's word, revealed first in the Bible, the Book of God's work or God's world, revealed for us in the world God's created. I think this is a really interesting and fruitful metaphor on the surface. It's even embedded in the BioLogos mission statement about God's word and

God's world. But like any metaphor, it will break down at some point when we start to push on it. So I'm curious here, as you've been trained in the sciences formally and have been working for, as you say, several decades here now and in theology, do you see any tensions or have any reservations? I'm just interested in talking a little more generally about how we understand these two different fields of study to come together. How has that worked for you? And what do you make of this two books metaphor?

Haarsma: As you say, I find it a useful metaphor. But it's, I find it's helpful to think about the proper methods in each discipline, when it comes to studying theology and hermeneutics of Scripture. What are the best methods that we have learned throughout the centuries for that, and then as we do science, what are the best methods there. And there are certain natural questions which are answered easily in one discipline, and not so easily or at all in the other. So it takes a little overarching work to put them together. I'm encouraged to do this, by my view of God's sovereignty. Just as biblical scholars say, you know, if two passages of Scripture at first seem to teach contradictory things you should dig into them, because we don't think God would actually teach contradictory things, but we may have to work at it a bit. And as scientists, we sometimes have theories, which at first seem to make contradictory predictions, but we trust there's a deeper underlying theory that unites them all. So I feel the same thing for sort of all of truth. If at first glance, Scripture and science seem to be pointing towards different ideas that are hard to reconcile, I trust there is an underlying truth, but I need to sort of follow the best methods of each discipline, to try and go deeper in each.

Jim: Let me, I want to push a little deeper into this method, into the metaphor and this methodology. I think it's really important for understanding the kind of work that you've done in the book here. The first explicit illusion that I've found to the created world as another book from God goes all the way back to the fourth century John Chrysostom who said, "if God had given instruction by means of books and letters, he who knows letters would have learned what was written, but the illiterate man would have gone away without receiving any benefit. This, however, cannot be said with respect to the heavens. Upon this volume, the unlearned as well as the wise man shall be able to look and wherever anyone may chance to come, they're looking upwards towards the heaven, he'll receive a sufficient lesson from the view of them." I think there's a couple interesting things about this I'd like to get you to comment on in first is that there's a reversal in the accessibility or at least the perceived accessibility of these two books today, because back in the fourth century, it was the minority who could read the book of God's word, right? Most people were illiterate. So there was a priestly class who had to interpret that for us. But everyone, says Chrysostom, could look at the heavens and get a sufficient lesson there of God's instruction. Now, however, I think that's reversed. Most all of us can read, but how many people can look at the heavens or nature in general and understand what they're seeing? And so we have the scientists as a new kind of priestly class to interpret the world for us. Is there anything interesting or important about this reversal? In accessibility of which of these books can lie more open to our view or to the view of the general public? Do you see anything interesting in there? Or is this just me?

Haarsma: It is interesting. Part of it is I think that when we look at the natural world, the part that is accessible to everybody, and doesn't require detailed scientific knowledge, is also somewhat general in what it says about God. As a scientist, I'm sensitive to the fact that when you have a limited set of data, your theories can, it can fit a lot of different theories. And so I think it is with the natural world. It points us to God. But if we only had the natural world to learn about God, it'd be very easy to draw wrong conclusions. So fortunately, God has given us special revelation. And I believe that theologians throughout the centuries have said that, certainly the main message of Scripture when it's explained or when it's read, should be pretty easily accessible. But they've also insisted that it's easy to get things wrong if you just approach scripture naively. So I think both in nature and in studying scripture, there are parts which are very easily accessible. But if you really want to dig into some hard, detailed questions, you need the help of specialists and a whole community to help you sort through the ideas.

Jim: Good. Expertise in both fields are a good thing, right? Well, that brings me to the second point that I was going to ask you about here related to this quote from John Chrysostom, which is the specialization of science. And whether that has, I don't know, maybe undermined to some degree the general population's ability to look at the natural world and see the lesson Christendom, and we could say, the apostle Paul, in Romans one, mentions as well that you can take from the natural world.

338

Has the sort of specialization or the detailed view of scientists looking at the world, has that disenchanted the world to some degree such that the rest of us are just kind of conditioned to see the world as so many mechanisms and gears and levers? Or what is the lesson that people can get from nature today?

Haarsma: So I would start with the lessons that were accessible from nature, way back 2000 to 3000 years ago, when Psalm 19 was written. Those are just as accessible as ever. Now, a lot of the detailed knowledge and specialization in science doesn't have a lot of obvious theological impact. Some of it does. It falls to the scientists and the philosophers of science and the theologians who learn some science and philosophy of science to sort of help the church in general say, and analyze these new discoveries and say, which of these do have implications and how do we sort through the the reasonable Christian understanding of these findings as opposed to some other religious or atheistic worldview spins that other people might put on those findings? So again, I think it's part of the community. It's part of the job of some specialists to help the general church community understand these implications at a level they can understand.

Jim: One more kind of question in this general methodology level of things, and then we'll get more specifically to your book. We in this business quite often talk about how these two disciplines influencing each other in this way. And I think, for many people, there's a kind of worry that most of the influence flows just in one direction, that science makes some new discovery. And theology has to adjust itself to that reality that science gets to say, this is the way the world really is. And then theology is scrambling to try to reinvent itself to some degree to fit with that. What's wrong with that picture? And maybe can you give any examples of that direction of influence flowing the other way of theology actually influencing science or our understanding of science in some way.

Haarsma: There are at least two really big examples of how theology has a huge impact on our study of the natural world, and the things we learn by doing science. The first is that Christian theology has had an influence in the very foundational ideas of science. historians of science like to write about, sort of the foundational ideas that helped get science going a few centuries ago, ideas about the regular repeatability and understandability of cause and effect, and how the world isn't full of nature, spirits that have to be manipulated by ritual, and some foundational assumptions, which all scientists today share and can really trace the roots in many of the original scientists to their Christian theological beliefs. So science owes a huge debt to Christian theology for some of its foundational beliefs and practices.

Another really important thing, I'd say this is perhaps the most common expression of theologies influence on the way Christians look at scientific results is, it's very often the case that there's a result in science that allows for multiple different worldview or philosophical or religious interpretations. So for example, I can tell you that the sun is running a nuclear fusion and it has enough fuel to last for a few billion years, and it'll burn out. Okay, scientists of many different religious views can agree about that. But what are the implications? Now there you can run into many different interpretations, some of which are compatible with Christian theology, and some of which are not. So on a whole host of scientific results where scientists have consensus, there are many different philosophical, theological spins you can put on it. And there, for Christians, a good theology is very, very helpful in sort of saying, what are the range of Christian theological interpretations that makes sense?

Jim: That's fascinating. Well, good. There's some degree of that going on here in your book now, where you're taking some if we, if we may say data points from the natural world and data points from Scripture in the Christian tradition, trying to then like stake out the territory or define the edges of possibility space within which we might still give an explanation for when sin entered God's good world, how it came to infect the rest of creation. So you mentioned earlier that the data typically you didn't use this phrase, but the philosophers say, the data under determines any theory we bring to it, right? So there are several kinds of possibilities here. Is this a fair one sentence description of your project? Or would you like to give it a more proper introduction of what you're trying to accomplish in the book?

Haarsma: That's a very good summary. I've read many books by theologians that I've found and by scientists who have been very helpful to me where they say, here's my understanding of human evolution and the science. Here's how I think we put our theology with it. Here's how I think sin entered the story. They've offered a lot of different ideas. In most of the books, the authors sort of say why they think their particular favorite scenario works best. But when you look at the wide range of possibilities, you realize, yeah, the data of science and the data of theology and church tradition actually allows for quite a wide range of possible scenarios, which I would say are still compatible with everything we know about what science is telling us and still compatible with the core doctrine of original sin. So a big part of my book was trying to sort of lay out that range and talk about what are some of the pros and cons of various possibilities.

Jim: Good. So you've, you've settled on or distilled down to four different scenarios that you mentioned as the main options for answering the question. When did sin begin? And how did it, what were the implications of that? So let's walk through these briefly noting some of the pros and cons of each of these as you see them. So the first to appeal to Adam and Eve as real historical individuals. But they're not quite as the flannel graph from Sunday school may have portrayed them right? The first two people created by God six or ten thousand years ago, from whom all of humanity descends uniquely. What's wrong with that story, and what has to be done to save the core of that story at least?

Haarsma: Well, there we have learned a lot of information about human origins and how God created human beings through a long process. And that process appears from all the data, from many independent lines of data, to include common ancestry with animals, and a population which was always many more than two individuals and fossils going back hundreds of thousands and millions of years. So a number of people have looked at that data and said, well, that doesn't mean we can't have some sort of historical Adam and Eve, but they would have to be part of a larger population. They could have been particular individuals chosen by God, given a particular revelation. There was a particular important theological event. Sin entered the world through, for the first time, through their disobedience. But they weren't the sole ancestors of human beings, they were a part of a larger population and their descendants then mixed with others who were alive at the time. So they were particularly important theologically. Biologically, however, they're part of a larger population. And we today are descended from them, but also from many others. And the genetic information in the fossil information, all sort of points to the idea that our human ancestral population was always much larger than two individuals.

Jim: So then give some possible dates here of the way this could work for Adam and Eve appearing in actual history, along with the kind of context or environment they would have found themselves in, and how the important parts theologically of this story could have played out. And everybody knows we're speculating here, right? We're extrapolating beyond what the data is forcing us to, but we're trying to imagine possibility space here. So give us a couple of these ways that Adam and Eve could have been real people, in a real space time in our ancestry, and how sin from them would have transmitted to the rest of us.

Haarsma: So there's a lot of questions you can ask and dozens of different scenarios you can imagine. But I'll focus on two questions you asked. One is the when question. Some people like to push that back quite a long ways, hundreds of thousands, perhaps millions of years. Back when our ancestors were living in small groups, with simple stone tools, but self consciousness, self awareness was just beginning to really take hold in human understanding. When it first became possible for our ancestors to think of themselves as persons and think of the person next to them as a person and realize that they had a choice of helping or hurting that person next to them, and that there would be consequences. So that's sort of one extreme, you could sort of say, as early as humans began to have a certain level, and it's hard to define exactly what level but it could have been, you know, a few million years ago, a certain level of self awareness and moral awareness, that also became possible to be spiritual awareness and awareness of consequences beyond the immediate good or bad I do to myself and the people around me.

Jim: Just to clarify there, when you're using the term 'human', several million years ago, we're not talking about Homo sapiens. Is there anything significant in that? Do we lose something by Adam and Eve not being the same species that we are?

Haarsma: I don't think so. I think there's a continuity if we trace our ancestors back through Homo erectus, possibly back to Homo habilis, even because of the continuity of culture as well as genes, because what each generation passes on to the next isn't just genes. It's also culture and practices and understanding and upbringing that there is from whenever sin entered the world. And if it entered a very long time ago, there's a continuity to us today. Now there is another extreme to the when question.

Jim: Yeah, give us the other one.

Haarsma: Yeah, we could imagine that our ancestors were living in groups and developing technology and living through the Neolithic and even beginning to develop agriculture, even beginning to develop reading and writing. And at some point, maybe fairly recently, I don't know perhaps 10,000 years ago, by then humans, Homo sapiens, were spread all over the earth. But maybe, from God's point of view, people were sometimes being nice to each other and sometimes be nasty to each other, but God didn't count it as sin because God hadn't yet given a particular type of special revelation, which would be necessary for God to count it as sin and hold people accountable. So perhaps somewhat recently, a few thousand years ago, there were particular individuals chosen by God given a very particular special revelation. And at that point, clear disobedience to God's commands is what made it possible for us to say, now there's disobedience, now there is sin. Now, between those two extremes of a few million years ago, and a few, and 10,000 years ago, there's a lot of possibilities. And there are good books advocating for a variety of options in between.

Jim: So, understanding Adam and Eve in these ways doesn't contradict anything science has shown about history. I guess I'm curious if they preserve enough to be recognizably the Adam and Eve of Scripture that we're hoping to hold on to. I've talked to some people who think these kinds of efforts to save a historical Adam and Eve are starting to feel a little bit like epicycles, put on an earth-centered cosmos in order to save that understanding. Is that an unfair comparison, you think?

Haarsma: The way I like to approach these different possibilities, the ways of seeing Adam and Eve as historical individuals out of a larger population, or alternatively, seeing Adam and Eve as more literary or symbolic figures, representing many individuals, is that there's pros and cons to each of these possibilities. For some people, people whose books I've read, and people I've talked to at conferences, they see too many theological difficulties with seeing Adam and Eve as symbolic or literary characters. They understand that there are some theological challenges to having Adam and Eve as historical characters as part of a larger population. But they see some theological strengths to that point of view. So it's almost a matter of preferences, which strengths and weaknesses do you feel are more important than others.

BioLogos: Hi listeners! On this podcast we hear a lot of stories of young people who consider leaving the church because of the tensions they find between science and faith. It doesn't have to be that way. That's why we developed Integrate, a teaching resource, designed for classroom teachers and home educators. It seeks to equip the next generation of Christian leaders to be faithful, informed, and gracious voices engaging with the hard questions raised by science. To learn more just go to biologos dot org slash integrate.

Alright, back to the conversation.
Interview Part Two

Jim: Okay, we want to get to talking to some of those non-historical options you have here. But let me make sure we're tracking with your four different options. You keep coming back to here, because the first two of these have Adam and Eve as particular historical individuals. But you don't then separate these according to the time periods in which Adam and Eve lived, but the method by which sin was transmitted to the rest of us, right? So talk a little bit about the difference there, and these two different possibilities in particular?

Haarsma: Yes, in early stages of writing this book, I wondered if I should make a grid laying out hundreds of possibilities. And I rejected that idea in favor of summarizing four. But then I had to make some choices as to which questions, I thought carried the most theological weight in terms of separating different groups of possibilities. And so on these historical ones, one group of possibilities I said was, Adam and Eve were representatives of humanity. And as soon as these particular historical individuals sinned, because they acted as representatives in a spiritual sense that the rest of humanity was then declared to be okay, we're all in this together, we are now all sinners, because our representatives failed to obey God. And so...

Jim: Let's hash that one out a little bit more. So let's say this is 10,000 years ago, Adam and Eve are in the Middle East somewhere and sin. But as you said before Homo sapiens are already all over the planet. So at

344

that moment, there are groups of people living in South America that all the sudden realize this, or they don't necessarily realize that something drastic has happened. What do you imagine, how do you imagine that working exactly?

Haarsma: That is, I would classify that as the hardest most challenging question for this particular group of scenarios. Those authors who have advocated this way of talking, this way of thinking about the entrance of sin, point to examples in the Old Testament where you know, one person acts and the whole community suffers, that may or may not be a satisfying theological answer for everybody. They point to the fact that everybody leading up till that point, had the benefits of general revelation and that people knew when they were being nice and when they were being nasty. Everybody was already doing combinations of niceness and nastiness, but God wasn't necessarily holding them accountable. You might quote a line from the Apostle Paul about sin being in the world but not being held to account until the law was given. So I still think there's real serious theological challenges to this view. But one could defend this idea with that sort of approach and saying, there was already rebellion against God's general revelation. But now once Adam and Eve disobeyed God's special revelation, now God sees all of humanity in this new way, and we're all in this new relationship to God.

Jim: So the rebellion against general revelation, in your view, you're not counting as sin.

Haarsma: Some would say, my own reformed background puts pretty strong emphasis on general revelation. So I personally find this particular view challenging. But there are those who write and say, in order for it to count as sin that is held to account by God, some kind of special revelation must come somewhere into the story.

Jim: And maybe this representative way works better if we put Adam and Eve in the much more distant past where we haven't spread all across the globe. Or maybe there's a bottleneck of a few thousand people where the representation seems a little bit more like it would have an effect immediately on everybody.

Haarsma: Indeed, there are some who write that way. And that I tend to agree, the theological difficulties, queasiness you might feel, about this first scenario, this representative scenario, if you make Adam and Eve very late in the story seem easier if you do it earlier in the story of humanity.

Jim: Okay, moved to number two then. Sin spread through culture or genealogy. How does this work?

Haarsma: The idea here is that, well, let's do the cultural one, that knowledge and understanding of sin requires some sort of knowledge and understanding of God and knowledge and understanding of who other people, thinking about who other people are in certain ways. This information can spread quite quickly. So not over the whole world in a decade or so but from group to group, from individual to individual over time. We all know that sin, in our day, spreads from group to group and person to person, through culture, through contact, through behavior. My sinful choices prompt other people to behave sinfully. And on and on it goes. So the idea here is that from the first sinners, Adam and Eve, knowledge of God and knowledge of their rebellion against God, then began to spread culturally, to the rest of humanity so that after a few hundreds or thousands of years, that knowledge has spread to the rest of the population.

Jim: So what do we do with those people during those few hundred our thousands of years before that had spread to their populations, what is their theological status?

Haarsma: That I would identify as one of the hardest questions for the second set of scenarios. [laughter] You're putting your finger right on it. In my book, I try to point this out. Part of my job in this book is to point out to advocates of particular scenarios, are you aware of these really hard questions that your favorite scenario raises? I would call that one of the hardest ones. What is the status of those individuals while sin is spreading? Why should some be held accountable and some not? Now we can always say, we are not the judges. An advocate of this scenario can say, this is an old question, what is the status of people who live good lives but never particularly had a chance to hear the gospel of Christ? Well, we're not the judges. Christ is the one who is the advocate for humanity and who will, God is the judge of these situations. We don't know how God makes these judgments precisely. So we can leave that in God's hands. But it is a hard theological question. It's worth puzzling over I think, trying to come up with as satisfying as possible answers.

Jim: Fair enough. Let's keep moving through your options here. So we get to all of them with giving sufficient attention here. So your third one is Adam and Eve is a highly compressed history. What do you mean by that?

Haarsma: Well, there's many parts in early Genesis you could call highly compressed history. You know, languages spread throughout the whole world over a very long period of time. But we have a compressed theological story in the Tower of Babel. Agriculture and musical instruments and iron smelting occurred in human history over tens of thousands of years, widely dispersed regions. But in Genesis four, it's all highly compressed. So we could imagine that Genesis two and three is an inspired story to tell the story of many human rebellions against God over a long period of time. The idea here is that from time to time in human history, we don't know exactly when it started, God began to make himself more fully known to particular individuals who are ready for it. Each one of these instances held the possibility of greater obedience and greater disobedience. These ancestors again and again and again, chose disobedience. Every act of disobedience pushed themselves and then all the people around them further and further away from God. So yeah, there may have been a first particular historical sin. But the important theological point is the accumulation of disobedience and the effect of disobedience of many individuals and the impact they had on everyone else over a long period of time. Until at some point, we arrive at the point where all of humanity is now in this state, we call being in a state of original sin where no one can be righteous.

Jim: So we may press into that a little bit further here. But I'd like first for you to distinguish that from your fourth option, which you call Adam and Eve as symbolic figures. What's the difference between taking the Adam and Eve story as a compressed history, versus taking Adam and Eve as symbolic figures?

Haarsma: It's a little hard to distinguish the third and fourth scenario, but in my mind, there's two important differences I had in mind. For the fourth scenario, I was thinking about all of humanity together. So not particular individuals receiving some particular revelation, but all of us in this together. So in the third scenario, I have a much stronger emphasis on some sorts of special revelation coming to particular individuals. Whereas in that fourth set of scenarios, I'm thinking about general revelation, and to a certain extent, special revelation, but everybody being responsible for whatever level of revelation they have received.

Jim: So in the third, though, you're not saying that there was a historical Adam and Eve that were the recipients of some of that special Revelation?

Haarsma: I'm saying it's not theologically important in that third scenario to try and pick out particular individuals at particular points in time. That there is a special role for special revelation when it comes to rebellion against God. But it was, you know, spread out over many individuals over time and an accumulation of events. Whereas with the fourth scenario it's more of an emphasis on everybody's rebel rebellion against God for whatever level of general or special revelation they may have received in their lives, and it's all of our ancestors together.

Jim: So what do you make of special revelation in that fourth scenario?

Haarsma: Well, it happens. Special revelation happens. I don't know when the first special revelation happened, before Moses, before Abraham, how far back and what form it took. Special revelation can come in many forms, from a burning bush to a still small voice, to the word of a teacher whom God is using to prompt us to the voice of conscience within our mind, the Holy Spirit acting in a particularly forceful way, in our thoughts at a particular time. I don't know what sorts of forms the first special revelation happened, but it did happen. So it's part of the story. In the fourth scenario, what I emphasize is that general revelation also is something that everybody has at some level, and that is certainly enough to make people accountable.

Jim: So let me see if I can put my finger on the hard problems here. There may be a couple of worries. Some people worry that the gospel might itself fall apart without a historical Adam and Eve who have seemed to have this place in the Bible. I actually don't think that's the hard question, though. I think that question can be answered by noting that, look, all human sin needs to be saved. We don't have to know the origin of something to recognize its present state and realize that

348

something needs to be done about it. But rather, the harder problem to my mind is pushing further to ask about the origin of sin with respect to the conviction that God created a good world. How does this come into play at all? If God has made this good world and it's not coming down to a specific decision of two people, the way the flannel graph version of the story tells, how does sin come to infect God's very good creation in the first place?

Haarsma: Yes, I agree. These theological questions are some of the hardest. I think there are hermeneutical questions that people want to answer. What do you make of Paul's saying sin entered through one man Adam? What do you make of Paul's and other writers' connection between death and sin? These are hermeneutical questions. And I think advocates of these scenarios three and four have answers for them. But some of the hardest theological questions are what you identify as, what do we say about sin entering the world and not making God responsible? A lot of the doctrine of original sin is trying to avoid two extremes. One is just to say, okay, so God made us sinners and God, you know, that's just it. God created us as sinners. We want to avoid that. God is not the author of sin. We want to avoid another extreme, and St. Augustine was worried about this one, the extreme of saying, well, okay, so in theory, it's possible for somebody to be righteous without Christ, that sin is just a particular choice that any individual makes. It's not a condition which humans suffer; it's just choices. So maybe somebody could choose rightly their whole life. Well, we want to avoid that extreme, too. We want to acknowledge that sin is a condition in which we are all in. And none of us can be righteous apart from Christ. Now, how did we arrive at this situation? Saint Augustine offered one possibility, other theologians have offered other possibilities. How do we make that work? How do we avoid those extremes? In scenarios like scenarios three and four, where we view Adam and Eve as representative or symbolic of many individuals, I think we can still emphasize revelation and choice for any particular individual at any particular time. There are choices that an individual makes, and this would have been true of our ancestors too, that they chose rebellion again and again. And God honored those choices by letting them live out the consequences of that rebellion, and that the consequences of rebellion were passed on then to the people around them and to their descendants. And so now we are in a situation in a culture in a spiritual state where none of us can be righteous apart from God, apart from Christ's redemption. That's an accumulated effect of all of the rebellions made by our ancestors.

Jim: Let me ask the same sort of question this way, which I think I wonder if lies at the, is kind of an assumption here at all of these different scenarios and asking when does sin begin. I remember being at a conference in Chicago that was talking about science and the Bible, you may have been there too, and a charge of concordism came up. For our listeners unfamiliar with that term, it's usually understood as the attempt to mesh scientific theories with what the Bible is saying. So that, say, the days of Genesis one, for example, correspond to or are in concordance with what science says about the history of the universe. Anyway, there was one fairly prominent scholar there who said he's not a scientific concordist with respect to the Bible. But he is a historical concordist with respect to the Bible. I'm curious what you make of that distinction. And whether your project, *When Did Sin Begin*, assumes a historical concordism, with the primeval history of Genesis 1 through 11? Or whether there has to be a first sin in the world? Is that the kind of—are we making a category mistake when we ask, when did the first sin begin? Or does it have to be a punctiliar event of some sort? What do you think about that?

Haarsma: Well, for scenarios in which Adam and Eve are historical individuals, one can certainly point to a time before and a time after, if you like, the sort of the fourth scenario where sin enters that where Adam and Eve are symbolic of all of our ancestors, one can still say that, presumably there is a time before sin is part of the story. But you have to go a long way back. I'm presuming here that animals don't sin. And therefore, at some point, our ancestors who may have been just as nasty and nice to each other as we sometimes see in the animal kingdom, that it wasn't counted as obedience or disobedience to God. At some point, our ancestors began to understand that what they were doing had moral consequences and spiritual consequences for the relationship to God. I don't know exactly when that happened. So even in this sort of forth scenario where Adam and Eve are symbolic of all of our ancestors, there is an entrance of sin into the story. It's diffuse. It's spread out. And that raises some theological questions. But I still think it's fair to say, that's the beginning of sin.

Jim: So what could we say the same thing of any person growing up any individual growing up today? There, they had their first sin?

Haarsma: Yes, I sometimes give this analogy to audiences I'm talking to. Little babies are very self focused. We don't call that sin. But at some point, we see a toddler do something naughty, and we look at, we see the look in their eye, and we say, yeah, that was willful sin. But where was the first willful sin? What was the nature of that first willful sin of that individual? I do not know. I probably missed the point at which it happened. God presumably knows when it happened, and what its nature was. But I don't. But I do know it happened at some point.

Jim: So I guess what I'm asking is whether evolution has rendered this problematic in the sense of, can we ask when was the first Homo sapiens? I mean, there's definitely a time before there were Homo sapiens. And there's definitely a time now. But this sort of evolutionary thinking has made that something of a category mistake to try to pinpoint. And here's the first one. As though a non Homo sapiens gave birth to a Homo sapiens, right? That's just not how it works biologically. And so given that our biology is so fundamental to who we are, is there a sense in which to that, say, the doctrine of original sin, the way Augustine formulated it at least, seems like it's fairly dependent on that kind of historical punctilinear time that maybe if we were, if we had just the data points today without that tradition of Augustine understanding of the doctrine of original sin, say of when did sin begin, would we be asking the question differently? Or have we painted ourselves into a corner here conceptually, somehow that our history and traditions here have done for us?

Haarsma: I think we've opened up some possibilities here. I think we can think, and we are invited by the data to think of the possibility that maybe the entrance of sin into the human story is a much more gradual thing, and is analogous to what you talk about in a growing child, that very first sin, can we identify exactly when the first sin was of a child? And is it even necessary to do? Is it important to do so? That is certainly a possibility. If we were trying to develop the doctrine of original sin today, in light of what we know about human evolution, that is an approach we can and should consider deeply. Of course, in my book, I also offer the other possibilities where it was a peculiar event, for particular, historical individuals. But that, as you mentioned earlier, raises other hard questions. So whichever way you go here, there's some hard theological questions, and you sort of pick which ones you find the most intriguing to make possibility for progress.

Jim: So can we pin you down and ask, all right, you've done all this study and organized these things and these different scenarios, which one do you find most compelling?

Haarsma: I do have a favorite. And I will tell you in private conversation. In my book, I deliberately don't. Here's why: one of the primary messages of my book is that there's a range of possibilities. Therefore, you Christians don't have to be afraid of this topic. It's not that there's just one type, one possible answer and if you don't like it, then you're in trouble one way or another. There's actually, there's something comforting in finding that, when we look at all the science, when we look at church tradition and theology, we find that there's quite a wide range of possibilities. You can probably find some that you find intriguing and plausible and I want to leave it there, at least in regards to my book.

Jim: Okay. This is an exciting time to be a theologian that's engaging with science. In this regard. I wonder, though, whether you can project the future, and surmise at least whether these possibilities will be narrowed down for us in some way, or they're going to be, can we even think of what kinds of discoveries that could be made that would start to close down some of these options and get us to get us to converge on on one of these scenarios?

Haarsma: It's certainly possible. In science, it often happens that we have a set of data, which under determines the theory, as you say, and later discoveries close down certain options, and maybe open a few more. But eventually, you sort of narrow down. And theological history has similar possibilities, similar stories, if you think about the development of the doctrine of the Trinity, for example, that took a while and there was a lot of options on the table. But the church kind of settled through reflection through the leading of the Holy Spirit, to a fairly a much narrower range of options on the Trinity, then there were in the very early church. So it's possible that this will narrow down.

Now there's another possibility if you think about the doctrine of the Atonement, there's quite a few theories of the Atonement out there. And the church, many parts of the church, and many theologians are saying, you know, we need multiple theories of the Atonement. The Atonement is such a huge event, such a huge action by God that it really doesn't make sense that one human analogy would capture every element of it. And Scripture speaks of it using multiple analogies. So probably we're never going to settle on one theory of atonement for the whole church. So it may be with the doctrine of original sin. If you think of everything God had to do, to deal with a problem of sin with the incarnation, and Christ's life, and Christ's suffering and death and resurrection, all of that, in order to deal with the problem of sin, maybe we will find ultimately that we need multiple possibilities, multiple analogies, multiple theories to deal with this very big topic of sin, and will have a range of possibilities, but we won't be able to narrow it down. Because no one theory, no one analogy can capture everything about it.

Jim: Yeah, I think that's a really interesting way of understanding theology and pushes toward what some in my discipline in philosophy, philosophy of science, question, you know, realism in a direct sense that, perhaps our theories, and we have to remember that theology is our attempt to make sense of what God has done and revealed to us, that perhaps our theories are limited, and we're not going to be able to give the exact literal realistic description of how all of this works. Well, we, as the church, have been at this for a good long time. And you and I, here now we've been at it for almost an hour, our time is about gone. What are the next topics you think you might apply yourself to in trying to understand here in the space of science and religion?

Haarsma: I might want to spend more time with people who have written books or reading articles on this particular topic and really try to pin them down. What is your favorite scenario for the entrance of sin? And why? And have you thought through all the pros and cons? But there's another possibility I'm thinking about and that has to do with the last long chapter of my book, 'Whose Fault Is It?' is the title of the chapter. And it has to do with God's self revelation in Christ as being particularly a self revelation, of self-giving love. I think there's really strong connections, which is why I wrote a whole chapter on this, between the entrance of sin into the world and God's revelation in Christ, of self-giving love being a particular part of what God wants us to understand. And particular connections to how God created the world, this vast world, using natural processes, in which beings like us evolve, who are capable of understanding, self-giving love. So I might choose to spend more time in that particular topic, that particular area of understanding the connections between what we see in the natural world and how God created the world, and God's self revelation as someone who gives sacrificially to his creatures.

Jim: Well, I look forward to it. The current book, though, is again, *When Did Sin Begin: Human Evolution and the Doctrine of Original Sin* found wherever good books are sold. And this has been a fun conversation, Loren. Thanks for talking.

Haarsma: Thank you very much, Jim.

Printed in Great Britain
by Amazon

20586741R00212